The Snow Skier's Bible

The Snow Skier's Bible

Peter Shelton

DOUBLEDAY

NEW YORK   TORONTO   LONDON   SYDNEY   AUCKLAND

PUBLISHED BY DOUBLEDAY
a division of Bantam Doubleday Dell Publishing Group, Inc.
666 Fifth Avenue, New York, New York 10103

DOUBLEDAY and the portrayal of an anchor with a dolphin
are registed trademarks of Doubleday, a division of Bantam
Doubleday Dell Publishing Group, Inc.

Library of Congress Cataloging-in-Publication Data

Shelton, Peter.
  The snow skier's bible/Peter Shelton.—1st ed.
      p.   cm.
  ISBN 0-385-26540-9 : $8.95
  1. Skis and skiing. 2. Cross-country skiing. I. Title
GV854.S5156   1991
796.93 -- dc20   90-24858
                                 CIP

Printed in the United States of America

First Edition

Contents

At play in fresh powder above timberline at Arapahoe Basin, Colorado. *Bob Winsett/Keystone Resort*

Introduction

In the beginning, skiing's family tree was a slender, utilitarian, Scandinavian stalk. Skiing was transportation, simple and unadorned. From one house to a neighbor's, from farm to market, from village to village through the long, snowbound winters. Swedish and Norwegian armies fought on skis. Norse hunters ran down game on their long, wooden "snowshoes." Over time that single trunk sprouted many branches, each with its distinctive fruit.

Perhaps the most instantly recognizable these days is the alpine skiing branch, developed in this century in the mountainous terrain of central Europe (the Alps) and America. Alpine equipment evolved to maximize control on downhill runs. It is characterized by wide, stable skis, relatively stiff, high boots, and fixed-heel, safety-release bindings on which skiers swoop down lift-served, often machine-groomed slopes. Alpine begat the rush of downhill racing, the hyper-kinetic dance of mogul skiing, the languorous whoosh of powder skiing and the radical surf moves of snowboarding. Alpine is also the sport of bright fashion, of glamorous resorts, and of a legendary camaraderie that goes back to the days when skiers first walked up hills for no other rea-

son than to slide back down them. Alpine is a child of the recreation revolution, sport evolved out of transport.

Out of the old rootstock came what we now call cross-country or Nordic skiing. A part of northern man's pre-history, this branch of the family is revered as national obsession in the snowy (if not quite so precipitous) Norse countries. Elsewhere in the skiing world it is enjoying an unprecedented renaissance.

In its purest form, cross-country is just what its name implies, a crossing of the landscape on skis: up, down, and around under your own power. But cross-country also begat ski jumping, ski running, ski skating, the elegant, bent-knee telemark turn, the secret soul of a tour through an untracked forest. Today it may take the form of a wilderness crossing of Antarctica or a civilized stroll around a wintry city park. Cross-country skis are narrower and lighter than their alpine brethren, and are used with "free-heel" boots and bindings that facilitate the natural movements of walking and running.

Some skiers specialize. Others become generalists, sampling the different sets of tools and the environments for which they are made. In the end, every turn through snow, whatever its heritage, adds to the alchemy of experience and makes a better skier. Every skier, whatever his persuasion, joins a family of mountain lovers. The sensation linking them all is gliding. Gliding over snow with an ease and grace of movement impossible to duplicate on dry land. This is the lure, the romance. A feeling of flying without having to leave the ground. Skis as wings.

This book seeks to acquaint you with all of the fruits on this marvelous winter tree, while focusing most particularly on the venerable patriarchs, cross-country and alpine. No book can substitute for the wind in your face, for the rush of gravity and the soft hiss of snow underfoot. My intent is to inspire new skiers, and encourage a branching out among the ranks of the already smitten. I doubt it is necessary to reinvigorate lapsed skiers. There are surely very few of these. As Lowell Thomas, for four decades the voice of CBS radio news and an inveterate skier, used to say, "Once a ski fan always a ski fan. When the sport gets you, it gets you forever."

Let's go skiing

ACKNOWLEDGMENTS

My thanks to the following, who all contributed, in one form or another to this book: Kerry Manion at the Keystone Resort, Shannon Besoyan at Sun Valley, Byron Hetzler at Winter Park, Bob Chamberlain, Burton Snowboards, Mount Bachelor Resort, Wade McKoy and Bob Woodall, Margaret and Richard Durrance, Knox Williams, Peter DeLong of Uhl Illustrations, Jerry Roberts and Barb Wheeler, Linde Waidhofer and Lito Tejada-Flores, Tom Lippert, Ed Pitoniak at Ski Magazine, Lori Adamski-Peek, Franz Berko, the Auburn Ski Club and Wester America SkiSport Museum, the National Ski Hall of Fame, Cloe Shelton, and Seth Masia.

I

ALPINE SKIING

Early skiing in the Alps. *Bohringer*

1

The Alpine Story

Although alpine is a relatively new shoot on the skiing tree, it is today the most visible and popular type of skiing around the world. The word alpine refers to the Alps of central Europe, to the iconographic peaks and villages of every skier's imagination: the Matterhorn, Mont Blanc, St. Anton, Zermatt. But the beginnings of alpine skiing go back many thousands of years before there were skis in the Alps.

It begins 1,000 miles further north in central Sweden where archaeologists unearthed a 3½ foot-long by 6-inch-wide wooden ski, preserved in a peat bog near the village of Hoting and dating from approximately 2500 B.C. The Hoting ski is the oldest known so far, though there is every rea-

son to believe Scandinavian and northern Russian hunters and warriors were skiing long before that. Cave drawings in both Sweden and Norway depict stick figures sliding along on curved-tipped, astonishingly modern-looking skis.

Skis were strictly utilitarian then, for transportation over the protracted winter distances, and for war. (Although one can't help imagining even warriors delighting in the rush of a downhill glide through freshly fallen snow.) One of the most famous images from skiing's early centuries, preserved in a painting by K. Bergslien, shows a wartime scene from the year 1206. Under siege, the two-year-old son of Norway's King Sverre is borne through the night from Gudbrondsdal to

A 4,000-year-old rock carving from Roday in northern Norway. *Courtesy Oslo Ski Museum*

Two-year-old Prince Haakon Haaksonsson borne to safety by Birkebein-
ers, or Birchlegs, during the Norwegian civil war of 1206. Paintinq by K.
Bergslein. *Courtesy Oslo Ski Museum*

safety in Osterdal by the Birchlegs, loyal soldiers
in snowproof birchbark leggings. Norwegians still
commemorate the event with a 35-mile ski race
each winter known as the Birkebeiner. The
course follows the original flight to safety, and
participants must carry a pack weighing at least
12 pounds to represent the infant.

The American Birkebeiner, laid out between
the Wisconsin towns of Hayward and Cable, has
long been the premier ski marathon in this country, drawing up to 8,000 entrants each year.

The evolution of skiing from transportation to
sport occurred relatively rapidly beginning about
150 years ago. Scandinavian immigrants to the
New World brought along their "snow shoes"
(often single planks of hickory up to 12 feet long).
Many found work as miners in the mountains of
California and the Rockies, and when the digging
slowed under the deep winter blankets of snow,
the "snowshoers," as they were known, challenged
each other to downhill and jumping contests.

The first documented ski clubs and racing teams
were formed in the winter of 1850-51 in the California gold camps.

Informal competitions were becoming quite
the rage in Christiania, now Oslo, and Stockholm
as well. In 1868 a somewhat indolent forty-three-
year-old carpenter's son named Sondre Norheim
from the Telemark region of Norway beat the
gentlemen of Christiania at all four of their competitions—style, jumping, track skiing, and free
running—and in the process personified the
change from utilitarian necessity into sport.

Norheim's ability to turn his skis in a kind of
prayerful kneeling crouch (later to be dubbed the
telemark turn) astounded his rivals. He also fashioned his own skis, and he built them two feet
shorter than the norm of the time. His were
about seven feet long and commensurately easier
to maneuver. He radically improved his control
over the skis by adding heel anchors of twisted
willow twig. Before, skiers had depended solely

on leather toe loops, which allowed the heel free movement to approximate the motions of walking but were sloppy at speed and on the downhills. Norheim's were the forerunners of the alpine, fixed-heel binding concept.

He also drastically improved the tracking and turning characteristics of his skis. He found that by "waisting" the ski, giving it a side curve (widest at the tip, narrowest under the foot), it held a better straight line *and* curved more easily when put on edge. All told, an astonishing number of technological advances for one man in one lifetime. It's no wonder Norheim is considered the father of modern skiing, not just by the Norwegians, but by skiers everywhere.

With Norheim skiing could be said to have split for the first time. On one side were the traditional runners and jumpers, the straight line skiers. And on the other were the vanguard of modern alpine, or downhill, skiing. But the acknowledged father of alpine, that is skiing in the Alps, didn't come along until about thirty years later.

SKIS COME TO THE ALPS

Norwegian expeditions brought the first skis to central Europe in the 1880s, to the Monastery of St. Bernard in the Swiss Alps. Almost instantly,

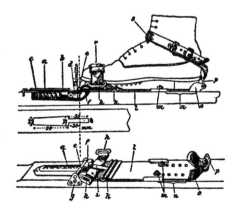

Matthias Zdarsky invented the stem turn and improved on Norheim's fixed-heel binding.

Turn-of-the-century Ski-Laufens (ski-hiking or running) in the Alps.

skiing proliferated throughout the region. Then in 1896 an Austrian hermit by the name of Matthias Zdarsky published the first book of ski technique, and alpine skiing was "officially" born.

Zdarsky was a dark-bearded eccentric who lived in the hills near Lilienfeld, and he had a problem: how to get to the village and back from his remote hermit's cabin. He was inspired to try skiing (as were many others of his age) after reading about Fridtjof Nansen's Arctic explorations on skis. Using skis and bindings based on Norheim's designs, he still found the going difficult. The way to town was quite steep and Zdarsky had trouble with the telemark turn, so he invented a braking/steering maneuver he called the "stem christiania." Zdarsky stemmed one ski to the side, angled it in the direction he wished to go and steered around with his weight on that outside ski. He used a single, long wooden pole which he dragged to the inside of each turn. The technique and the book he wrote about it became the basis for all alpine ski maneuvers to follow.

Interestingly enough, the British, with no real alpine mountains of their own, were instrumental in the development of skiing around the turn of the 20th century. They had no mountains, but the Brits were the world's foremost sportsmen and vacationers. An oft-mentioned seminal event took place in Switzerland in 1864. St. Moritz innkeeper Johannes Badrutt made a bet with four English guests which changed the nature of vacationing, and of skiing.

It was fall. As Badrutt was bidding farewell to his guests he said it was too bad they had to return to the cold and damp of London when he would be experiencing sun and fine weather, stripping off his coat by noon most days. He bet the Englishmen that if they returned at Christmastime, they would be so enchanted they would wish to stay 'til spring, and he Badrutt would accommodate them free of charge.

So heretical was this notion—no one in England had ever considered journeying to the mountains in the depths of winter—that the Englishmen took up the bet. Coming in to St. Moritz over the pass in a horse-drawn sleigh, the sun off the snow nearly blinded the astonished travelers, and they were indeed obliged to remove their heavy fur robes. Badrutt's bet was won, and the Brits returned home in the spring fit and tan and bubbling with enthusiasm for a new kind of winter tourism.

Skiing was soon included in the pantheon of British alpine amusements, and in the 1920s a fellow named Sir Arnold Lunn decided to organize informal competitions. He stuck small flags in the snow in a zig-zag pattern, checked his stopwatch, borrowed a word from the Norwegians, and invented slalom. His signal Arlberg-Kandahar race in 1928 elevated alpine competition to world status. By 1930, the International Ski Federation (FIS) added slalom and downhill racing to the already established running and jumping competitions. In 1936 they were included for the first time in an Olympic games, at Garmisch-Partenkirchen.

The First Ski Teachers

With the explosive growth of winter tourism in the Alps (and in the United States), the need arose for skilled ski instructors. Hannes Schneider of

Hannes Schneider, founder of the Arlberg School and technique, the first widespread ski teaching method. *Ski Magazine*

Gary Cooper was one of many Hollwood stars who regularly visited America's first destination ski resort, Sun Valley, Idaho.

St. Anton in the Arlberg region of Austria filled the need so well he became a kind of ski god. Schneider's Arlberg technique, based on Zdarsky's stem and a rotating upper body to apply steering force to the skis, became the world standard. Schneider himself was a charismatic proselytizer, a tall, hawk-nosed, empathic prophet who sent protégés to start ski schools around the skiing world. (In 1928, Schneider disciple Sig Buchmayr started the first ski school in the U.S. at Sugar Hill in Franconia, New Hampshire.) In 1939, freed from a Nazi jail with the help of American ski enthusiasts, Schneider made his triumphant way to the United States, to Mount Cranmore, New Hampshire, where he walked off the train and through an emotional gauntlet of raised ski poles.

THE UPHILL REVOLUTION

While Schneider's teaching advances signaled the beginning of the era of controlled skiing, technical advances in ski lifts and equipment revolutionized the sport even further. Before 1932 one still had to hike up the hill in order to enjoy the schuss back down. True, in Switzerland and to a lesser extent in the eastern U.S., one could hop a train that rumbled deep into snow country, hop out and find skiing right on the spot. The Swiss even had a few funiculars, or cog railways, that ground their way up steep passes, in the process opening up the longest "lift-served" skiing in the world at that time. (Ernest Hemingway rhapsodized about such skiing in his Nick Adams stories. In "Cross Country Snow," for instance, Nick finishes a swooping run to the valley off a funicular and says, "There's nothing can touch skiing, is there?")

Then came the uphill revolution. In 1932, the first rope tow, powered by a four-cyclinder Dodge, went up in Shawbridge, Quebec. (The car was set on blocks and the rope looped around a rear drive wheel.) It was followed in 1934 by the infamous Ford-powered tow on Bunny Bertram's pasture hill at Woodstock, Vermont, a ride that historically rivaled the downhill schuss for excitement and exhaustion. T-bars, platter pulls, Poma lifts: Various other contraptions for towing skiers up hill sprouted like winter wheat everywhere there were skiers and white hills.

Nineteen thirty-six was a red-letter year in the lift story. That winter railroad magnate Averell Harriman opened the Sun Valley resort in Idaho, and with it unveiled the world's first chair lift. Harriman's design engineer modified a system originally used for loading banana boats in Central America and came up with a sit-down conveyance for skiers complete with a lap blanket for the cold days. Sun Valley became the ski area of the stars. Gary Cooper, Clark Gable, Sonja Henie, and Ingrid Bergman, among others, frequented the resort.

Chair lifts proliferated like snowshoe rabbits throughout the late '30s and '40s. They popped up at such diverse places as Alta, Utah, Mont Tremblant, Quebec, Aspen, Colorado, and Gunstock, New Hampshire. Surface tows sparked the sport's first real participation boom. Chair lifts made skiing easy, made it glamorous, put the resorts that had them on the destination map.

With lifts came the elimination of need for free-heel bindings. No one had to walk significant distances on skis any more. Cable bindings held the boot heel firmly down on the ski. Skiing was no longer up and down; it was all downhill. The separation of alpine skiing from nordic became complete.

EVOLUTION OF EQUIPMENT

In the decades since, technology has brought steady change to the alpine world. Each advance made skiing a little friendlier, easier to learn, safer, more glamorous, or extended its season.

Bindings

Skier safety was greatly enhanced in the postwar years with the invention of the first truly releasable bindings. It happened after a man in the Pacific Northwest named Hjalmar Hvam broke his leg jumping off a cornice on skis. Under ether in the hospital, he had a dream, and when he awoke he asked for pencil and paper in order to sketch his idea. It was a releasable toe iron that would open when a strong twist was applied through the boot. Hvam marketed his binding—promoted with the slogan "Hvoom with Hvam"—into the 1960s, by which time much more sophisticated bindings were on the market. But all of them, then and now, operate on the same Hvam-inspired principle of the twist-out toe piece.

With the advent of releasable bindings, that

classic skier's badge of courage, the leg cast, began a steady decline, until today broken legs are a nearly forgotten memory. The most pervasive ski injury of the 1980s was the sprained thumb, caused by ill-advised attempts to brace against a fall.

Skis

The evolution of the ski itself couldn't be said to have affected safety, but it certainly changed the way we ski and the ease with which we learn. Up until the 1930s skis were a single plank of wood, often hickory, curved at the tip, but very heavy and very stiff. In the mid-30s, a Norwegian named Marius Eriksen (who is best known now as the father of Stein Eriksen, Olympic and world champion, and the quintessential skiing stylist throughout the boom decades of the 1960s and '70s) built a laminated wood ski that was more flexible and more durable than the old one-piece skis. Steel edges became the norm rather than the exception, allowing better control on hard snow and steep slopes.

In the early 1950s, Howard Head, a Baltimore

Aircraft engineer Howard Head built the first successful metal ski in the late 1940s, ushering in the modern age of design innovation.

aircraft engineer, turned the ski business upside down with the introduction of his aluminum sandwich skis (plywood was the core ingredient). They were thinner, lighter, and significantly easier to steer than their wooden predecessors. They were so slinky, in fact, they were dubbed "cheaters" by the happy masses who made the switch from wood.

Metal skis were not accepted by the racers until after the 1960 Winter Olympics at Squaw Valley. At that seminal event Frenchman Jean Vaurnet stunned his fellows with a victory in the downhill on a pair of aluminum Rossignols. Since then, ski racing has been the crucible from which virtually all of the technical advances in ski gear has emerged.

Fiberglass skis, which were far more durable and resilient than metal-only constructions, made the scene in the 1960s. High-density foam cores made for a lighter ski in the 1970s. High molecular-weight-polyethylene base materials rendered yearly varnishing and daily waxing obsolete. In the 1980s space-age materials like kevlar, carbon fibers, and ceramics—all many times stronger than steel by weight—were added to ski recipes to increase liveliness, absorb shocks, and reduce weight.

Modern skis have made the sport far easier to learn than it was in Alf Engen's early days. The long-time director of the ski school at Alta remembers the formative years in the early '40s: "By gosh, the skis were just planks then, so big, heavy, and stiff. We had to ski very fast to get them to turn." Now, thanks to fifty years of material and design evolution, you can carve turns as slowly as you please, cling with confidence to steep ice, and glide almost friction-free through deep powder.

Plastic Fantastic Boots

Ski boots made similar design leaps over the same span. Leather lace-up boots gave way to the Henke Speedfit buckle boot in the 1950s. In the '60s American Bob Lange developed the first plastic boots, and leather went the way of the all-wood ski. Plastic was waterproof, of course, and completely maintenance free. The new boots were warm and came in designer colors. But the real revolution was in control. Suddenly, skier-generated turning forces were transmitted much more powerfully, more precisely to the ski. Exag-

The evolution of the alpine ski boot (from left): a converted hiking shoe from the early days of this century; a box-toed leather boot from the 1930s; a 1950s lace-up model; the world's first buckle boot, the Henke Speed Fit; and an early Lange boot, from the company which made the first plastic ski boots. *Boots courtesy of Colorado Ski Museum in Vail*

gerated body movements could be toned down. Subtlety replaced muscular effort as the name of the game. Control and comfort soared to new levels.

Today's boots often come complete with the following "bells and whistles": adjustable forward lean, adjustable forefoot and ankle fit, adjustable flex, adjustable footbed angle, and adjustable side cant for custom fitting boots to legs which are naturally knock-kneed or bow-legged. Colors are wilder than ever. And the link between skier and ski has never been so complete.

PREPARING THE PISTES

Two big changes at the ski areas themselves, besides the advancements in lifts, contributed mightily to skiing becoming easier and more predictable. The first was snowmaking. Who would

have thought, back in the 1930s, that anyone but God could create a snowflake? Skiers accepted the fact that some years would be bountiful and others would be lean. Then area operators began experimenting with blowing mixed air and water out of high-pressure hoses onto the trails.

Now you don't absolutely have to have snow from heaven. Almost every ski resort in the eastern U.S. blows snow onto its slopes. Resorts in Colorado and California, which originally felt themselves immune to the East's snow worries, have in recent years jumped on the band wagon, to guarantee early-season openings and as a hedge against nature's inconsiderate, warm-and-dry tantrums. And the technology of snow making improves yearly. Now the "seed" for a snow grain is an innocuous bacteria, developed in the lab, which allows crystals to form at temperatures considerably above freezing.

So snow is virtually guaranteed. The other big

change is in how that snow, natural and man-made, is prepared as a ski surface. Used to be everything was powder until skiers themselves, by walking up and sliding down, packed it into packed powder. All snow was ungroomed snow. Alf Engen remembers days when the unpacked snow was so pervasive all he could do was traverse people one way across the hill, lay them down on their backs, flip their skis up and around, and traverse them back the other way. Skiers packed slopes, machines didn't.

Enter one Steve Bradley at the Winter Park ski area in Colorado. Bradley was looking for a way to smooth out the VW-sized bumps, called moguls, created when skiers turned repeatedly in the same places. (An innocent in a ski school class once asked me where the ski area stored the moguls during the summer months.) Platoons of employees armed with shovels were just too expensive and impractical. So he built himself an odd-looking contraption, a kind of cutting wheel on an erector-set frame, that could be steered by one man on skis. The Bradley Packer effectively shaved the bumps and, the inventor soon learned, also did a fine job of packing out fresh snow. Smooth, tamped trails were easier to ski than powder, and paying customers flocked to areas where grooming was emphasized.

Today the same job is done by fleets of quarter-million-dollar "snowcats," sophisticated, diesel-powered machines that can create ballroom-smooth pistes out of yesterday's bumps or last night's heavy snowfall or last week's pile of man-made.

To be sure, some of the adventure has gone out of skiing as a result of these modern guarantees. But the trade-off has resulted in easier, safer skiing for the vast majority of part-time enthusiasts.

Before the invention of the Bradley Packer in the mid-1950s, all snow was ungroomed snow. Here America's first ski Olympian, Dick Durrance, cuts up the powder at Alta, Utah. *Margaret Durrance*

The world's first grooming machines, the Bradley Packers, at work on the slopes of Winter Park, Colorado, in the mid-1950s. *Winter Park*

More skiers reach a higher level of proficiency sooner than ever before. And more older skiers will be able to stick with the sport longer, as the graying of America continues into the next century.

SKI FASHIONS

I should mention one more revolution that changed skiing forever: the introduction of fashion to the sport—specifically, the invention of the stretch pant.

In the 1930s and '40s skiers dressed in whatever worked: big puffy parkas, knickers, riding breeches, or baggy pants that flapped like gabardine flags in the wind of descent. A handful of firms worldwide sewed tailored woolens for the smart set (the Sun Valley/Hollywood crowd foremost among them), but the sport still lacked a

real skier "look." To the rescue came Willy and Maria Bogner. In Munich, they experimented with new fabrics, wool and nylon blends, that could be pulled any which way and still return to their original shapes. In 1952 they introduced the body-hugging stretch pant. They were warm, water resistant, sleek and fast. Marilyn Monroe modeled a pair. So did Ingrid Bergman. So did the Shah of Iran. Henry Ford ordered fifteen pairs. SKI magazine reported: "Overnight, skiing had been transformed into a sexy and very visible sport."

BACKLASH AND DIVERSITY

All of these advances have had their price. The dollar-a-day or ten-cents-a-ride lift pass is long gone. A single high-speed guard chair may cost a

Modern grooming machines "snow farming" at Keystone, Colorado. Such packing and smoothing has changed the face of alpine skiing, making more terrain more accessible to more skier's. *Keystone Restort*

A contemporary family ski day. Advances in clothing and equipment, lifts and grooming have made the sport easier than ever. *Wade McKay*

ski area millions of dollars to install. As will a new snow-making system or a couple of new grooming machines. High-fashion ski wear and exotic fiber skis, poles, boots and bindings don't come cheap. The price of progress is always passed along to the skiing customer. And although the cost of alpine skiing still compares favorably with golf or sailing or visiting Disney World, many alpine skiers have come full circle, seeking their sport's simpler roots. In the 1970s and '80s skiers in droves took up cross country again. The gear was light and relatively inexpensive. You didn't need a lift ticket or a fashionable ski suit. All you needed was a nice day, some like-minded friends, a rucksack lunch, and fields of snow rolling away for as far and as long as you wanted to go.

This backlash led to the rediscovery of the telemark turn, left slumbering for fifty years during alpine's dominance. (See Chapter 5: The Cross-Country Story, and Chapter 7 on telemark skiing.) It also spurred the invention of alternative tools for sliding on snow, like the monoski and the snowboard. The proponents of both have brought back the kind of radical, formative excitement that suffused skiing's early decades. Today there is a resurgent interest in alpine touring, that branch of the sport where skiers link villages or resorts over backcountry trails known as high routes, after the French *hautes routes*.

Far from hurting alpine skiing, the new diversity has reinvigorated the sport to its roots. Alpine skiing is flowering like never before, in ways that old Matthias Zdarsky, at the turn of the century, could never have imagined.

Skiing is a lifetime sport. The learning never stops. *Keystone Resort*

2

Alpine: A Basic Progression

First steps on skis can be an odd sensation, like the feeling of walking to the sea in scuba gear. The boots feel large and stiff, encasing the ankle, and the skis feel like slippery slats. But no matter. Very soon you will be *sliding*, the name of the game, the use for which this clunky gear was designed. As the sea supports the diver and transforms his equipment into something weightless and efficient, so too does ski gear, with motion, become elegant and functional.

How do you go about choosing the right equipment for starting out? The answer is, let a qualified rental shop make the decisions for you. There is no reason for a beginner to buy his or her own gear. Rent for the first few days—perhaps even the first season—and see how you like it. Later you will want to consider buying your own. At that time, you will know better what you want and how to shop for it.

BOOTS: The Essential Link

Boots are the most important and most individual piece of equipment. They are the controlling link between skier and ski, and they must be comfortable enough to wear all day. They should provide a natural stance; the tilt of the footbed should neither rock you too far forward nor too far back. The boots should be flexible enough to allow your ankle some movement, the better to walk and absorb changes in terrain. Rental shop boots, while they may not come with all the "bells and whistles" (current jargon for the adjustable functions) of higher-end boots, usually fit the bill quite nicely.

When it comes time to buy, purchase the best boot you can afford and save money on the other things, the skis and bindings. Rock-bottom for a skiable boot may be $200 or more. But if it takes another $100 to get you in a pair that fit well, by all means, spend it. Boot fit is absolutely critical to skiing pleasure and rapid progress.

Finding a good boot fitter is the key. You're probably going to have the best luck with a professional at a specialty ski shop. Mass merchants (the big chains and sporting goods stores) may have a slightly lower base price, but the time and care taken in ensuring a good fit make the specialty shop easily worth the $10-$20 difference.

Experience tells us there is no such thing as an average foot shape. But the economics of manufacturing (it takes about a million dollars to tool up a new set of molds at the boot factory) means that each boot line aims at a theoretical average foot. A good boot fitter will know that historically Koflach and Dachstein, for example, build on a relatively wide last, while Raichle's top-end models have traditionally fit narrower feet, and that Nordica, the world's largest boot seller, has always tried to hit the middle of the bull's-eye. A good boot man will also be able to modify or adjust the fit after your purchase, if necessary.

Without expert help, it simply wouldn't be possible to pick among all the models put out by Alpina, Dachstein, Dolomite, Dynafit, Heierling, Koflach, Lange, Munari, Nordica, Raichle, Rossignol, Salomon, Sanmarco, Strolz and Technica. And that is an incomplete list. Without help you probably wouldn't even hear about smaller companies like Salt Lake City's Daleboot, the only U.S. manufactured alpine boot. (The Daleboot has a number of unique custom fitting features that make it a popular boot with tinkerers and hard-to-fit feet.) Most of the other boots are molded in Italy, though the companies represent virtually all of the alpine nations of central Europe.

The point is, even with help, finding the right boot takes a commitment of time and effort. Do take the time. Establish a relationship with a good boot fitter, and try on as many different models as you can. I'm not going to recommend or even list specific appropriate model numbers here because it won't mean a thing to your feet, and because the life cycle of such things is never more than three years at most. Specific models become obsolete, not the technology so much as the "look," the color, the dictates of marketing. So this is where you trust your boot fitter to be current as well as conscientious.

Variable versus Fixed Volume

To give you a brief head start, however, you should know that there are two basic boot designs and two fit system theories. (Both systems incorporate leather or synthetic inner boots with an outer plastic shell.) The older of the two fit systems is the variable-volume shell usually associated with an overlap shell design and front-entry, like a sneaker or a hiking boot. Adjustable buckles (most often four of them) close the shell around the foot. The tighter the buckles, the smaller the inside volume. The other system is the fixed-volume shell. These are most often referred to as rear-entry, after the most common shell design, though we are now seeing top-entry and mid-entry variations. Fixed-volume shells secure the foot by means of internal adjustable instep plates or cables which press the foot in place.

At the beginning levels, arguments about which performs best, overlap or fixed-volume, are pointless. Comfort is really the only consideration. I have my personal prejudices in favor of overlaps—I like the way they snug the foot in a direct, low-volume link to the ski—but overlaps take a more careful initial fitting than do fixed-volume boots. More problem feet find a happy home in fixed-volume models and the rear entry feature (like opening a door and sliding your foot into an open-back clog) is decidedly more convenient. Alpina, Sanmarco, Heierling, and Koflach (among others) offer overlap boots in the lower-end price range. Everybody (except Strolz, a family company in Lech, Austria, which makes only overlap boots) has at least one fixed-volume design. Nordica has nearly twenty. Salomon, which pioneered the fixed-volume, rear-entry idea, makes no overlap models.

Remember, the operative word is comfort. Try the boots on using a single pair of thin socks. Modern plastic boots provide all the insulation most feet need. In fact heavy socks, because they hold more moisture against the skin, tend to work against warm feet. Sometimes too-heavy socks contribute to an overtight fit; this too can lead to cold toes. Wear the boots around the shop for a while, at least twenty minutes if the initial fit seems good. You want snug. A boot that feels tight in minute number one will probably feel bigger after time. Sore points at the toes, ankles, or shins may indicate the need for a larger size or a different brand with a different last.

A final word about cost. Suggested retail is a complete fiction. Don't be scared off by prices in the fall magazine buyers' guides. The price of ski gear has a lot to do with when you buy it. Avoid buying anything in the four weeks preceding Christmas. Shop instead at the spring, or better yet, the fall sales. Suggested retail will often be cut in half.

Beginners—even those who've stopped growing—are better off renting equipment for the first few days on skis.

SKIS

Having said it once, I suppose I should repeat it: Beginners really don't need to buy. The quality of the gear at the rental shops will be identical to what you can buy at the low end of the spectrum. But if you insist . . .

The first question is always, How long? A beginner should start with skis 10-20 centimeters shorter than his height. In the 1950s and '60s the rule of thumb was to reach as high as you could, then fit skis to the level of your wrist. No more. Shorter skis are lighter, softer, easier to maneuver and learn on.

Most ski schools now teach a form of GLM or Graduated Length Method. As you progress you go to a longer ski, perhaps head height as you reach the intermediate level. Then, as you become more and more proficient (and want to ski steeper terrain and more varied snow conditions), you may move up to so-called "full

size" skis: 195-205 centimeters for most men, 185-195 cm for most women. Longer skis are slightly more difficult to manage at slow speeds, but they make up for it with stability and edge hold at higher velocities. It's certainly no accident that downhill racers, who reach speeds as high as 80 mph, choose 220 cm skis, and speed skiers, those daredevils who hurtle straight downhill in search of new speed records (the current best is over 130 mph) wouldn't think of pushing off on anything smaller than 240 cm.

Beginners need a shorter ski because you want greater leverage over the tools on your feet. You need a fairly wide ski (for easy balance), a fairly soft and straight ski (not a lot of side curve) for easy swiveling and skidding in your first turns. As you progress, and become more adept at carving your turns (see Chapter 3), you will want a ski that responds more eagerly to edging and pressure. But for now the soft swiveller is the ticket.

The problem is the cheapest skis are pretty cheap. They have low-quality cores and extruded polyethylene bases. (Extruded bases are relatively slow and soft; they cut easily. Sintered bases have much higher molecular weight, resist scratches, and slide much better over the snow.) Avoid injection-molded skis. They are the cheapest and most likely to warp. Hold out for a ski with a wood core. They hold their shape and are more durable.

Buy a brand-name ski. The cheapest skis in each manufacturer's lineup, known as special makeup skis, often bear the name of the sporting goods chain where they are sold. Skis with the actual brand name on the topskin are likely to be better. And they will come with a full (usually one-year) warrantee. Beware of super inexpensive skis that may have come to this country as gray market goods. When skis don't sell in Europe one season, they are sometimes shipped here the following season, but not through normal distribution channels, and not often with a warrantee.

There are even more ski makers than there are boot makers. A partial list: Atomic (Austria), Blizzard (Austria), Dynamic (France), Dynastar (France), Elan (Yugoslavia), Evolution (U.S.), Fischer (Austria), Hart (U.S.), Head (U.S.), K2 (U.S.), Kastle (Germany), Kazama (Japan), Kneissl (Austria), Lacroix (France), Nishizawa (Japan), Olin (U.S.), Pre (U.S.), Research

Dynamics (U.S.), Rossignol (France), Salomon (France), Streule (Switzerland), Tyrolia (Austria), Volant (U.S.), Volkl (Germany), Yamaha (Japan). The large number of U.S. companies is somewhat deceiving. Only K2, Volant, and tiny Evolution actually manufacture their skis in this country. All of the rest are made in European factories.

So how do you choose? The answer, once again, is to place yourself in the hands of a specialty shop. If you were happy with the boot fitter, reward him by buying skis from him as well. The sensible thing is to choose a ski-and-binding package, which can often be had for less than the retail price of the skis alone. (This tells you how much maneuvering room the retailers have while still making a profit.)

BINDINGS

With rental bindings, of course, you don't have a choice of name brands or model numbers. But rest assured, rental bindings are almost invariably first rate; the ski shop in this litigious age wants them to work as safely and efficiently as you do.

When buying a ski-and-binding package, the only thing you need to know is your DIN number. DIN stands for Deutsche Industrie Normen or German Industrial Standard, a worldwide system of measurement for binding performance. A child of 70 pounds might need a DIN setting of 2 or 3 to be safe. Where a man of 170 pounds might require a DIN of 10 or more. Strength and ski ability figure into the equation too. The faster you go and the more force you can safely apply to your legs, the higher your DIN. The higher the number, the more force it will take to twist out of the binding. You needn't guess at the numbers yourself; every ski shop has a chart and someone with the experience to interpret it.

Different models within a company's line come equipped with different springs. The size and stiffness of those springs determine the DIN range for that model. A true child's binding will have a DIN range of 1 to 5. An intermediate adult binding might have a range of 3 to 9. And a binding designed for experts will most likely go from a DIN of 5 all the way to DIN 14 or 15. The numbers mean the same thing no matter the company or country of origin.

Choosing a binding by company name would be as hard as choosing a ski that way. The list includes: Atomic/ESS V.A.R. (Austria), Geze (Germany), Look (France), Marker (Germany), Salomon (France), and Tyrolia (Austria). You can't go wrong with a binding from any one of them. The most expensive bindings in a company's line will have aluminum housings (for durability and torsional stability), big springs and custom paint jobs. They cost about half what a top-end ski commands. Cheap bindings ($100 or less) have plastic housings, molded-in color and lighter springs.

But across the board, all bindings work pretty much the same. For the simple reason that they are all asked to do the same two things, two complex and contradictory things: a) keep you rigidly affixed to the ski so you can control it, and b) release you from that appendage when there is a good chance its long lever could do you damage. A great deal of sophisticated engineering goes into modern bindings. And they work. That most common accident of bygone (non-releasable) days, the broken leg, has nearly dropped off the ski injury charts.

For bindings to do their multiple jobs correctly, you should have them checked once a year at the beginning of the season. And, most importantly, you must make sure your ski boots are free of dirt and snow when you step into the binding. A snowy boot can sometimes impede the proper release function.

POLES

Once skiers moved from the single long pole of Zdarsky's era to twin sticks (as the British refer to them), proper pole length has varied little. Function dictates the best length at about elbow height.

Almost all poles are made of high-strength aluminum. The days of bamboo and fiberglass are over. Beginners should pay no more than $15 or $20 for new poles. In fact, $3-$5 poles at a ski swap or garage sale will do fine. With a hacksaw and a vice you can remove the grips and cut down too-long poles. Chances are, starting out you wouldn't be able to feel the difference with your eyes closed between a $3 job and a $60, ever-so-slightly lighter luxury pole.

LEARNING TO SKI

ON SNOW: Natural Stance

All of skiing's moves stem from a balanced, natural stance. Feet flat in the boot, weight evenly distributed along the centerline of the foot from toe to heel. Ankles flexed slightly. (All modern boots have a certain amount of forward lean built in, so the ankle at rest will be slightly bent.) Knees and hips similarly flexed to allow the upper body mass to rest comfortably directly over the feet.

The whole idea is to assume an alert but relaxed ready position, as one might in returning a serve in tennis, for example. It's extremely important that the skeleton do most of the work of holding the body up and not the musculature. A forced stance—too far forward or back—inevitably results in poor performance and overtired muscles.

WALKING : Finding the Fall Line

No mystery here. It may take a little while to get used to the idea that you can't cross your feet over to change direction—you have to take small, incremental steps to one side or the other—but basically, walking on skis is similar to walking anywhere. You'll use less energy if you slide the advancing foot forward instead of picking it up and placing it.

The difficulty—and the fun—comes when the skis begin to slide on their own. Walking on the flat is easy. What about on a hill? You'll need to walk about quite a bit on variously angled slopes during your first day, getting from here to there and practicing first turns before riding the lifts.

In the beginning, the slightest incline seems to invest the skis with minds of their own. They want to slip forward or backward, depending on the slope, and without any permission from you. To stand still on a hillside, it is necessary to stand *across* the hill, perpendicular to the fall line. This is an extremely important, if somewhat subtle concept. The fall line means, simply, down the hill, the direction a ball would roll or water would flow from where you are down the slope. Point your skis in the direction of the fall line—even a few degrees off the perpendicular—and they will slide ahead. But stand directly across the pitch, and you will not move.

Maneuvering uphill on gentle gradients is as important in the beginning as learning to control the downhill slide. There are two basic uphill walking strategies, the sidestep and the herringbone step. You may need one or both to get to ski school lineup, to ascend a lift line,

A balanced stance is neither too far back nor forward, but centered over the feet (*center*). Let your bone structure support you, not your leg and stomach muscles.

A natural stance: feet shoulder-width apart, head up, hands forward and spread slightly for balance. The skier is relaxed yet alert, similar to the ready position in tennis. *Tom Lippert*

retrieve a dropped mitten, or climb to the lodge for lunch.

To sidestep, first find the fall line and stand perpendicular to it. Then take small parallel steps to the side, up the hill. The uphill edges of both skis tilt slightly into the snow, preventing you from sideslipping. You can walk up anything with a side step as long as you keep the skis across the fall line.

The herringbone is faster but more strenuous and works best only on moderate pitches. Facing up the fall line, spread the ski tips apart, into a broad V shape. Thus turned out (as a dancer would say) walk uphill, taking care to maintain the V and setting the skis down each time on their inside edges. The edge angle keeps the skis from sideslipping. A skier doing the herringbone up a hill leaves a distinctive set of tracks, like the weave in a herringbone tweed.

THE STRAIGHT RUN

First runs are most successful where there are no worries about turning or stopping. Find a slope with a broad flat at its base or better yet a gentle counterslope to stop you. (Here, as in all phases

Sidestepping is the easiest way to walk uphill. To avoid sliding forward or backward, skis must be kept perpendicular to the fall line. Note how the uphill edges of both skis are set into the slope.

Climb gentle inclines with the herringbone step. (Note the pattern similarity to a V-shaped tweed.) Grip is provided by the inside edges of both skis. Poles push back for support.

of learning to ski, terrain selection can spell the difference between fun and frustration.) Glide forward with the feet shoulder width apart, weight centered between the skis and balanced fore and aft: the natural stance. Relax, keep your hands ahead of your hips, and look where you are going. Resist the temptation to look at your skis; they will still be there when you stop. Focus instead on the sensation of gliding, the feel of the snow underfoot, and on maintaining a comfortable balance. Climb back up the hill and do it again. And again. And again.

Sooner or later you will need to apply the brakes. You will use what used to be called the snowplow, but which ski instructors now prefer to

Gliding (*top*) and braking wedges. The broader the wedge (or snowplow) shape, the more friction the edges create, the greater the stopping power. The gliding wedge is the basic turning platform. *Tom Lippert*

call the gliding wedge. While gliding forward, push the skis into an A shape, sliding the tails out away from you while keeping the tips together. The wedge naturally puts the skis up on edge, like an inverted herringbone, increasing friction, and slowing your speed.

Practice all manner of wedge shapes, from skinny ones barely off the parallel and barely brushing the snow with the inside edges, to wide, muscular ones, where the edges bite into the snow and bring you to a power stop.

Try long straight runs in which you alternate wedges and parallel glides. Press out into a wedge, then relax, stand tall, and let the skis drift back to parallel. Push out into a wedge again, taking care to feel the tails of the skis brushing across the snow, smoothing it with their edges. Think about your skis as big butter knives, and you are spreading soft margarine or cream cheese on a very large slice of bread.

WEDGE TURNS

A gliding wedge is the perfect platform for initiating first turns. In this position the skis are just itching to turn. The right ski is already pointing to the left, the left ski is already pointing right, and both skis are tilted up slightly on their inside edges. All you need to do is shift weight from your centered (straight running) position to one ski or the other.

Shift most of your weight to the right ski, for example, and that edge will engage, turning you in the direction the ski is pointing, to the left. Simple. Transfer your weight to the left side and you go right, as long as the ski is edged and your weight continues to ride there.

Edging and weighting the edged ski are two of the three components that go into all turns, not only these first wedge turns but the most effortless (appearing) expert turns as well. The third element is the steering force you apply to the ski through twisting the foot and leg. You are steering when you brush the tails out to form a gliding wedge. You want to continue steering when you weight the turning ski. You want to continue spreading that soft cream cheese in an arc, continue driving the ski in the direction you wish to go.

Troubleshooting

Edging. Pressure (or weight). Steering. Together they constitute the recipe for turning. Leave one ingredient out, or add too much of another and the cake will go flat. Here are three typical problems learning skiers encounter with their wedge turns.

Little or no weight shift. This is the most common one. First-time skiers sometimes don't trust a weighted ski to turn them. They're hanging back on their heels and trying to muscle the skis into a turn. Or their instincts may say that to go to the left one must lean to the left. This is a natural enough response but a counterproductive one. Skiers must fight the tendency to lean. Instead, you want to maintain a tall, balanced stance, one from which you can apply pressure to either ski without leaning.

So often, troubles come back to the basic stance. It's difficult to weight the ski if you are not in balance to begin with. And to learn that basic stance, to really feel it and trust it while you're moving, requires practice on nonthreatening slopes. I'll come back to this point again and again: appropriate terrain is the key to all learning. Trying to learn something new on frightening terrain is like trying to bake that cake in an oven with no controls. You must control the environment or the alchemy hasn't a chance to work.

If you're having trouble weighting the turning ski, go back to a slope where speed control isn't a factor, a slope where you needn't "hold on" to the hill at all. From a gliding wedge with your weight in the middle, between your feet, think about pressuring one ski edge. Bend that knee slightly and lower your weight onto that foot. Do it one turn at a time until you groove the sensation of that weighted ski coming invariably around the corner.

Too little or too much edge. Too much edge is the more common mistake. It happens if your wedge grows too wide. The further out you push your heels, the sharper the edge angle will be to the snow. A beamy wedge is good for slowing down quickly, but it is problematic when it comes to turning. It's tough to get your weight out there onto the turning ski. And it's difficult to steer a ski, to make it skid in the turn, when its edge is dug sharply into the snow. The solution: ski in a

A

B

C

D

The wedge turn. In a gliding wedge (A), the skier weights his right ski (B), presses the inside edge (C), and steers (D), twisting the foot and leg in the direction of the turn. *Tom Lippert*

narrower wedge. Stand up straighter, bring the skis underneath you where the edge angle will be flatter to the snow.

Frightened skiers over-edge. They tend to lean up the hill away from the fall line and the turning ski. In the process, they pretty much guarantee that they will not turn. It's a vicious circle. And the only answer, once again, is to retreat to terrain where fear is not a factor. Begin again with straight runs and gliding wedges on slopes which end in flats or counterslopes. Try small, briefly weighted "foot turns." Step from one foot to the other (in your wedge), to create a snaky, wiggly descent. Then try longer turns at very slow speeds until the instinct to shy back from the hill is overcome.

Under-edging, or skiing with the skis too flat to the hill, is rare, but it does happen. It happens to people who are bowlegged. If you are bowlegged, ask the ski shop about "canting." Modern boots and bindings can be tilted in or out to compensate for lower-leg bowleggedness and its opposite, knock-knees.

More often under-edging is caused by the skier standing too aggressively over the turning ski, leaning too far down the hill. The weight is there but the ski is too flat on the snow to grip and turn. No friction, no change of direction.

If your ski is too flat, whether from bowleggedness or an unbalanced stance, you solve the problem by flexing the knees and actively moving them toward each other. Adduction of the knee toward the center axis of the body will roll the ski onto its inside edge. Add pressure and steering and away you go around the corner.

Insufficient steering is the third common problem. Let's say you've got your ski on edge. You've got your weight on it, and it still won't turn. Its course seems set in a groove of its own making, and it just goes straight. Usually this happens in combination with other problems: too severe an edge angle and/or an unbalanced (possibly fearful) stance that prevents your steering the ski.

Practice twisting the foot and ski while you are stopped. Brush it lightly across the snow as you point the tip in the direction you want to steer. Feel the smoothing/spreading sensation of the edge. Now ski again. Brush your ski into the turn. Make it skid the way you've seen police cars skid around corners in movie chase scenes.

In any discussion of steering, it is important to stress that all of the steering action takes place below the waist. Sometimes you'll see beginners turning their arms, torsos, and shoulders in an effort to make the skis follow suit. It doesn't work. In fact, it often has the opposite effect. The goal here is to ski with a very quiet upper body and do the requisite twisting and edging with knees and feet. This independence of upper and lower body makes for easy balancing during a turn, lets you stand up and see where you are going, and uses the fewest muscles.

If you are over-twisting your upper body, try this. Set up your gliding wedge straight down the fall line. Aim for the lodge, or a tree, or a friend. Fix your eyes and chest on that object and lock on, as if by laser beam. Hold your hands out in front of you as if you were carrying a tray of drinks. Lock them on. Now begin a turn, to the right say, by pressuring and steering the left ski. Complete the turn to a stop without ever relinquishing your stare or the orientation of your drink tray. Work this exercise to both sides and you will find that your skis turn more readily and your balance on them will be improved.

TURNING AND SPEED CONTROL

Turning is speed control. Steer a turn far enough and the changing slope angle will slow and eventually stop you. The act of turning generates ski/snow friction and slows you to some extent. But by far the greater slowing force comes from your having turned away from the fall line, away from the pull of gravity. Good skiers use both the shape of the mountain and the friction of skidding skis to scrub off speed when they need to.

Beginning skiers should practice both techniques too. We've already talked about the braking properties of the good old snowplow, or wedge. There are times when nothing but a wedge will do. When you're on a narrow road or cat track, for instance, where there isn't room to turn. Or in a lift line with a downhill tilt. Or any congested situation that requires caution and a minimum of flailing around. Small children sometimes settle into a wedge and stay there for the entire ski day. It gives them a wide, stable base and instant braking with either foot. I would encourage grown-ups to learn the attributes of the braking snowplow, but then as quickly as possible to move on to the beauties of terrain skiing.

Try this. From a gliding wedge in the fall line initiate a turn to the left. Weight and steer the right ski gradually. Try not to brake with it, but just wait and watch as the arc carries you out of the fall line, across the hill and even slightly *uphill* to a stop. Try the same thing to the right, driving with the left ski. Again, try not to brake. Try instead to make your path a partial circle, ever curving until the hill stops you. When you can do this consistently, when you can use the terrain to control your speed, you are ready for grand things.

HEADING UP-MOUNTAIN:
Riding the Lift

When you can turn and stop at will on the practice slopes (sidestepping back up the pitch is often the hardest part of the drill), you are ready to ride the lifts and put in some mileage. At some areas your first lift will be a surface lift, a rope tow, T-bar, or Poma. Other areas have replaced their surface lifts with slow-speed chairlifts for novice skiers. Either way, all that sidestepping will be behind you.

Rope tows were the original uphill transportation in this country. The famous ones at Shawbridge, Quebec and Woodstock, Vermont were powered by old trucks on blocks with the rope looped around a rear drive wheel. Modern ones are a little quieter but work much the same way. The rope is a continuous loop. It never stops. You must walk up to it, position your skis in line with the rope's direction, and slowly squeeze the moving rope with your hands. If you grab the rope too abruptly it will pull your upper body over before your skis have a chance to match the rope's speed. That's the goal: to engage the rope the way a clutch gradually connects engine and drive train.

Once you get the hang of them, rope tows can be a lot of fun. For one thing, you get to ski uphill as well as down. That's good for your overall mileage. There's definitely a lot of learning going on as you scoot up the track: balancing, steering, riding a flat ski (which is a form of edge control in itself). Pomas and T-bars provide the same practice. They differ from rope tows in that the cable loop travels overhead, and you are pulled up slope by contraptions suspended from the cable. A T-bar can pull two people at once; the Poma just one, on a small disc that fits between your legs. These lifts save a lot of wear and tear on the hands. (In fact, if you know you will be riding a rope tow frequently, consider sacrificing a pair of tough leather work gloves in lieu of your nice ski mittens.)

The chair lift is the easiest of all to ride and a nearly effortless, quiet, floating component to a ski day. Suddenly, you are king of the air and all that you survey. The exciting parts are the getting on and off. Beginner chairs are usually quite slow-moving, but it helps to alert the operators that it is your first time anyway. They will help position you in line with the oncoming chair and then make sure you are seated before it scoops you up and out over the snow. At the top you have but to stand up at the marked spot and ski down the ramp away from the lift. Sometimes the transition from sitting to skiing without having stopped in between throws beginners off balance; their skis are moving before their bodies are. This is normal. After a couple of rides you will get the knack of pushing out of the chair and projecting forward down the ramp.

LINKING TURNS

Up to this point I have talked only about executing one turn at a time, and that's the way you should start out until you feel comfortable with the slowing power of your turns. The next step is linking turns together in a smooth, serpentine descent. There are no new mechanics to learn, just a pattern of movement to ease the transition from one turn to the next.

That pattern takes the form of up-down-up movements, or, thinking of it in terms of pressure, light-heavy-light. At the beginning of each turn you should be standing tall with your skis in a relatively narrow wedge and flat to the snow, not tilted way up on their edges. You are light on your edges, light on the snow. From this position it's easy to steer the outside ski into the turn, get it started in the new direction. (Some skiers may be more familiar with the terms "uphill" and "downhill" skis when talking about turning, but I find these problematical. The ski that does the turning in every case begins as the uphill ski and finishes the arc as the downhill ski. It's simpler and more accurate to refer to the outside, or turning ski and the inside, or unweighted ski.) In fact, in a tall gliding stance, you will notice that your ski tips will drift toward the fall line on their own, helping to initiate your direction change for you. As you steer you begin to feel the edge, and you pressure that ski to give the edge purchase and drive it around the curve. To apply pressure, flex at the knee and ankle and let your weight sink to the turning ski. This is the heavy phase of the turn.

When the turn has done its work and you are across the hill again, speed under control, it's time to stand up once more, releasing your hold on the mountain, getting light, letting the skis drift down the hill and steering, with the opposite leg this time, into the new turn. Up-down-up. Light-heavy-light. Ski technicians, who like to break movement down and give everything a name, call these three parts of every turn initiation, control phase, and finish, which leads seamlessly to the next initiation.

Finish is an important word here. It's quite common for novice skiers to begin linking turns and find themselves accelerating down the hill rather than maintaining a constant speed. The acceleration comes from a failure to finish, or complete, each turn in turn. Incomplete linked turns look like a set of wavy arcs deviating only slightly from the fall line. Picture the same linked turns with fuller, rounder arcs, bringing the skier back across the hill each time. He speeds up through the beginning of each turn, but he controls that speed through the round finish of the arc. In this way you can ascribe to your turns another pattern: slow start, fast middle, slow finish.

Troubleshooting

Problems linking turns usually have to do with initiations, getting started, giving in to that moment of acceleration, committing to dive, however temporarily, into the fall line. If the hill is too steep no amount of verbal methodology will help. Move to terrain on which you feel comfortable. This is the only way to overcome the holding back. In a relaxed stance, as opposed to a defensive crouch, the skis are easily steered into and through the fall line. Work up to speed in small increments, so that acceleration in a turn doesn't come as a surprise.

Second, it's tough to initiate a direction change if you don't have confidence in your ability to slow down. Work on turn endings one at a time to a stop. Master the finish, and the beginning will come easier.

OUTSIDE SKI/INSIDE SKI

What is happening with the *other* ski while you are concentrating on steering and weighting the outside one? In wedge turns, the inside ski does nothing to actually turn you around the corner. It acts as a second balance point, though it should carry very little weight. And yet sometimes that inside ski—if it is too far up on edge or is carrying too much of your weight—can hinder the turn; it gets in the way of your steering. The solution to this problem is also the key to reaching the next level of skiing prowess. When you begin to steer your inside ski as well as the outside one, you are knocking on the door of intermediatedom.

Your goal, once you have found the knack of steering the outside ski in a wedge turn is to *match* your edges, to get both skis on the *same edge* and turning in the *same direction*. A turn that finishes with the skis thus aligned, that is, no longer in a wedge (opposing edges) but parallel (same edges), is called a christy, after Christiania, the ancient name for Oslo, Norway, where parallel, skidded turns were first practiced about a hundred years ago. A christy turn can be initiated any number of ways: we have wedge christies, stem christies, parallel christies and step christies. All of them end with inside leg steering as well as outside leg steering and with the skis on matching edges.

How do you steer the inside ski? With the same twisting movement of the leg and foot that you use to steer the outside ski. Try a holistic approach first. On very gentle terrain where speed control is not a factor, begin a series of shallow, foot-steered turns, back and forth across the fall line. Try, without dissecting the movements in your head, to steer both feet at once. Because of the gentle slope angle you should be using a narrow wedge, and your skis should be quite flat to the snow, making for easy pivoting of both feet.

If this works right off the bat, great! You are standing well and you are ready to try matching skis on slightly steeper terrain. If the inside ski

A wedge christy begins by steering the outside (in this case, left) ski into a wedge turn (A and B). With all the weight on the ouside ski, the skier is free to steer the inside ski as well (C), knee to the inside and steering the foot, matching edges and direction through the finish of the turn (D and E). *Tom Lippert*

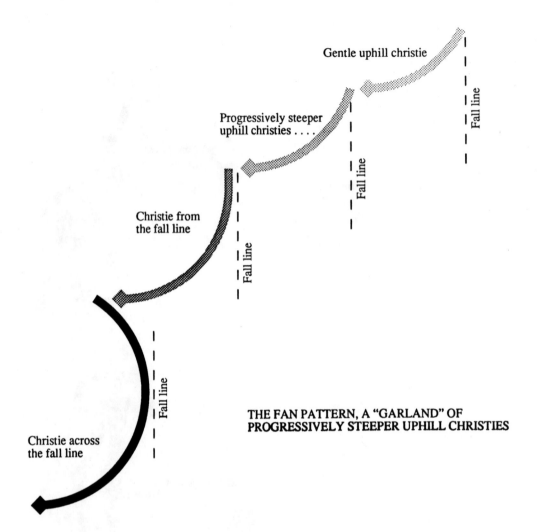

Gentle uphill christie

Progressively steeper
uphill christies . . . .

Christie from
the fall line

Fall line

Fall line

Fall line

Fall line

Fall line

**THE FAN PATTERN, A "GARLAND" OF
PROGRESSIVELY STEEPER UPHILL CHRISTIES**

Christie across
the fall line

gets stuck on its edge, you are standing too knock-kneed. Roll that inside knee away from the body's centerline—abduct—to flatten the ski on the snow. Now it should steer more easily.

Move up to slightly steeper terrain and try matching skis in turns where speed control is a factor. At first match skis only at the end of your turns. Once you are well across the fall line, roll the unweighted knee up the hill, away from the body's centerline, until both skis are slicing ahead on the same edges. That is, both right edges if you have just completed a right turn, or both left edges if you have just made a left turn. This period between turns where you are moving across the hill is known as *traversing*.

The sequence again: From the traverse, stand tall, push out into a wedge, drift toward the fall line, weight and steer the outside ski, now steer the inside ski as well, matching. A good exercise

for practicing matching is a *garland*. On a slope with plenty of room side to side, begin a series of turn initiations. That's right, initiations, but no follow-through across the fall line and around the corner. It goes like this. Traverse. Stand tall and begin the drift toward the fall line. But then instead of transferring your weight to the new turning ski, steer back up the hill and match with your inside ski at the same time. Stand tall and drift. Then sink and steer both skis back up the hill. Your path will show a series of christies, half turns in a scalloped line from one side of the slope to the other. Naturally, you'll want to turn around and practice your garlands back the other way, matching with the other inside ski.

As you get better at matching you'll start steering the inside ski earlier and earlier in the turn. The balance is easier, more natural, and controlling the arc of the turn is easier when the

The basic parallel christy differs from the wedge christy only in the initiation. Here the skier stands tall in the basic stance (A), lets the skis drift toward the fall line (B), inclines his body (to edge the skis) and at the same time applies full weight to the outside ski (C, D, and E) for a strong, steered finish. Note in *E* the bend in the weighted ski, while the inside ski carries no weight. *Tom Lippert*

skis are working in concert. To facilitate early matching choose your terrain carefully. Look for small rolls in the terrain and start your turns just as the hill falls away off the top of the roll. That momentary lightness of being as the pitch drops away makes the matching/christy phase that much easier.

Ski enough rolly shapes and you may find yourself dispensing with the wedge altogether. This is great! It is enough to approach the crest of a hump in a tall parallel stance then sink and steer both skis into a christy on the down side: the basic parallel turn.

In decades past skiing "parallel" was a badge of high achievement. It still is. But it shouldn't be your primary goal. We now know that there are many serviceable (and elegant) ways to begin a turn. Some use simultaneous (parallel) leg action, while others use sequential leg action (wedge, stem, or step). None is better than any other, and each has its place in every good skier's bag of tricks. As you grow in skill and mileage, you will find yourself using the parallel initiation more and more. Not for its style so much as for its ease. The truly important thing early in the game is that you master the christy phase of the turn, the control phase, with the skis matched and parallel.

CENTRIFUGAL FORCE

Skiing is a game of conscious resistance and equally calculated letting go. In a well-balanced turn, all or almost all of your weight is riding on the outside ski. In any turn, once the curving begins, centrifugal force is pushing your weight out there. Your turn is like a centrifuge; the force is from the center out. This makes weighting the outside ski easy, IF you give in to the force and let your weight settle on that foot. This is skiing's essential leap of faith: To make the skis work, you have to give in to the force that would pull you down the hill. You have to trust that pressure on that outside ski; while it may feel precarious at first, it is just what's needed to control your descent.

At the same time, to make effective turns we have to resist centrifugal force. If we went limp and gave in completely it would pull us over our feet and down the hill. So while the outside ski finds its arc through the snow, we have to find our balance on top of it. We have to lean just enough to the inside to stay in balance and still drive the ski. Lean too far to the inside, of course, and you create a new set of problems, including loss of balance and ineffective steering.

Everybody's seen the photos of the ski racer carving around a slalom gate. The skis are edge up on their sides, biting into the snow. And the racer's body is angled significantly to the inside of the turn, braced against the force that would pull him off line. Recreational skiers rarely generate these kinds of forces and therefore don't assume these extreme positions, but the equation holds for every turn: The faster the speed (or the sharper the turn), the more centrifugal force is generated, the more the skier has to lean against it.

This is the heart of skiing balance. We embrace a seeming contradiction, letting go and resisting both at the same time. We must allow centrifugal force to pull our weight to the outside, the scary side, so that that ski will do its thing and turn us. And then once the weight is settled on that turning ski, we resist any further pull, as if we were the solid spoke of a wagon wheel. It takes constant adjustment and realigning. And it is what makes skiing such a satisfying internal contest. Every turn is different from every other. And every moment requires a fine tuning of the elements of balance.

I should note that few skiers, even the great ones, actually think about all this in the middle of a run. The body responds naturally with patterns of learned movement. But they are learned patterns. And sometimes it is valuable to understand the mechanics of what you are trying to do as you seek to establish those good habits.

FREEZING, FATIGUE, AND FEAR

None of the three Fs should get you if you use a little forethought and if you are lucky enough to have a good teacher. I heartily recommend ski school for beginners. A morning, or a few mornings, with a certified instructor will help you sidestep the pitfalls that seem inevitably to befall self-taught first-timers. (More on this in the section on fear.) But do ski on your own as well. Beginners need mileage. And sometimes watching and listening to your own internal voice is the best path to advancement.

Freezing

Skiing can give you the cold shoulder (not to mention toes and hands and face) if you are not prepared. But if you are well covered and you keep moving, there aren't many days when it's too cold or nasty to enjoy your sliding. Being out in the cold, playing in it, and being comfortable, even snug, inside your man-made cocoon, is part of the romance of skiing.

There are two ways to become cold, underdressing and overdressing. Underdressing is self-explanatory. You haven't enough insulation or weather protection to stay in the comfort zone. Overdressing is the one beginning skiers don't often think about. Skiers sweat, even on cold days, and beginners more than most as they hike the hill for first turn practice. In fact, as a beginner you'll work harder at almost everything from putting skis on and off to figuring how to get up after a fall. If you sweat and that moisture stays next to your body in a layer of clinging cotton underwear, for example, you will feel cold, and when you stop exercising, on a chair lift ride or for lunch break, you will be cold.

The answer is to layer your clothing and avoid cotton fabrics next to your skin. Technology has made great strides in skiwear in the last decade—in bright color and fashion, but more importantly in cold-weather function. Synthetic-fiber undergarments, made of polyester or polypropylene, will not absorb moisture; instead, they transfer it out to your next layer. Your skin stays dry, and you stay warm.

So, layer one should be a nonabsorbent set of long underwear. Next you need insulation. Wool is a classic choice. It's warm and keeps at least some of its insulating properties even when wet. The high-tech equivalent of wool is a synthetic pile, lighter and warmer for its thickness than the old classic and an even better insulator when wet. Wool or pile sweater on top; wool, pile, or synthetic blend sweat pants on the bottom. (The days of skiing in Levis, while the fashion statement may be emphatic, are, thankfully, over.)

Finally, for the outermost layer you need a weather-resistant shell—jacket and pants or one-piece suit. Most high-count nylons these days are windproof. (This is important; even on windless days you generate your own serious breeze.) The best quality garments are windproof, water-resistant, and somewhat breathable. Fabrics and fabric treatments like Gore-Tex and Entrant allow body moisture to evaporate while preventing larger water and snow molecules from penetrating.

So, the three-layer system should include: a wicking layer next to the skin, a layer (or more, depending on the temperature and your own comfort threshold) of insulation, and a weatherproof layer on the outside.

Keep your head warm with a wool or polyester hat or headband. Forty percent of the body's heat is dissipated through the head and neck. On really cold days wear a fuzzy neck gaiter that can be pulled up around your ears and chin. And on

Intelligent weatherproofing means wearing a hydrophobic (or "water hating" fabric like polypropylene) underwear layer next to the skin; a wool or pile insulating layer (sweater or turtleneck, sweatpants or tights); and a windproof, waterproof/breathable outer shell—in this case, a one-piece suit. Acrylic neck gaiter, warm hat, and mittens complete this cold-weather outfit.

really really cold days, when the temperature is well below zero Fahrenheit, consider wearing a full face mask, either of silk or polyurethane. On these bitter days regularly stop and check your skiing partner's exposed skin for the telltale white patches that indicate frostbite. If you see one, place an ungloved hand on the spot until it turns pink again. Don't rub. And look for a place to get out of the cold for a while.

Hands and feet, being the farthest from your central heating system, are often the hardest tokeep warm. Modern boots are waterproof and well insulated. If your feet are cold, your boots may be too tight, cutting circulation to your toes. You may be wearing too many socks. Or, you may simply have popsicle toes, in which case you might consider buying electric socks or boots with battery heat packs.

To my knowledge, there is no such thing as electric gloves, though there may be. In general, mittens are warmer than gloves. If your hands get cold on the trail, stop and swing them around like a propeller one at a time. The circulation should soon return.

Goggles are a good idea in cold weather; they keep the wind off a good portion of your face. Goggles or glasses with 100 percent ultraviolet protection are a must when the sun is out. The combination of high-altitude solar radiation and the reflection off the snow can burn eyes painfully in the course of an unprotected day.

And while we're talking about sun, you'll want a good sun block cream for your exposed skin, SPF 15 or higher. Sun burn, and its unsavory long-term effects, comes quicker in the thin atmosphere on a ski mountain.

All of this careful dressing and closing of gaps should add up to what a friend of mine calls "the inside inside, and the outside outside." The inside stays in, snug and more or less impervious to the elements, while the outside stays out, though it may tap on your goggles and rustle your nylon outer skin. If you've done it right, there's nothing quite so pleasant as coursing through the cold, through a storm even, secure in your personal bubble of comfort.

Fatigue

You're going to get tired. When you do, stop and rest. If you don't listen to this internal message,

you risk becoming cold and/or sloppy and accident-prone.

There is one-third less oxygen in the air at 9,000 feet. Shortness of breath is a natural response. How do you prepare in advance for skiing's rigors? Fitness and acclimatization. Most important is to get in shape before you go skiing. Running, cycling, rowing, tennis—any regular aerobic exercise will help get the cardiovascular system in shape. To be effective, you should be working out two or three months before skiing, not just a couple of weeks before, although anything is better than nothing.

Skiing-specific exercises include bicycling, skating, rollerblading, weight work (particularly quadriceps), and running in the forest. These develop leg strength and agility.

Stretching should be a part of every skier's day. Stretch the legs, groin, back, shoulder and neck muscles. You will ski better and be less prone to injury and sore muscles. The hot tub may be the greatest American contribution to après ski, but even a long soak will not completely vanquish the soreness after a hard day on the slopes.

There's nothing you can do about altitude except respect it. If you're going to be skiing at high elevations in the Rockies or the Alps, consider giving yourself an extra day at a mid-elevation stop like Denver or Geneva. Ease into it. Barring that, consider not skiing your first day at altitude, or at the very least taking it easy. Stay hydrated. And drink alcohol in moderation. After a couple of days, your body should substantially adapt to the thinner air.

Fear

Everyone at some time or other is afraid. As a beginning skier, it's only natural to be a little frightened of the white, tilted plane, of the slippery boards on your feet and the seeming abdication of control that goes with them. But a good teacher should lead you through the steps outlined in this chapter. He or she should lead you from one success to another and give you the tools to overcome those first, natural inhibitions. And he should do it gently and with attention to your specific needs. If he doesn't, you got a bum instructor. Demand another one. No learning skier deserves to be placed in a scary situation, the definition of which can include riding the lift before you are ready or skiing terrain that is too steep for your level of skill.

A good instructor will blend easy terrain with slightly challenging, but not threatening practice shapes. Skills for handling intermediate slopes, for instance, are acquired on novice pitches. The learning takes place within a certain comfort zone. And then it is reinforced again and again until it is habit, again in the comfort zone. Only then do you test it on the intermediate blues. And so you move up the scale, step by step.

No learning happens when your muscles clutch in fear. So, communicate with your teacher. Let him or her know what feels good and what doesn't. And make sure you go to the places that feel good. There you will learn to ski.

TIPS & TALES: Learning

The classic horror story around ski schools is the boyfriend story. It goes like this. Boyfriend brings his girl skiing for the first time. He doesn't bother to enroll her in a beginner's class. He simply takes her up the lift to the top of the mountain. After all, this is how his friends taught him to ski. The terrified young lady, beyond tears, spends the rest of the day inching her way down the hill, or perhaps she just takes her skis off in disgust half way down and walks. If she has any brains, she never speaks to the boyfriend again.

If this is a worst-case scenario, what's the best way to learn to ski? The answer is there is no best way for everyone. First-time beginners should, as I've said, start in group ski lessons. But what about skiers who are beyond the beginner stage and want to improve, intermediates who want to break through to expert skiing, very good skiers who want to master a new medium, like ice, or moguls, or powder?

First, there are no shortcuts, no quick fixes. Many days and many miles on skis go into the making of a better skier. Quickie lessons, half-day, or even worse, one-hour private lessons, are usually less than useless. There simply isn't time in an hour or two to change old habits or ingrain new ones. So, if you really want to see a jump in your progress, consider a week of all-day lessons at a resort that features them, like Taos, New Mexico or Killington, Vermont. (All-inclusive ski weeks, with lessons topping the list, used to be the only

Positive imaging and mental practice have a lot to do with successful learning.

way families took ski vacations. Now, sadly, they are a rarity.)

One of the most intensive is the Vic Braden Ski College on Buttermilk Mountain in Aspen. Braden, of course, is the celebrated tennis coach, but here he has formulated a saturation ski course, primarily for weak skiers seeking to leap into the intermediate ranks. The fact is, anyone can benefit from the intense focus, repetition, video work, and encouragement.

Women skiers (some of them the resurgent victims of the boyfriend story) have made women's ski seminars popular. Started by Squaw Valley ski instructor Elisa Slanger in the mid-1970s, special women's multi-day courses have spread across the country. Based on the theory (certainly true some of the time) that women respond poorly to machismo in male-lead ski school classes (or husbands/boyfriends), these classes combine relaxation, stretching, video feedback, and gender support along with sound teaching basics to reach their goals.

With these or any similar multi-day clinics or

seminars (studies have shown adults do not like the idea of going to "school," even ski school), it's important for you to identify what kind of learner you are. Do you respond best to visual examples which you then try to replicate? Or are you primarily the intellectual type; must you understand, verbally, the skill to be learned first before you try it? Or are you the sort of person who learns best by trial and error, a doer rather than someone who puts the pieces together visually or intellectually? Most of us are combinations of all three. But one usually dominates, and if you know yourself and can communicate your needs to your instructor, he or she can tailor the exercises to your learning strengths.

Finally, keep in mind these three practice-time rules. Always work on new skills first where the skiing is easy for you. The brain cannot absorb new material—say, a parallel initiated turn—when it is concentrating on survival. After a while move to the terrain where you would ski most of the time and groove the new feelings—turn them into good habits*— with a lot of mileage.

Don't *work* on your skiing all the time. Skiing is play. Give yourself a break. Ski two or three fast-and-free runs for every one where you slow down and practice movements from a lesson.

Last but not least, whenever possible follow behind a better skier. Not off onto terrain that is too difficult for you, but over shapes that fit in your comfort zone. Follow close on your guru's tails, your track right on top of his or hers. Forget what you look like and what you are or aren't doing to make the turns, just lock in behind, match the track and let your leader sweep you down the slope. It's the sincerest form of flattery, and it's the fastest way improve your skiing.

3

Alpine: Intermediate

With today's sophisticated equipment, groomed slopes and teaching methods, most skiers can make the jump rather quickly from novice to the intermediate level. Turning becomes less intellectual and more instinctive. Speed increases. And a much bigger sweep of the mountain opens up for exploration. Intermediates begin to swoop and soar, to partake of the real freedom and expression of alpine skiing.

The same skills hold for all levels of skier: edging and steering the outside ski, and learning to balance on that ski through the full arc of the turn. That's it in a nutshell. Beginners do it at slow speeds on relatively gentle playgrounds using a wide stance or wedge. Intermediates use the same tools (somewhat refined from the first swiveling beginner turns) with more speed, more bravado, and on a wider scope of mountain shapes. Experts have mastered these basics to the point where they are second nature on any slope in any snow condition.

Being an intermediate is not an end in itself or a stop on the way to expertdom; it's a broadly defined phase, for lack of a better word, in what should be a continuous honing of these skills.

CONTROLLING THE TURN

A simple way to define an intermediate is one who skis comfortably the majority of "blue" marked runs at ski areas. Almost all ski areas in the U.S. have adopted the same difficulty rating system. Trails marked with a green circle are "easiest." Trails marked with a blue square are "more difficult." And "most difficult" trails are designated with a black diamond or two black diamonds. Double diamonds, they're called. And their names ring out like a litany of the steep: Spiral Stairs at Telluride, Goat and Starr at Stowe, Aspen's Bell Mountain. Intermediates often feel princely on green runs and bereft on double diamonds. Theirs is the vast landscape in between.

These color codes are relative designations within a given ski area. A blue run on Aspen Mountain, for example, may be steeper or otherwise more difficult than a blue run at Vail. It depends on the natural shapes they have to work with, the snow quality and amount, the ski area's clientele, and so on. But generally speaking,

A big mountain world opens up to intermediate skiers. *Tom Lippert*

wherever you are in this country you can gauge your comfort zone by color.

In Europe they have color codes too. But, unfortunately, they're not universal and the colors don't always mean the same thing. In Switzerland, for example, blue is easiest, red is intermediate and black is expert. France seems to be going to the U.S. system, but not at every resort. Read your trail map and ask questions if you have any doubts about what terrain is appropriate for your ability.

My definition of an intermediate is someone who is expanding his or her horizons (in terms of where on the mountain it's comfortable to ski) through controlling the shape of his turns. You need more than one arrow in your quiver. You need long, carved turns for gentler slopes and higher speeds. And you need to be able to call upon slower-speed, tighter-arc turns where the going is steeper, bumpier, or wherever the snow conditions merit. Occasionally you'll even need to throw your skis into a 90-degree skid, to avoid a sudden object or come to a quick stop. And in between, you want to be able to steer deftly through traffic, steer around small moguls, steer to slow down and steer to gain momentum—you want to begin, in other words, to play the terrain.

In order to develop this variety in the circumference of your arcs you will need to work on three groups of skills: edging skills, weight transfer skills, and rhythmic skills. Each of these, with the exception of rhythmic skills, was introduced at the earliest stages of beginnerhood. They will be with you to the Olympic team, if you get that far. And in addition, you'll need miles and miles on snow (the fun part) to develop the kind of judgment that tells you what arc is called for in a given terrain situation. I call this a sense of *line*.

This chapter will explore these four concepts and how to put them to work.

INTERMEDIATE EQUIPMENT

Good equipment can't make you a good skier. But poor equipment can hold you back. As I stated in the last chapter, beginner skis and boots are designed to make skidding, swiveling, slow-speed turns easy. This they do. But as you progress to higher speeds, steeper slopes, and different shapes of turns, a beginner ski can impede your learning. A better ski (and/or a better-fitting, better-performing boot) will bring more sophisticated capabilities to the task, match your growing skills.

Skis

Don't go looking for a full-bore race ski, even though that is what the best skiers in the world are riding on. You don't go learning to fly cast with a thousand-dollar carbon-fiber rod, and you don't learn to drive in an Indy car. Race skis are too stiff and demanding for most intermediates. It takes a lot of force (speed plus weight properly applied) to bend them. And if you can't bend them, they won't turn. (I once had the opportunity to flex a ski used by U.S. Olympian Phil Mahre. It felt like a 2X4. But then Phil's thighs are tree trunks, and he generates tremendous forces in his turns on a race course.) These skis are at the other end of the spectrum from too-soft beginner skis, and they too can put a damper on your learning pace and pleasure.

A good intermediate ski will initiate turns easily, will forgive you your minor balance mistakes, and will carve a turn for you when you are ready. (See Carving below.) Chances are it will be a soft slalom model (it may be called a "recreational" slalom or a "sport" model) in the $300 to $400 range. (Once again, list price is deceptive. You can probably get them on sale for at least $100 off.)

The slalom designation does not necessarily mean it is a race ski; it refers to the ski's shape. (Check the fall magazine buyer's guides or a specialty shop expert for advice on which slalom models are real race boards and which are "recreational" slaloms.) Generally speaking, slalom models come out of the narrowest molds and have the most pronounced side geometry (sidecut). They bend easily and turn quickly. Giant slalom models are made for longer turns and higher speeds. They are generally heavier and have a more stable feel.

Every manufacturer has at least one soft slalom in its line. Three that have been exceptionally popular and versatile are K2's TRC, Rossignol's Quantum series, and the Dynastar HPI. While these model names haven't changed for several years, they no doubt will in the future. Underneath, though, in construction and performance, their successors will likely be very similar.

All three of the above skis come with sintered bases, a feature that adds $10 to $20 to the price. It is well worth it. Sintered polyethylene bases are much tougher and faster than their extruded cousins. The higher molecular weight of the sintered base makes it much more resistant to rock gouges. They need less frequent tune-ups and glide better on the snow. Interestingly, the harder bases are also more porous. They will absorb much more wax, and deeper, than the softer extruded plastics. The only negative to this porosity is that the bases will dry out more readily during the summer months. It is necessary to keep them waxed (regular hot-waxing during the winter and one coat at the end of the season) in order to keep them from oxidizing.

Boots: Finding the Flex

The same boot-buying axiom holds true for intermediate/advanced skiers as for beginners: buy the best boot you can afford. Scrimping on the feet only leads to disappointment. The only caveat is to buy a boot that is appropriate for your size and strength. Lighter people need softer boots. Stronger people will be able to flex a stiffer boot than someone who skis more delicately. In that sense you could probably tie your DIN number, the release tension you require to stay in your bindings, to your boot flex. The higher the DIN, the stiffer the boot you should be shopping for. Unfortunately, boots don't come with a set of flex numbers.

If flexing the ankle is so important to a proper stance, why have stiff boots at all? For the same reason that Phil Mahre rides a stiff ski (and a stiff boot): he wants his every movement transmitted instantly and precisely to his ski. The boot is the (more or less) stiff link in that chain of command. We want our signals transmitted right now, with authority (stiffness). But at the same time, we need to remain supple enough atop the ski to ride comfortably and in balance over the terrain (flexibility). The trick is to find a boot that gives you enough of both.

Boots: The Fit Is It

Fortunately, there are zillions of models to choose from. Nordica, the number one boot company both in terms of models available and total boots sold worldwide, alone has dozens. Again, a boot fitter at a reputable specialty ski shop is your only hope. He or she can also steer you through the tangle of measurement systems out there: metric, French Mondo Point, English, Euro, men's and women's Brannock, and U.S. street shoe. It's a maze. So far, the industry's attempts to come up with a single system acceptable to all has only resulted in more new systems. You may use three or more of them in one sitting with your fitter.

Try on as many different boots as you possibly can. Take the time to get the best possible fit. And consider having some custom fit work done on the boot you do choose. Most people can benefit by custom work of one kind or another. Custom-molded footbeds can stabilize your foot inside the boot, solidifying the link between knees and skis (from Peterson Laboratories or Superfeet for about $130). *Canting* can solve certain edging problems brought about by bow legs or knock knees. Sore spots in an otherwise good-fitting boot can by solved by *sculpting* the inner boot or heating and reforming a spot on the shell. Conversely, sloppiness inside the boot—caused by petite ankles, for example—can be alleviated with additional *padding* in the right places.

Chances are a solid mid-range boot (which will sell for approximately two-thirds the price of your skis) will come with various performance adjustments (bells and whistles in current boot talk) built in. Most models now have uppers, or cuffs, with several forward lean positions to help you find your natural stance, whether it be nearly upright or more aggressively forward. (Everybody has a different natural stance, depending on his shape. The idea is to have your center of mass riding comfortably over the center of the ski. If the boot shaft is tilted farther forward your center of mass moves forward and vice versa.) There will also likely be forward flex adjusters, for a stiffer or softer feel; rear spoiler adjusters, to dial in how far back the boot will let you go; and side cant adjusters, to fine-tune for lower-leg alignment (knock knees, etc.). Less common are adjustable footbeds, to raise or lower your heel inside the boot.

All of this makes it possible to fine-tune the performance characteristics of your boot, not the fit. Go for the fit first, then the bells and whistles.

For a more complete discussion of the two main fit systems, variable and fixed-volume, see the equipment section of Chapter 2. Remember

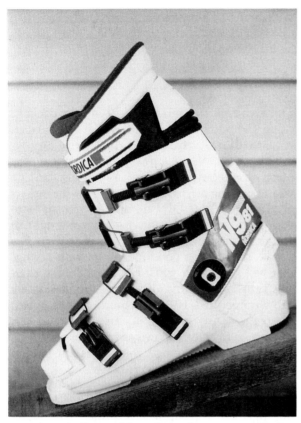

Overlap-shell/variable-volume boots are still the favorites of racers and expert skiers for their lower volume and better snow "feel."

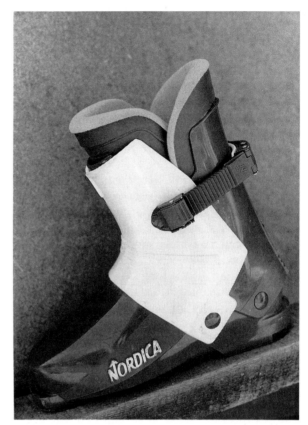

Rear-entry/fixed-volume boots are the favorites of occasional skiers for their comfort and ease of entry and exit.

that variable-volume, overlap-shell boots require a more careful initial fitting. Fixed-volume shells, with their internal straps and so on for holding the foot in place, are easier to fit and tend to work for a larger percentage of feet without further customizing.

More racers and top skiers still prefer overlap boots for their lower volume and closer "feel." But some rear-entry boots, most notably Salomon's pioneering efforts, have made steady inroads in performance characteristics, and have developed a loyal following. Rear-entry models are the overwhelming popular favorites with occasional skiers over the last decade due to their comfort and the ease with which they come off and on.

Women's Gear: Function or Fashion?

In recent years skis and boots targeted specifically at women have proliferated. The argument is made in industry literature that women are built differently than men, they ski differently than men do, and therefore they should have equipment designed specifically for them. There are two problems with this. One, are the assumptions correct? Do women really ski differently than men do? And, two, are the new skis and boots really different and/or better?

The answer to the first is, yes, women are certainly built differently than men, but, no, a competent woman skier is doing nothing differently to turn a ski than is her male counterpart. There is no evidence that a woman's wider hip structure or her slightly lower center of gravity (these are averages) dictate a different set of design criteria. Generally speaking, women are lighter than men, so it follows that most women should choose softer-flexing skis and boots. The women's skis on the market are soft-flexing, all-terrain, intermediate models with "feminine" paint jobs. The same ski, with a different top skin, no doubt appears in the recreational line as something else. Women's skis are, for the most part, a fashion statement.

The same is not true, or shouldn't be true, of women's boots. Women, on average, do have narrower feet than men, B width or narrower. If they wear high heels, their Achilles tendons are significantly shortened. And many women have a lower calf-muscle structure than men. Women's ski boots, then, should be built on narrower lasts with lower, wider cuffs than men's boots. Mostly, this is not the case. It costs so much money to tool up a new shell last that most manufacturers simply pad the liner of a soft-flexing mid-range boot and call it a women's model. And, of course, women's boots (like Model A Fords) come in any color you want, just as long as it's white.

Three companies do claim to have built their shells specifically for women's feet: Dachstein, Sanmarco, and Technica. Their boots are worth checking out.

All women's models are soft-flexing. This is fine for most intermediate and even some lightweight advanced skiers. But once a woman crosses over into the realm of the expert, women's boots just don't have enough gumption to meet their needs. These women have traditionally had no other choice than to try to find a fit in a men's high-performance boot.

Bindings

Once you go beyond the ski/binding package stage (which should be soon for any serious intermediate), you'll be faced with buying bindings separately. Don't panic. It's the simplest piece of equipment to buy. You really can't go wrong, as long as you choose one with the correct DIN range. Your DIN number will go up with your skill and speed. And with your weight, if you are still growing. Again, check the chart at the ski shop. It's a good idea to go with a range that will grow with you. For instance, the chart says your DIN now is a 5. Get a binding with a DIN range of 4-10. The binding works best when the spring is lightly compressed, and you have room to crank it down as you get better.

Other than DIN range, you are making fashion choices: color to match your boots and skis, or a brand name with which you identify for whatever reason. Does it make sense to use Marker bindings because the Mahre brothers do? Are

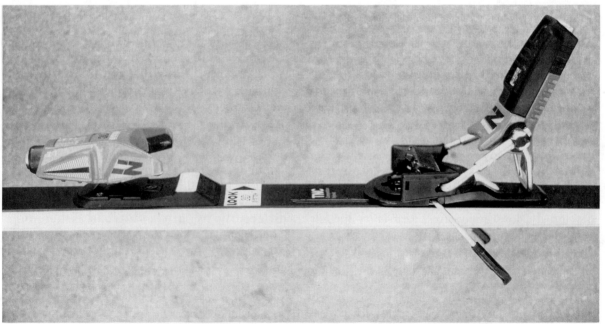

A modern turntable binding. Any binding will perform its dual function—that is, fixing you to the ski and setting you free of it under enough duress—only if the DIN is right for your size and ability.

Looks better because Olympic gold medalist Alberto Tomba uses them? Does Franz Klammer's name and his glorious gold-medal run in Innsbruck in 1976 mean that Tyrolia's are the best? No. Of course not. But this is the way the world works.

There is one functional difference in some binding heel units. (Toe pieces all work pretty much the same.) Everybody makes so-called step-in heels; two companies, Look and Marker, make a different kind of heel piece called a turntable. With turntables, the whole heel piece swivels in a lateral release. Some people think this makes for a smoother exit with less strain on the tibia. On the other hand, turntables must be cocked by hand before stepping back in. They suffer slightly on the convenience scale, but devotees consider them the safest bindings going.

Expect to pay about $150 for a set of mid-range bindings, $200 or more if you want die-cast aluminum housings, which are more durable and slightly more torsionally stable than Delrin (a DuPont plastic) housings.

INTERMEDIATE TECHNIQUE

We could no more do without edges than an ice skater could do without his blades or a wood-carver his chisel. They are the sharp link between skier and snow, the elegant curved tool, the direction adjusters, the brakes.

At one end of the performance spectrum, we want to learn to make the edges *carve*, to work the edges the way an engraver carves a line into a piece of soft wood. The opposite of carving is *skidding*, brushing the snow surface with our edges the way a knife smooths jam onto a piece of bread. It's still edging, just the flip side of the coin. Call it de-edging, or reducing the angle of the ski to the snow. With the one you are cutting a precise, circular arc. With the other you are skimming the snow sideways. Both are valuable tools. Most turns fall in the middle, employing some of each, carving and skidding. By trying for the extremes, we expand our range of options.

Carving: The Precision Tool

First, an experiment. Stand on a very gentle slope pointing down the fall line. Roll one knee to the inside, tipping that ski on edge. Weight this ski

Edge angle : Top, the skier is upright, the skis are relatively flat to the snow; this facilitates skidding. Below, the skier angles his knees and hips up slope to put the skis sharply on edge for carving. *Tom Lippert*

These curving lines (I call them sidecut turns) are simply the result of ski shape. Edge and weight your ski and it will etch a similar curved (not a straight) track. *Tom Lippert*

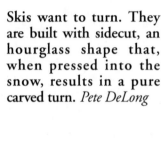

Skis want to turn. They are built with sidecut, an hourglass shape that, when pressed into the snow, results in a pure carved turn. *Pete DeLong*

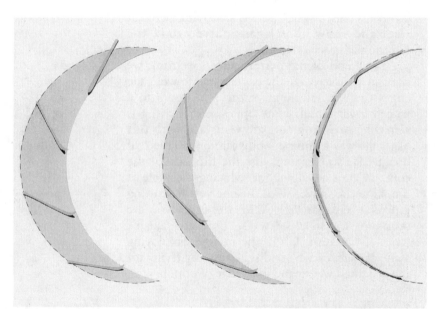

A carved turn (right) leaves a narrow track as the ski moves forward on its curved edge. A skidded turn (left) results when the ski is pivoted and the edge brushes sideways across the snow. Most turns are a blend of carving and skidding (middle). *Pete DeLong*

and glide slowly down the pitch. Your path will not be a straight line but a long curve etched on the snow by the built-in curved shape of the ski. In its purest form, this is carving. Every point on the edge has passed over the same point on the snow.

Skis want to carve because of this curved shape. Look at a ski. The tip is wider than the tail and both are wider than the waist. When this hourglass shape is pressed into the snow you get a turn. Built in. The more you bend the ski in a turn, the tighter becomes the arc. This is the ultimate turn racers are forever trying to engrave on steep race courses.

Sidecut Turns

Pure carved turns, or sidecut turns, as I call them, are very much within the realm of possibility for intermediate skiers. But they aren't very practical. (Neither does a racer achieve this kind of perfection very often in a race course.) With a radius of 80-100 feet, the sidecut turn just doesn't make sense for most turning situations. Most of the time we need to control speed and direction by adding skid to the ski's built-in turn. We pivot around the tips, the ski's edges wash across the direction of travel, leaving (if you can see your tracks in the snow) a broad swath where the pure sidecut turn left only a curving line.

Skidding isn't bad, as we shall see in the next section. But an unrelieved, undisciplined pivot-swivel turn is often the mark of a stalled intermediate, one who cannot seem to make the move to true expert skiing. Carving is the goal. Carving is the precision instrument.

Practice the sidecut turn whenever you can: on roads, across flat spots in the terrain, any place where you have lots of room and speed control isn't a factor. As a pure exercise it develops your edging skills, the movement of your knee and ankle rolling the ski up on its inside edge. It also develops balance. To stay balanced over a long, continuous arc like this takes real concentration and practice. You'll find in the beginning that balance shifts back and forth between your feet. Notice that when the weight shifts over to the inside leg, the curving action stops, the ski goes straight. You need weight on that inside edge for the sidecut to turn you. Keeping the weight there continuously is an acquired talent.

You'll find as you get more adept at etching sidecut turns that you'll use them more and more often. I find it unstable, for instance, to schuss straight down almost any hill—no matter how short the pitch or how reassuring the runout below—unless I am edging one ski or the other. By edging the ski and standing against it, there is none of the wobble, none of the precariousness of schussing with the skis flat to the snow. Flat skis at high speed are susceptible to deflection, from "snow snakes," lumps in the snow, any irregularities in your path. But an edged ski, slicing along its sidecut path provides a stability, a surety that makes higher-speed cruising a comfortable feeling.

Carving Exercise 1: The Crab Walk

So now how do you incorporate this carving, this strong edging into your turns? One thing to keep in mind is that it is much easier to add skidding to a carved turn than it is to add carving to a turn that is already substantially pivoted. In other words, it's much easier to feather your edges mid-turn and soften their grip on the snow than it is to do the opposite. So, all else being equal, think about starting your turns with strong edging, then, if you need to tighten the radius through skidding, you can.

Interestingly enough, one of the best ways to practice the feel of carving is in wedge turns. There's nothing retrograde about wedging! Racers do this exercise all the time. They call it the "crab walk."

Start down a gentle grade in a wedge, both legs flexed at the knees and ankles. Edge one ski strongly—let's say the left—so that it cannot skid at all but instead follows its own cut groove in the snow (essentially a sidecut turn). The right ski is brushing the snow in a skid. (It obviously wouldn't work to have both skis strongly edged in opposing directions.)

Now switch actions. Relax the edge hold on the left ski and dig in with the right. You'll find you are controlling the action with your knees. You drop one knee to the inside to edge while you push the other knee out over the ski to reduce its angle relative to the snow.

Do the crab walk at slow speed. You'll find that switching the edging emphasis from left to right and back again, results in rather dramatic changes in direction. The strongly edged ski carries the day. The side-to-side motion feels the way a crab must feel, darting, darting, more sideways than forward. The more abrupt the shift, the more instantaneous the direction change. At greater than walking speed, it's hard to ride in balance between the direction changes, so keep it slow. (Back in the early 1940s, some powder skiers, most notably Alta's Dick Durrance, used a similar technique for skiing the deep snows. They called it the Dipsy Doodle because of its bounding, acrobatic look. One observer described Durrance's body as bouncing back and forth between his wedged skis "like a ping pong ball.")

Besides getting your juices flowing at the top of a run, the crab walk develops strong knee action, both abduction (to the outside of the body's centerline) and adduction (to the inside), the key skill in learning to carve. And you begin to develop a feel for the skis's response to your edging, and de-edging. Beyond these, it's fun being a ping pong ball now and then.

Carving Exercise 2: Carved Wedges

While the crab walk may seem to be a pure exercise with no direct application to your skiing, it can in fact lead to very practical new control. By changing your emphasis slightly, from hard edging and abrupt, straight-line direction changes, to smoother, more rounded turns, you gain valuable carving experience.

Again in a wedge, and again at slow speeds— but this time on a little steeper pitch than the pure crab walk—pressure the left ski and steer it into a turn. Think of the ski tip biting into the snow and leading the way into the turn. You can increase the tip's natural tendency to do this by actively applying pressure forward, by flexing at the ankle and pressing your shin against the front of your boot. The boot/lever transfers this effort to the front of the ski. Thus pressured and edged, the tip begins a carve to the right. Keep the pressure on and the ski well edged, and you have—not just any old snowplow turn—but an aggressively carved wedge turn. A big difference.

The carved wedge turn feels crisper, more precise, comes around sooner and surer. If you can see your track, you'll see that the carving ski leaves a narrow crescent gouged in the snow. The other ski, the drifting, unweighted one, leaves no mark at all.

Try it on the other side, driving the right ski,

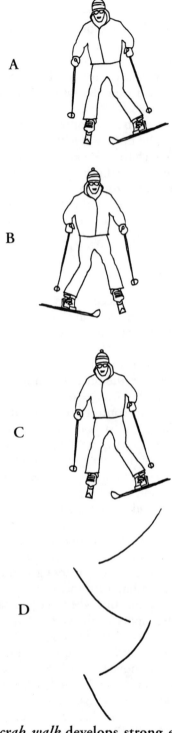

The *crab walk* develops strong edging skills. This skier carves the left ski (A) by moving the left knee in and tilting the ski way up on edge, while the right ski skids across the snow. Then he switches legs (B), carving on the right, and then back again on the left (C). The edge ski will leave sharply etched lines in the snow as in drawing D.

pressure forward at the outset, into a well-edged arc. Once the ski begins to turn, strong edging makes it "hold," where not enough edging (or too much de-edging, however you like to think of it) would result in the ski skidding out in a softer, wider arc. Try to feel the ski bend under your weight. Try to keep pressure on the center of the ski until the arc is complete and you either come to a stop or you are ready to change feet and change direction. Keeping the pressure on is a matter of refining your balance so that you can stand on one foot at a time through the full arc of the turn. I'll come back to this again and again—most specifically in the section on weight transfer in this chapter—but it can't be overemphasized: *good skiing is like loping down a hill, we balance on one leg at a time, controlling direction and speed, one foot, one leg, one ski at a time.*

Link these slicing, carving wedge turns together, one right after the other: left foot, right foot, left foot. Each turn should be a clean crescent moon. Vary the the radii. Try them in short crisp bursts, like clipping down a long stairway, one you have known for years. Look well ahead and project your momentum out in front of your feet. This is always important. Stand straight and relaxed, head up, eyes forward. If you find yourself hunched over and watching your feet, the effort, while well-intended, is somewhat wasted. Good balance, and therefore quickness and precision, flows from an erect stance, eyes roaming the terrain ahead.

Try carving longer turns from a wedge too. You'll find the wedge itself, the displacement of your ski tails to the side, will be smaller; you don't need a large head start for the direction change. On longer turns, the pressure is applied more subtly and over longer duration, and the steering, or twisting, will be muted. No desire here to crank the skis around sharply.

Lengthen your turns enough—and you are back to the sidecut turn we talked about earlier, where the curve of the ski, weighted and edged in the snow, is all you need to effect a turn. Stay balanced and the ski does all of the work.

Be sure to match the terrain to the shape of your turns. Practice side cut turns and longer wedge turns on open, relatively gentle pitches where you have room for big arcs and where you won't acquire too much velocity. Try the shorter radius carved wedges where it's steeper, where speed control is necessary and where gravity will

help you feel the edge biting in, scooping out the turns. Finally, try these turns around slalom poles, known as gates, if you get the chance. Gates do one thing; they force you to turn here, turn here, turn here. The added discipline, and often the additional effort required to "make" the gates (get around each one in order), can do wonders for a slow day or a seemingly stagnant progression.

Carving Exercise 3: Garlands

Some people will be able to make a seamless transition from carved turns in a wedge position to carving without a wedge. Skiing parallel, in other words. It's a short step from balancing on one ski through a long radius wedge turn to balancing on that same ski in a parallel stance. The ideal progression would seek to gradually reduce the wedge angle in all turns until it vanished and you were simply stepping from one carving ski to the next, one inside edge to the next. That's the ideal.

In practice there's often a useful intermediate step, and that is doing carved-turn garlands. These are exercises that strengthen the carved finish of your turns, leading, by increments, to full carved initiations. The term garland comes, I believe, from the scalloped tracks the exercises leave on the snow. You start with shallow arcs across the fall line and gradually progress to more and more complete arcs (bigger sections of the circle), closer and closer to the fall line. And finally to full turns (full half-circles) across the fall line.

The ideal terrain for a set of garlands is a long sidehill—the side of a gully, for example, or any prolonged side slope—where you can link a series of partial turns all in the same direction. Begin with the barest finish of a turn. From a shallow traverse, skis parallel and about hip-width apart, pressure and steer the downhill ski (let's say it's the left one) into a turn to stop. Like the carved wedge turns, try to feel the ski tip leading the way, drawing the rest of the ski along in its path. Flex at the ankle and press lightly into the tongue of your left boot to weight the inside edge at the tip.

Try another right turn, this time from a slightly steeper traverse. Pressure and edge the turning ski, still the left one, while the uphill ski glides along on its matching edge (remember matching?) supporting little or no weight. Edge aggressively and feel the ski hook around in a clean, carved arc. Do it to a stop each time. Don't worry about linking turns just yet.

As your traverses get closer and closer to the fall line, you will be carving an ever larger section of the theoretical semicircle. (Think of a pure carved turn as scribing a 180° half circle on the snow.) Start tall, weight centered over the full length of both feet, big toe to heel. Flex at the ankles, pressing into the left boot tongue, weighting that ski exclusively. *Drive* that ski— as opposed to thrusting it sideways or pivoting it— through the partial circle. In this way carved turns take advantage of the tendency of skis (very much the point of ski design) to go forward on a curved path rather than rake the snow crossways.

The beauty of the garlands is that you can focus on just the one ski at a time. The other one is just there, just in case, a kind of matching outrigger, but not a factor at all in the controlling arc. Also, you're not changing your edge to initiate the turn. All the action takes place on the same set of edges. Try to build up to the point where you can balance the full arc on the outside ski.

When you have worked a series of garlands on both sides, right and left, so that you can carve them from a start right in the fall line, it's time to try it from across the fall line, a full turn so called, because in the process you *change* edges from one set to another. Terrain selection is very important here. As I mentioned in the last chapter on basic parallel turns, a roll or fallaway is a good place to start. As the pitch drops away beneath you, the edge change is made simple, almost automatic.

Picture it this way. You have just completed a turn to the right. Your weight is solidly on the right edge of your left ski. You drop over the roll, shifting weight as you go to the right ski, the new outside ski. You flex at the ankle, edge and press the right ski into its natural curve. The only difference between this and the partial-curves in the garland exercise is the changing of the edge, the rolling of the knee, in this case the right one, from one side of the ski across to the other side.

Of course, there is also the fact that you made a *weight transfer*, from the left foot to the right. That's the other element in a complete turn. Edge change and weight transfer. But for the moment let's just concentrate on the edging. In the garland, it's the edging, and properly applied

pressure, that results in a carved arc. Generally speaking, the more edge, the tighter will be the resulting turn. Less edge and the turn shape will be longer. In the wedge turns, too, it's the edging and pressure we use to make the ski work. (In wedge turns, by definition, there is no change of edge; both inside edges are already slightly engaged and ready to go.) We'll get to initiations (the various ways to bring about weight transfer) later in this chapter. What I'm most interested in at this juncture is how you make the ski work on the snow, on developing that good carving action through the control phase of the turn.

Carving Exercise 4: School Figures

The international body governing figure skating recently did away with the school figures part of each competition. This is a shame. Although television didn't consider the slow, precise, almost dowdy etching of circles on the ice to be exciting enough to show its audiences, I loved the few glimpses I have had. The skating was reduced to its most basic elements. Flash counted for nothing. The skaters wore no sequins, just their warm-up togs, like dancers in rehearsal. The only things that mattered were the marks on the ice: how exactly the contestants drew the prescribed figures, how symmetrical were their circles, how clean their lines, how close to mythical perfection they were able to come. The ones who were good at it showed exquisite slow-speed balance and the ability to direct their momentum in smooth, sinuous arcs.

They were craftsmen in the way that I believe skiers need to become craftsmen, to use the tools on their feet as those tools were designed to be used. It's this kind of craftsmanship, and not a quick tip from a private instructor or the mastering of the current "in" technique, that will lead intermediate skiers into the realm of the experts.

One of the best exercises for developing the carving craft feels the way I imagine the skaters felt doing their school figures. It involves, quite simply, scribing very long turns at very slow speeds. Find an open patch of nearly flat terrain. (You can do this where the hill is pitched up a little steeper as well, but it is harder, and better for you, on the near-flat where momentum is not a factor in helping you balance.) I like to do this

"Drive wiz zee hips" is the key to balance, French great Jean-Claude Killy once said. With head up, hands out front and hips directly over your feet, you are in control of the arc. *Tom Lippert*

right off the top of the chair lift, if the terrain is right and not busy with bodies.

At not much more than walking pace, begin a turn to the left. The only point of this turn is to draw a round line. Balance as completely as possible on the right foot and eke the turn around, ever so slowly until there is little momentum left to carry you. Immediately begin the same action on the left foot and ski. Take care not to pivot the ski on the snow. Stand on it, and apply, as subtly as you can, the steering forces you've practiced up to this point. The object here is not to *make* a turn but to walk a long (as excruciating and delicate as you can make it), curving tightrope.

Draw it out as long as you can, then repeat the mirror image on your right side. At first you may find it hard to balance all the way around on one foot. You may find your balance shifting from the outside foot to inside and back again. That's okay. Just remember the goal is to develop your balance to the point where you can stand on that one turning edge for the entire hemicycle. Stand

upright over your feet. Keep your hands out in front of your hips. And most important, keep ankles flexed so that your hips stay centered over your feet.

This is the key to all balance. The great French racer Jean-Claude Killy once gave a tip to a visiting journalist: "Drive wiz zee hips," he said, and the message stuck with me. Drive with the hips. If your hips are right over your feet, the pressure of your combined weight and your centrifugal force flows directly to the center of the ski. You are in control of its arc, driving the ski. If, however, your hips are over your heel or behind your foot altogether, the pressure is on the back of the ski, you are "in the backseat," as they say, and driving the ski becomes a more difficult and a more exhausting task. More exhausting because in this position you are no longer held upright primarily by your skeleton but by the large muscles in your thighs.

Of course, every part of the body contributes to its overall balance. Hips are absolutely essential. Hands and eyes are keys as well. Keeping the hands out front is one very good trick to keeping the hips forward. As skis accelerate down the hill, hands leading the way down slope help to counter the natural tendency to shy back on the heels. Head up and eyes forward is another balancer. A lot of people seem intent on following the action of their feet, as if they could possibly get away. Their bowed heads and small-world focus limits not only their balance but their sense of the terrain at large, their ability to project themselves over and through that landscape. In other words, it seriously reduces their sense of *line*.

Carving and Line: Playing the Terrain

The most important epiphany in my skiing life involved the notion of line, or the path one takes down the mountain. It happened when I was following a superior skier, a woman who would later become my wife but who, at that time, was first and foremost a teacher by example. Following close on Ellen's trail through changing terrain forced me to see the mountain through different eyes. Where I had been straining to make perfect turns without regard for the shapes underfoot, she sublimated her efforts to the natural design before us. Where the shapes were round and serpentine, she drew soft, round arcs. Where the hill dropped away suddenly, she went with it, spreading her arms like wings in acceptance of the gift of flight. Where the slope was convex, like the insides of a dish, she stood tall and leaned against the sides like a surfer and let the banks swing *her* around. Here was the art I'd suspected but never understood.

Everyone's sense of line will be different. It's a function of character and mood as well as the givens on the mountain: the shapes, the quality and consistency of the snow, the traffic, and so on. The idea is for you to use the terrain instead of letting it use you. Begin direction changes on fall-away forms, where friction is reduced. Control speed by controlling the shape of your turns, short-radius, semicircular arcs where it is steep, long-radius, open crescents where there is no need to hold on. Shoot up a steep bank to dissipate some of your speed instead of throwing on the brakes. Use the spoon-shaped troughs between moguls to jet around the corner (like banking a turn on a bobsled course) instead of making a turn. Play the terrain.

An awareness of line is the best antidote for the number one trap in skiing: obsession with The Turn. Doing it Right. Getting it down Right. Thinking that by somehow mastering the details of The Turn, all else will fall into place. (It might be a ski instructor's perfect turn that you saw, or one of Stein Eriksen's stylish feet-together sweepers, or just some vague image of grace or beauty.) This is unfortunately common and self-deceptive thinking. There is no Turn. Exploit the terrain harmoniously and creatively, and the turns will take care of themselves.

The best way to learn about line is to shadow a good skier, your track on top of his (or hers). Ski smooth but variable terrain in which you feel comfortable, not overly challenged. Forget what the bodies are doing, and concentrate instead on what your leader sees, where he goes, and how he gets there. Thereafter, at the top of each run, imagine your line through the first turns. Picture it exactly. Take the time to let it sink in. Racers memorize every gate on a racecourse, sometimes as many as sixty turns, before they run it. Sometimes you'll see them at the start or on a chair lift heading for the start, with eyes closed tracing wavy lines in the air with their hands. They're preplaying every turn, the short and quick, the long and hard, in sequence in their minds. We can't often, nor do we need to do this. Spontaneity and reacting to what we see is part of the fun of a ski run. But imaging is a powerful learning tool. Start each run with a few well-imaged turns and the rest of the trip will be more enjoyable. You have to be able to see it before you can do it.

Skidding: Learning to Let Go

Skidding is the opposite of carving, the soft caress as opposed to the knife edge. Skidding is letting go of one's hold on the snow in order to gain a different kind of control.

Ski instructors across the land occasionally needle each other with the rhetorical question, "Are you skidding me?" Turning the skis sideways has gotten a bad rap in the past because ski pros, like the top racers they were emulating, were doing their darndest to achieve better carving action in their turns. The best skiers, it appeared, were trying mightily to *eliminate* skidding from their turns. If carving was the most precise, the most accurate and fastest way to ski, then skidding was the bad guy. Right?

Wrong. Skidding is just as important a tool as carving. When the great racers come to a stop in the finish area, throwing geysers of snow into the air as they go from sixty mph to zero in three seconds, what are they doing? Skidding. When a good skier adjusts his line mid-turn to miss a rock or drop below a misshapen mogul or a patch of ice, what is he doing? Skidding. No one can carve all the time. Slipping sideways comes in handy in traffic, where it is the most effective way to scrub off speed. It's essential on steep slopes where pure carving would lead to big arcs and excessive velocity. And it's an important part of good powder technique where slipping through the resistance is as important as pushing against it. Besides, slipping is fun. When you know how to skid efficiently you have more tricks in your bag. When you don't feel like an engraver, you can give

Sideslip position: **skis perpendicular to the fall line, edges set into the hill, hips and hands and shoulders facing down the hill in anticipation of the movement. By rolling the knees down the hill, the edges will release and sideslipping commence.** *Tom Lippert*

the mountain a gentle shave.

Everyone should seek to master both skills, carving and skidding. They are not mutually exclusive. In fact, there is skidding in every turn, except one, the pure sidecut turn. If the sidecut turn is pure carving, then pure skidding would have to be a straight sideslip, skis at right angles to the direction of travel, your path marked by a swath exactly as wide as your skis are long. Every other turn results from a combination of forward movement along the curved edge (carving) and sideways displacement (skidding). How you mix these elements will determine the shape of the arc you lay down.

Skidding Exercise 1: Sideslip

This is the classic edge control exercise, and it hasn't been improved upon, really, for fifty years. Pick a smooth, steep patch of snow off to the side of a trail and stand skis perpendicular to the fall line. Your edge angle, the tilt of your skis relative to the slope, is what keeps you from slipping down the hill. Your edges are set. Now, gradually, soften that edgehold by rolling your knees downhill. When the skis begin to sideslip, set the edges again and stop. Repeat the sequence. Roll your knees down slope, feel the skis begin to slip, and reset your edges to stop.

Gradually extend the length of your slip. You want to be able to balance comfortably over your feet—and stay in balance—as you move sideways. If the slipping comes in jerks and starts, and weight shifts back and forth from one foot to the other, consider this about stance. Rather than standing square to your skis—that is, hips and hands and shoulders facing the ski tips as you would do in a straight run—try turning slightly and facing the direction of travel, down the fall line. Give the uphill ski a slight lead on the downhill ski, say half a boot length. This will turn your hips slightly toward the fall line (and keep the uphill ski from crossing over the downhill one). Now turn your shoulders and hands, and most important, your head to the direction you will be slipping. Flex normally at the ankles and knees. Now slowly release your edges and slip. In this position it should be much easier to both control the edging and stay in balance over the slipping skis.

This position, with the upper body turned slightly out of line with the skis, is called anticipation. It is a key concept in rhythmic skiing, in linking one turn—especially short, quick turns—to the next. In sideslipping exercises an anticipated position is primarily a balance tool, a way to keep the body's center of mass in dynamic balance over the feet, which, as you will have felt, are trying to slip out from under you down the hill.

Troubleshooting

Suppose your skis behave independently. The downhill ski begins to sideslip, but the uphill ski stays put creating an awkward straddle. To correct this, bring your skis fairly close together at the outset, no more than hip width. Stand as you would in any turn, with 95-100 percent of your weight on the downhill ski. Assume the anticipated, downhill-facing position. Now as you roll your knees to flatten the edge be sure the uphill knee matches the motion of the downhill knee. Both skis should release and slide together. Similarly, when you set the edges again, your knees should be moving in concert.

Another problem: try as you might, you can't seem to sideslip straight down the fall line; your path is always to one side or the other. You'll find, in this instance, that your weight is slightly fore or aft of center, either the tips or the tails of your skis are leading the way. This is not a problem so much as a challenge to your centering skills. Center your weight between your big toe and heel—experiment—and you'll find that place where you can keep the skis perpendicular to the fall line and moving straight down it.

Skidding Exercise 2: Falling Leaf

You can use this fore/aft balance experiment in another, delightful way, in an exercise I call the Falling Leaf. As you sideslip, purposely apply pressure forward in your boot and steer the skis uphill to a stop. Just as you are about to stop, shift your weight back to neutral and let the skis describe a similar arc backwards, also to a stop. With your tips now pointed down the pitch, begin the sequence again: sideslip forward; steer up to a stop; sideslip backward; steer up to a stop. Once you get the hang of the pendulum motion, your arcs will have a lilting, rolling feel, like that of a dried leaf rocking down the air on a still fall day.

Do this on both sides, of course. And mix in a lot of skiing between sessions. Look for steep pitches to do your sideslipping; you'll find it's quite difficult to slip at slow speed on a flat or gently tilting plane.

Skidding Exercise 3: Hockey Stop

One way you can skim over flat or near flat terrain is to use the technique called the hockey stop. You've seen skaters throw their blades sideways and skid to a halt. This is the same braking maneuver ski racers use, in a plume of spray of their own making, to slow down after the finish banner. And the same one skiers of all stripes have used for decades to show their style and playfulness. While I'm not recommending zooming down and spraying your friends, I do recommend the technique, properly done, as a great way to fine tune your edge control.

Pick an open slope, gather some speed in the fall line, then throw your skis across your direction of travel and skid to a stop. Try to keep the skid going in a straight line (fore and aft centering) and try to maintain dynamic balance through the stop and beyond. Anticipation is the key to achieving both.

A strong sinking motion at the outset will lighten the skis and aid the pivot out of the fall line. But be sure to keep your upper body (use your outstretched hands as indicators) facing the direction of travel, while the legs and skis twist. Just as it does in the passive sideslip on steeper terrain, the anticipated position helps you to steer your skid and to stay balanced over your feet. Too often, the ending to a dramatic hockey stop is an anticlimactic tipping over into the hill. The skier is leaning in to get the edge angle he needs to stop, but he's way out of balance when the motion does cease. In an anticipated position, you can edge with your knees and stay in trim right through the stop, the way a tennis player always returns to a neutral ready position.

Carving and Skidding

Remember that carving and skidding are both forms of edge control, two ends of the same spectrum. Neither should be coveted at the expense of the other. Both are invaluable skills.

Try making some runs with your primary aim

to carve the cleanest, sharpest lines you can. Engrave the snowy shapes with arcs that most closely resemble the curved shape of the ski itself. Put the ski well over on its side and try to eliminate all traces of pivot/skid from your turns. Then take other runs where you attempt to keep your skis as nearly flat to the snow surface as you can. Skim the snow as if you were edgeless. Swivel the skis where you can. Let the shapes pull you where they will. Ride sideways, backwards, like a falling leaf. Both ways have their pure satisfactions. Both will teach you edge control, and add tricks to your quiver for down the road.

WEIGHT TRANSFER

The difference between an intermediate who has stopped progressing, who has "plateaued out," and the ever-improving advanced skier is the ability of the latter to stand on one foot at a time. Yes, we've got two legs, most of us, and two skis, but in fact, good skiers are using only one at a time. Some theoreticians have gone so far as to boil successful skiing down to a formula like this: Stand in balance; stand on the inside edge of the outside ski. Simple.

It's not quite that simple, but almost. We know that that one edge, the inside edge of the outside ski, is the one that turns us. And we know that balancing on that edge, from the beginning of the turn to the end, is the surest way to control the arc, the speed, and therefore our line down the hill. It follows then that the one thing we absolutely have to do in order to change direction is transfer weight from one turning edge to the other.

Volumes have been written about the various ways to accomplish this. You have your stem initiations, your steps, your divergent steps, your skate and your parallel initiations. Every one of them has as its object the same core result: the efficacious transfer of weight from one ski to the other.

People mistakenly assume that parallel initiations are the goal of good skiers. True, good skiers more often than not begin their turns with parallel and (perhaps more accurately) simultaneous leg movements, but good skiers use all the tricks at their disposal. They may step to gain a higher line, skate through traffic, stem on a narrow road or to test the snow on the first run of the day.

Parallel initiations happen to be the easiest in a variety of modern conditions, particularly on groomed and packed slopes. Parallel initiations require the least active movement on the skier's part. But don't be fooled into thinking that graceful parallel technique is two-legged skiing. It isn't. Even with the legs and feet close together, the parallel skier is turning, and balancing, on just one leg at a time. That the other ski nestles in close (as in the stylish skiing of Stein Eriksen and others) is a matter of ease and style. In a sound turn the inside ski bears no weight at all.

Herewith, then, a compendium of different ways to effect the necessary weight transfer:

Initiation 1: Parallel

I'll start with this one because it is easy, and because too many old schools put it at the end, where it seems unreachable.

Appropriate terrain is always important; practice parallel initiations where you feel comfortable, preferably on rolling terrain where fallaway shapes can aid your direction changes.

Begin, not with a complete turn across the fall line, but with a half turn, the second half. From a steep traverse steer into an arc as if doing garlands. Try to time the turn so that you'll complete the arc at the top of a convex terrain feature, a knoll or bump. Remember to center your weight over the outside ski and to edge it by driving the knee forward and toward the center of the arc.

Now, at the top of the bump, stand up a little straighter, relax the edges, and STEP TO THE OTHER SKI. Commit to it. Stand on it. Now steer (edge and pressure with a little twisting) that ski through a full semicircle. Stand tall and square to your skis. Keep your head up and look for another roll. When you get there (sliding over the top and down momentarily lightens the load on the skis making it easier to change edges) simply step to the new ski, roll it on edge, and away you go.

This is an elegant medium-to-long radius turn. It takes time to unfold, but most groomed-slope skiing gives you the time and the space. The keys are good steering skills and good balance on the controlling ski. The most common problem is not with the initiation, with getting started into the turn, but with maintaining balance once

A

B

Use a parallel initiation when the terrain is fluid and easy. The weight transfer occurs at *B.* From there through the end of the turn, it's a matter of steering (edging, weighting, and twisting) that one ski. Note that the skier starts tall, transfers his weight to the left ski, then drives through the arc, flexing ankles, knees, and hips through the control phase of the turn. *Tom Lippert*

C

D

E

A

B

Use a step initiation to change your line in a race course, to step around obstacles, or to move quickly from edge to edge. The skier takes a lateral, parallel step (B) to initiate the turn. Balanced on the new outside ski, he steers through the control phase (C and D) and gets ready to step again (E). *Tom Lippert*

C

D

E

A

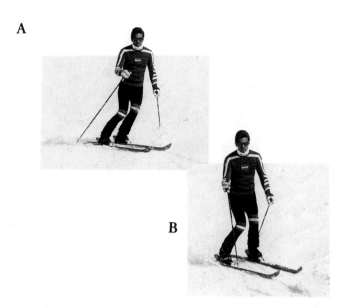

B

Use a stem initiation when testing snow conditions, when you're feeling cautious, or when you want to ski slowly. By pivoting and edging the outside ski (B and C) before weighting it (D and E), the skier achieves a head start to a sure direction change. *Tom Lippert*

C

D

E

you've stepped to the new turning ski. Turns start off okay but have jerky, straight-line patches where balance shifts to the inside foot and back again. Fallaway initiations will help. A good exercise is to pick the inside ski up off the ground as soon as you change feet and try to hold it there through the full arc. You'll see racers doing this while they're free skiing. It's a kind of visceral habit to reinforce the one-footed truth of carving turns. Do it where you can stretch your turns out long and slow. Soon your balance will grow to match your arcs.

Initiation 2: Step

Sometimes you'll see a skier begin a turn with a parallel step to the side, a slight variation on the basic parallel initiation. He may be stepping around an obstacle, stepping to gain a longer line, or stepping to more instantly place his body mass to the inside of the arc. You may see skiers step directly to the new turning edge or step up on the outside edge then roll the ski over onto the new turning edge.

Stepping is as old as the Dipsy Doodle, as practiced by Durrance and the Engen brothers in the '30s and '40s, and as new as the newest racing theories. The point of it is to gain a new line or a new balance where the basic parallel turn won't give it to you, or won't give it to you fast enough.

The two most useful applications are these. When you need to lengthen your line or start the turn a little higher, step up to the outside edge, find your balance, and steer into the turn. When you need to tighten your line, to start the turn a little quicker (because of traffic or the trail edge is coming up or because you're just slightly out of balance at the finish of the previous turn), step to the inside edge of the new ski. This kind of initiation can be extremely quick and positive. There is no gap at all between the strong edging at the end of one turn and strong edging beginning the next. Slalom racers, who are the quickest of the quick, darting around close-set red and blue poles, often use this technique. Seen from the front, their feet appear to be controlled popcorn, popping back and forth from one foot, one edge, to the other.

I also use the step initiation on one of my favorite mountain shapes, the dish-sided bowl or gully. There's one at most ski areas. Spar Gulch at Aspen is a classic. It's basically a creek bed, widened and smoothed, with high, concave sides that invite sweeping roller-coaster turns up one side and down, then up the other. The initiation takes place at the top of each sweep, with momentum fading and a long way to go to reach the fall line again. I find that stepping directly to the new inside edge guarantees my balance on the high banked sides.

Initiation 3: Stem

Even surer than the step initiation is the stem. In this case you transfer weight to a ski which is both tilted onto the new edge *and* rotated slightly into the new direction. By pivoting the outside ski and edging it, *then* stepping on it, you get an instant, sure reaction in the direction you want to go.

It used to be the stem was the first initiation taught to advancing novices. It has the obvious connection to the wedge turns most of us started with. But it had the drawback that many intermediates found it hard to break the stem habit, to learn other initiations including parallel. The stem developed a stigma.

It shouldn't have. The best skiers in the world stem, when they need a near-instant direction change, when they need a wide, sure-fire stance from which to test snow consistency or stability. Mogul skiers stem to place their skis just so in the troughs between the bumps. Patrollers stem when they are bringing a sled behind them down the hill. Ski instructors stem when threading a line of slower skiers on a catwalk. The stem is basic and nothing to be ashamed of.

Use it like this. At the completion of one turn, pivot the new outside ski (never both; a stem is not a braking maneuver) in the direction you will be going; a stem is like a head start toward the fall line. There is no weight on this ski, so the displacement should be easy. Slide just the tail away from you , then transfer all of your weight to the new turning ski, match edges, and steer through a normal control phase. Simple.

Of the three initiations, the stem is the oldest, going back at least a century to the stem cristiania. It is also the most conservative. Use it when you feel cautious or unsure of what's coming next. Use it at slow and medium speeds. At high speeds, the displacing of the ski and the instant direction change can be disruptive to both balance and line.

All three initiations serve to transfer your weight from one turning ski to the other. Stems and steps have a broader balance base, but they require more active movements on the skier's part than the parallel turn does. The parallel initiation is the subtlest, the most efficient in many instances. Thus its universality on the slopes. One of skiing's cardinal rules is to conserve energy, to never do more than you have to. As Alta pioneer Alf Engen put it: "When you ski down you're going to use as little strength as possible. I skied very loooose. [The Norwegian ooo sound is long and multi-syllabled, like cream pouring.] I wouldn't even hold my poles tight. Looose and easy. Looose as a gooose. Ya! That's the way to ski well."

Initiation Exercise 1: The Stork

I've already mentioned the one-legged turns, where you pick up the inside ski and hold it up and close-in, for the full arc of the turn. You can do other exercises to increase one-footed balance. Try traversing on one foot, flamingo-like, first the downhill foot as long as you can go, then the uphill foot. In some ways this is harder than balancing on one edge in a turn because you don't have the centrifugal force of the turn to lean against.

Initiation Exercise 2: The Skate

Probably the single best exercise for improving balance and edging skills (and therefore making all initiations more efficient) is the skate. Skate on skis whenever and wherever you can. It's fun, it's habit forming, it's very much like roller or ice skating, and it develops independent leg action and balance better than anything else I know.

Begin by skating on the flat. (Think of it as a gliding herringbone.) Push off a well-edged ski; a too-flat ski will slip away, it will not create the platform you need to spring from. Push off to the side onto the other foot. Glide as far as you can on that foot (a flat ski glides best), then edge it (flexed knee to the inside) and push off back the other way. Push off a well-edged platform, glide on a flat ski. Start with small motions and work up to bigger and bigger ones. Maximize the glide by bringing the unweighted ski in close (again, like the flamingo). Then, as momentum slows, point it off to the side (make a V of between 45

and 70 degrees), edge and stride off on the new ski. (For a more in-depth look at skating, see Chapter 6: Track Skiing, in the cross-country section of this book. The equipment is a little different, but the movements and the balance are very much the same.)

When you feel comfortable on the flat, try skating up hills, to the lift or to the lodge or back up to help a friend or to retrieve a lost pole. Uphill skating is a little tougher, but it will further refine your push-off and glide.

Finally, skate while skiing downhill, not on a steep downhill but on something mellow and rolling. It may seem redundant with gravity already doing the lion's share of the work. In fact, it may even be a little scary as you accelerate from push to push. But it is exquisite practice. Here you are refining one-legged balance at real skiing speeds. You'll find you gain the most control by skating onto the outside edge of the gliding ski, the way you would do on a step turn to the outside edge. A slight edge gives the ski directional stability. Then, when you are ready to stride back the other way, roll the knee over to create your platform, and push off.

When skating downhill, reduce the angle of divergence between your skis to anywhere from 20 to 40 degrees. Take smaller strides and project your momentum forward, down the hill. If you're skating on soft or newly groomed snow, stop occasionally and look back up your track. You'll notice the strongly edged skis leave curved lines in the snow (sidecut turns!), as if you were engraving your way, one foot at a time, down the hill.

RHYTHMIC SKIING

What do you do with your poles? Up to this point, you could probably get away without poles, though they have been useful in lift lines and in walking or climbing from here to there. (Children often learn to ski without poles, an approach I applaud and one I think could be extended successfully to many adults.) I have purposely not talked about poles to this point because I believe in emphasizing what's happening at the foot level. You ski with your feet, not with your hands and arms. But there comes a point when the poles become a real boon to rhythmic skiing, to linking turns together in a seamless flow.

Correct use of your poles will do two things:

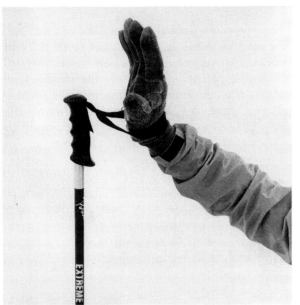

Grasping the pole and pole strap.

time the action taking place at snow level, and help to position your upper body in preparation for the coming change of direction.

Pole Plant: As a Timing Device

Use the pole plant to signal the end of one turn and the beginning of the next. The tapping of the point into the snow acts as a kind of trigger for the transfer of weight from one foot (and one turning edge) to the other. After a while the linking becomes automatic: plant your pole, a turn follows.

This is especially true when short-radius, rhythmic turning is called for. The ability to string together a metronomic sequence of turns can make life beautiful on steep slopes, for example, or in the moguls or in tight spaces like catwalks or along trail edges where you may be tightroping the soft snow between the trees on one side and the moguls on the other. A key ingredient in a successful series of turns is always the pole plant.

To begin with, carry your poles loosely (not in a death grip) with hands out in front of your body, about waist high, and the pole baskets lightly trailing behind. You want to be able to make your pole plants with a wrist action, not an arm-swinging, whole arm movement. If the hands are always in this forward, ready position, it's a simple matter to cock the wrist, bring the basket forward and plant.

Where you plant the basket depends on the kind of turn you are making. Long-arc turns on gentle terrain dictate that you plant the pole up near the tip of your ski. In short-radius turns on steep slopes, plant off to the side, opposite your boot and down the hill. In a short-radius quick-pivot turn, a pole plant near the tip might interfere with the turning skis. Conversely, wide-to-the-side pole plants on long turns pull your weight back and disrupt balance. Think of the option range as a quarter circle from your ski tip to a point roughly opposite your boot. The tighter the turn, the further back and to the side will be your pole plant.

Timing Exercises

Here are two ways to teach yourself the pole plant habit. One is visual, the other auditory.

Select a field of small or nascent moguls. Groomed slopes that are just beginning to grow back their bumps (like a two-day-old beard) are often good. The hill should not be so crowded with bumps as to make the skiing tricky, but you want to have enough lumps to use as turn targets. Try to make each turn right on top of a bump, and make a point to spear the crown with your pole to trigger each initiation. Keep your head up (looking for that next lump; it might be six feet away, and it might be fifty), and keep your hands at the ready, ready to bring the basket forward and go. If the lumps are coming in quick succession,

The pole plant links the ending of one turn with the start of the next. As the skier nears the end of one arc (A), he brings the pole basket forward (B) to be planted at precisely the moment he begins the new turn, stepping onto the outside ski (C). Note in C and D how reaching for the pole plant has positioned his upper body to anticipate the coming turn. *Tom Lippert*

A

B

C

D

bring your basket forward as soon as you step to the new ski. Have it ready to punch whether there is a mogul there or not.

Make a game of it. Choose some image of yourself—as a picador perhaps or as a marksman—deftly popping the snow at precisely the right spot. Make it a positive jab, though not disruptively so, and follow these imaginary bull's-eyes down the slope.

The other device works best where there are no bumps to tell you where to turn. Choose a smooth, regular piste where you can impose your own rhythm. Plant your poles to a steady beat, either inside your head or voiced out loud. Sing a song, cluck your tongue, or count out a cadence. (No one is likely to hear you, and if they do, what does it matter? Most people do something with their mouths while they ski: whistle or sing or talk to themselves. I either whistle or attempt facsimiles of the sounds my skis are making on the snow: whoosh, whoosh, whoops, whoosh.) Let each pole plant trigger a turn, whether stemmed or stepped or whatever. It doesn't matter. Just keep the cadence coming—be ruthless—and you'll find that the turns do too, as if you were pushing a button.

One more exercise to strengthen the pole plant and the foot-level reactions that follow. Pick a short patch of smooth, relatively steep terrain. Without using your poles, make as many turns as you can in a given space. Go back up and try it again this time with pole plants. Forget how you look, just face down the hill, plant down the hill opposite your boot, and work a rhythmic succession of turns. Count your turns to the finish line. You'll find that your score gets better and better, that the pole plant not only smooths out the timing but actually seems to generate turning power in short-radius, slow-speed turns.

Pole Plant: Positioning and Anticipation

That last exercise is a good example of how the pole plant not only times your turns but also helps generate turning power. Remember the rotated stance described in the section on sideslipping? I called it anticipation, where the skis pointed across the hill while the upper body, head, and hands were rotated toward the fall line. In this last exercise, the pole plant (wide and reaching down the hill while the skis were still turning the other way) plays a key part in the turning force created by anticipation.

Picture it this way. Suspend a sheet of paper in one hand. Twist the bottom 90 degrees with the other hand (this is your lower body finishing a turn across the hill). Hold the top steady (this is your anticipated upper body stabilized by a pole plant), and let go the bottom. The paper returns to square.

In the same way anticipation is a kind of winding up and releasing of tension. The pole plant works to stabilize the upper body so that the lower body can unwind against it. This principle is at work in almost all advanced-level turns: in the bumps, in powder, and any time the skier is stitching short-radius turns down a slope. The only time it doesn't come into play is in gradual, long-radius turns, where there is little or no pivoting and the body rides naturally square to the skis.

Anticipation helps link one turn to the next. It also allows the body's center of mass to remain comfortably to the inside of each arc the skis scribe on the snow. (If the center of mass were not inside the arc, we couldn't resist the strong pulls of gravity and straight-line momentum.) Anticipation means the upper body follows a more direct line down the pitch while the skis and feet take a more circuitous, side-to-side route. Again, look head-on at a good skier in person or on celluloid. Notice how the upper body doesn't move much. It keeps its orientation down the hill (these guys never have to turn their heads to look at the camera), while the skis zig back and forth controlling the line and the rate of descent.

The pole plant is absolutely key to maintaining that balanced anticipation. When the pole goes in at the end/beginning of a turn, the upper body is said to be blocked. The lower body, twisted against the torso, "wants" to return to square, wants to uncoil in the direction of the new turn. Thus the turning power generated by anticipation and the quickness with which a well-anticipated skier can change from foot to foot, edge to edge.

Assuming strong carving, skidding, and weight-transfer skills, anticipation is what separates the mass of advanced/intermediate humanity from the relatively few skiers who move on to the difficult slopes and wild snows of the expert.

Anticipation Exercise 1: Target Skiing

Pick a smooth section of terrain, and choose something at the bottom of your view—a tree or

Stein Eriksen has, since the 1950s, epitomized the notion of style on skis, but the characteristic (and much imitated) reverse shoulder technique shown here was an outgrowth of the equipment he had to work with. Stein skis much differently today.
Franz Berko

lift tower or another skier—to point at. Point your head and hands and shoulders at that object and make slow, tight turns toward it. Never take your eyes off it, keep your upper body oriented that way, and plant your pole each time in the direction of your goal. Feel your lower body turning, twisting independently of your upper body. It may feel a little artificial at first, but in time it will feel as natural as walking.

Anticipation Exercise 2: Hockey Stop

Another good exercise is to add a pole plant to the end of a hockey stop. Remember the hockey stop maneuver is itself an exercise in opposition, the lower body twisting against a steady upper body. If, at the end of the skid, you reach down the hill and plant your pole, just at the same moment as your edges stop you, you will have recreated the decisive moment in an anticipated turn. Reaching out and down with the pole as your skis slow will help groove your positioning. And planting the pole with authority at the instant of edge set will (even though you're not continuing

around the corner) establish the feeling of blocking. You should feel, when you stop the motion this way, the wound-up energy in your lower body, eager to release into a new turn.

Anticipation Exercise 3: Hands

My final suggestion is not really an exercise, it's a call to awareness. Good positioning seems to depend so much on the hands. They're so small and yet slight shifts in their placement can mean the difference between balanced readiness and complete loss of control. You've seen it in others, maybe you have felt it in yourself. When hands slip back behind your hips, your weight is back on the tails of the skis, control is difficult, and speed is an enemy. When at the end of a turn hands rotate around uphill, weight shifts off the outside ski, your edges don't hold and turns wash out. These are positioning problems which lead to edging and turning problems.

Some times the body is reacting to fear; you're in over your head terrainwise, and the thing to do is seek out more comfortable slopes. But where fear is not a primary factor, proper hand positioning can lead the way back. One rule of thumb is to keep your hands in sight at all times. If both are out front (not stiffly so, but relaxed and forward) where you can see them, chances are your weight will be centered fore and aft. Another trick is to pretend you are carrying a tray of drinks as you ski. This will keep your hands from flying around and help you toward a good anticipated stance. Offer the tray to someone down in the valley and you will tend toward the proper fall-line orientation.

TIPS & TALES: Personal Style

To many skiers the notion of style is mixed up with a vision, like one of Stein Eriksen. In many circles he doesn't even need a last name, he's just Stein, the elegant, wavy-haired Norwegian-become-American ski icon of the 1950s and '60s. Stein skied then, and still skis, with his feet and knees pressed together, with his body angulated in a graceful comma above his skis. Every movement, from the edges on up, seems calculated to add to the seamless effect. And indeed Stein has always equated skiing and gracefulness. "To me, gracefulness on skis should be the end-all of the sport. If I was going to ski just to rush down the mountain, I wouldn't get any satisfaction out of it."

Countless thousands have tried to imitate Stein's style. Few succeed even part way, and none succeed completely. For, in the end, Stein's style is his own. It's an expression of character, of inner truths that he and only he, given his upbringing, his body, the life he's lead, can express.

It's important to distinguish, I think, between style and stylish. The latter is about conforming to the fashionable standard, fashionably elegant, smart or chic. True style is original. If you want to ski with your feet close together, and it feels right to do so, fine. Just be sure that you, like Stein, can retain the efficiency of skiing on one foot at a time, of full weight on the turning edge, whatever your stance.

If on the other hand, your body type, your attitude and personality say that you should ski with your feet apart, then so be it. You should not feel pressure to conform to some prescribed standard. Everyone will have a different image of perfection, just as everyone has a different notion of the best line to ski down a given slope.

Can developing a personal style get in the way of learning how to ski? For a generation now ski schools have been shying away from even talking about style and, especially in America, teaching a very generic, purely functional methodology. The argument goes that by trying hard to look a certain way, skiers in the past were failing to learn the skills beneath the surface. There is some truth to this. But true style, as it is a function of personality, won't conflict with utility. Only stylishness is a danger.

Beware of mannerisms. I see young skiers holding their hands a certain way, close together in front of their belly buttons, poles out to the sides, because they have seen a racer they admire doing it. I see other skiers whose heads bob like pigeons with every turn; they're looking down at their skis to see (I suppose) if things are going stylishly enough down there. Mostly, I see people obsessed with doing perfect turns without regard to the terrain they are skiing. They are all wrapped up in The Turn. Doing it right. Doing it right. Hey, how'm I doing? They're so busy "working on their turns" they fail to see (and take a run at) the bigger picture. Good skiing, artful skiing has as much to do with seeing as it does with technical expertise.

Form follows function. All great skiers are technically sound. Put them on a race course where everyone's objectives are the same, and they will all look pretty much the same. But outside the race arena, technical proficiency is only important insofar as it is freeing. Carving, skidding, braking and balancing are tools to set the spirit soaring. They are, like the parts of speech are to language, necessary elements of expression. If you are willowy, agile, dainty, reflective, passive, extroverted, solid, aggressive, or determined, your style should reflect it.

Style is valuable in and of itself. A true style is an antidote to the modern throw-away credo of "just DO it!" Forget the trimmings, forget the nuances, forget history and ceremony and hard work, just DO IT! Well, after doing it a couple of times, throwing your body down a ski mountain, what have you got? What's next? The answer is, Doing it with style. Committing to a deeper learning. Developing skills to the point where personality and pride shine through the deed. Satisfaction. Only then can we approach perfection.

To the experts go the spoils. Freedom of choice for this skier means choosing deep powder in the trees.

4

Alpine: Expert Snow, Expert Skills

The world expands for the expert skier. Now there is the whole mountain, top to bottom, boundary to boundary. Choices multiply. Where to go when? The question becomes a matter of delicious alternatives: steep or not so steep, out in the open or in the trees, sun or shade, bumpy or smooth, wild snow or groomed. Not that expert skiers are never challenged or pushed to the limit and beyond. They are. But once the skills and the mileage accrue (it's kind of like a frequent flier program with freedom of choice as the benefit) you can go just about anywhere the snow has filled in over summer's rocky bones.

The primary difference between the expert and the advanced intermediate is the former's comfort level on steep slopes. The steep: where gravity's pull is less obstructed by intervening planes of earth, where there is a weightlessness, a sense of flying. There are other reasons to designate a run black diamond—an ungroomed blanket of moguls is the most common—but steepness is the classic litmus test, the crucible which separates the truly skilled from the pretenders. We'll talk about what it takes to tame the steep in this chapter.

The other distinguishing characteristic with experts is their handling of the range of textures found on the whole mountain. To whit: ice, powder, crud (a catch-all term for various incarnations of cut-up powder and wind- or sun-glazed snows), as well as the man-made pin-ball alley known as the bumps (moguls). We'll take a look at these textures and the particular challenges each provides. And we'll explore strategies for survival and even (dare we say) transcendence in the bumps.

And finally, we'll explore that wind-in-the-face, terrain-gobbling, mountain-shrinking phenomenon called speed. Some very good skiers spend all day at very slow speeds, in the powder, coursing through the trees, picking their way down the bumps. But all experts know how to go fast safely, and where, and when.

In short, we'll sample some of the tastiest fruits on the alpine tree. Some of these take a longer reach, a greater commitment and concentration, but when you make your way out the branch and do pluck them, their sweetness will bring you back season after season for more. It's no fluke that deep-powder skiing, for example, is compared (favorably) with the pleasures of sex. Devotees chase the stuff around the world from Canada to the Alps to the Himalayas of Kashmir. A few extraordinary fanatics have accumulated as much as 14 million vertical feet of helicopter skiing in British Columbia, at a cost of about $30,000 per million.

The more you learn, the less likely you are to contract a case of boredom on skis. Far from becoming complacent, accomplished skiers just seem to find ever more opportunities, for fresh

A

B

The key distinguishing factor between an intermediate and an expert skier is the latter's ability to balance completely on the outside ski, to ride that single, turning edge through the full arc. He may not always pick up the inside ski like this, but the balance is always there. *Tom Lippert*

C

D

patterns of movement, fresh ways of seeing and descending. Every run brings another chance for grace.

EXPERT EQUIPMENT: Skis

There is a dizzying array of skis at the top end. Skis for racing, for "recreational" racing, extreme skiing, high-speed cruising, "luxury" skis costing up to $1,000, specialty skis for moguls and powder. There is no go-anywhere, do-everything ski, though many have claimed the title. Most serious skiers have more than one pair. It's like fly rods or bicycles. You really can't take your big steelhead rod bushwhacking up a tiny creek. And you wouldn't think to ride your mountain bike on an in-town criterium.

Race Skis

You certainly don't have to specialize or develop a quiver full of different boards. At $450-$700 retail, many expert skiers get by with a single pair, thank you very much. Usually that single pair is a race-bred slalom or giant slalom ski. Here's why. Race skis are the highest-performance models in a manufacturer's line. They are likely to be the most durable skis in the line, built to withstand the bends and twists of high-speed, full-force skiing. They are the most responsive skis; load them right and they'll snap a turn in a blink or hold an edge on New England blue ice.

These are the skis that are most constantly being revised and improved by the ski makers. International racing is the testing ground. Features proven here—new shapes, new vibration damping systems, new materials—are incorporated next into mass-market race skis, then filter down the line (eventually) to sport and recreational models.

You still have to choose skis appropriate to your size and strength. Few skiers, even very good ones, would enjoy Phil Mahre's board-stiff race slaloms. You have to take into consideration the magnitude of the forces you generate in your turns, the turn shapes you prefer, and the kinds of snow you most often ski on.

Slalom skis are the cutting horses of the ski world, built for quick changes of direction and for carving short-radius arcs. They thrive on steep mountains, where short-swing skiing is the norm, and they are generally tenacious on hard-packed snows. *Giant slalom skis* are usually wider, sometimes softer, and always have a longer turn built in. Giant slaloms are often the ski of choice for cruising on big, smooth mountains. Their flex patterns and vibration-damping systems are designed for stability at speed. Some, though by no means all, powder-snow skiers prefer giant slaloms because their greater width helps them "float" better in deep snow.

Far more specialized than slalom and giant slalom models are the Super G and downhill skis. *Downhills* are like Indy cars, made to go fast on a prepared track. Most are over 220 cm long, heavy and straight (very little side cut). There aren't many places on today's mountains where you can really crank these up to speed, and their use is limited to actual racing. Super G's run from 208 to 215 cm long. They're a cross between a giant slalom and a downhill, are fun on the wide-open spaces when traffic is light. But they, like the downhills, are limited production skis, expensive, and rare.

Special Condition Skis

Mogul lovers should consider buying a special *mogul ski*. Every manufacturer has one. They usually come out of the slalom mold, but with slightly different flex patterns than a true slalom ski — softer in the tail for a more forgiving arc in the troughs between bumps and stiffer in the tip to ward off deflection. You won't find any metal in a bump ski as you will in most giant slaloms and some slaloms; when metal bends too far, it stays bent. Bump skis are usually pure, 100 percent, springy fiberglass or exotic derivative: carbon fiber, kevlar, boron, ceramic. The Dynastar Vertical and K2 Viper are two such glass mogul dancers.

Devoted powder skiers, likewise, will be tempted to spring for a special *soft-snow ski*. In very soft, fresh snow, almost anything will work —the medium is so forgiving. But sooner or later aficionados, including those planning a helicopter or snowcat powder trip, will consider a true powder ski. It will be wide, soft, and short. Wide so that it will plane ("float") near the surface of the snow. Soft because the bent ski itself, more than edges and side shape, creates a turn in the deep. And short (10-20 cm shorter than your full-length ski) because overcoming the added friction and weight in three-dimensional snow, of going up and down within it, is just that much easier with a shorter tool on your feet.

The Head Deep Powder, built in the 1950s and '60s, was the first great powder ski. A few diehards still bring theirs out when conditions are really deep. Unfortunately, few American manufacturers make powder skis any more, and the Europeans who do don't sell them in this country. The premier powder board here is the Miller Soft, produced in loving but minuscule numbers in Salt Lake City, Utah. Two Sun Valley-based companies, PRE (for Precision) and RD (for Research Dynamics) build good ones, the Extreme Powder and the Heli-Dog, respectively. Blizzard, Kästle, and Fischer make special powder skis, but most of the ones you'll see in this country were purchased in Europe.

Skis: How to Talk Tech in the Shop

When you go to buy a pair of skis, you will likely be flooded with tech talk regarding construction and performance characteristics. The best way to arm yourself is to study the fall buyer's guides in the ski magazines. While they don't allow you to flex and feel the products in your hands, they do usually do a good job of defining terms.

Briefly, you will encounter the three construction techniques: torsion box, sandwich, and now cap construction. The *torsion box* method takes a preshaped core and wraps a continuous sheet of fiberglass around and around, like a mummy. Sidewalls, top skin, base, and edges are added in the mold. The glues and resins cook, and a light, springy, often torsionally stiff (good for hard snow) slalom ski appears. Torsion box is not limited to slalom skis, and not all slaloms are built this way, but many are. Dynamic pioneered the technique in the 1960s. Head and K2 perfected it.

The *sandwich* is the oldest and most versatile construction. As the name indicates, one lays down precut ingredients in the mold—plastic base, fiberglass sheets, aluminum sheets, core, more fiberglass, more metal, top sheet, etc.—and, after curing, out pops a sandwich ski. The choice of ingredients and how much of each, determines the performance recipe. Giant slalom skis are

usually made this way. The metal layers make them quiet over the snow, stable but not quite as quick as a torsion box ski. Almost all of the Austrian skis—Atomic, Kästle, Kneissl, Blizzard, and Fischer—and most of the American lines manufactured abroad, are made this way.

The newest construction is the *cap*. In this one the top and sides of the ski are one piece, like a flat-top arch, glued in place over the base and core. Salomon's is molded of Kevlar, carbon, and fiberglass. They call theirs monocoque construction. Volant, a small American company which was the first with the technique, builds theirs out of stainless steel. Other ski makers will follow. The advantages of the cap seem to be in strength-to-weight; they can be made significantly lighter than traditional constructions. And they claim a more positive transmission of forces from boot to ski edge. We'll just have to see about that.

Inside the ski are an equally bewildering array of *cores*. Some are laminates of wood (durable, stable, relatively heavy), some are urethane foam (light, flighty), while still others employ various I-bars, Omega ribs, and air channels. The only ones to avoid are injection-molded foam cores, where the insides are squirted into a premolded shell. Generally, only beginner's skis are made this way. Of the rest, each has its virtues. Wood not only refuses to go away in the face of the new plastics, it's resilience and "alive" feel make it the core material of choice for many top-end skis.

And what of *vibration dampeners*, swallowers, absorbers, dissipators? Every ski maker has his theories. It has been shown that some vibration frequencies at some places along the edge are good (good vibes like good germs), while others are bad. That's why Rossignol put its Vibration Absorption System, or V.A.S.—little rubber and metal bad-vibe-swallowing sandwiches—at different places on their slalom and giant slalom skis. The science of it is complex, and maybe a little witchy, but there is no question that skis ride smoother and more precisely over the snow now than just a few years ago.

Skis come with either full-length or segmented "cracked" edges. I can't see that there is any performance difference. The manufacturer either wanted the steel edge to be a factor in the overall flex of the ski (full-length) or he wanted the edge to play no role in the ski's flex (cracked). Cracked edges are slightly more delicate; hit a rock hard enough and you can bust a segment out. You see them on some slalom skis, rarely if ever on giant slalom models.

Finally, the *bases*. Sintered is the only way to go. As I mentioned in Chapter 3, extruded bases are for beginner skis only. Sintered bases are much slicker and harder. And they're getting better all the time. P-Tex is the dominant brand name, though there are others. With P-Tex, the higher the number (P-Tex 2000, P-Tex 4000, etc.) the harder and faster the base. Black "Electra" bases have charged carbon molecules in them which seem to improve performance on warmer snow. Clear sintered P-Tex appears to be better on colder snows. Remember to keep sintered bases waxed. Their high-porosity causes them to dry out quickly.

Boots

Check out the boots on the feet of the World Cup racers. There's not a current model among them. Some even go back a decade or more. People who spend a lot of time in their boots find a pair they like and stick with them. Changing boots is much harder to do than changing skis.

The same is true for any dedicated skier. Find a boot that fits well, one that puts you in a natural stance, and stay with it. All the bells and whistles and new colors won't make up for comfort. Not that boots haven't gotten better. They have. (And more expensive. Expect to pay between $350 and $500 for top-of-the-line models.) But there aren't really any new technologies, new materials, ushering in the kinds of breakthroughs that have enlivened the skis themselves.

The improvements in boots have been in *entry systems* and personalizing adjustments. Entry systems first. For a long time overlap shell (variable volume) meant front entry exclusively. Fixed-volume shells equated with rear-entry closure systems. Now there are combinations. The Dachstein VC line, the Lange Mids, Nordica's Syntech line, and Dynafit's ETS line all have overlap fore boots and cuffs that unbuckle and behave like rear-entry models.

Rear-entry has traditionally been associated with user-friendly entry and exit, but the performance characteristics of fixed-volume boots were somewhat suspect (too stiff, too much room inside the shell). By the same token, overlap, front-entry boots were known as better performers (lower volume, more sensitive and "sneaker-like"), but they were a bear to put on and off, especially when cold temperatures stiffened the plastic shell. Now those once clear lines may be blurring.

There is no question that boots are more *adjustable* than ever before, and this is good. Once you have the shell you want, your boot fitter can measure you for canting (side-to-side shaft adjustments for lower leg angle) and for a custom footbed (highly recommended). From there, getting the boot to work perfectly is a matter of trial and error. Only you can tell, on skis and on snow, how much forward lean you want to set your stance at neutral. Only you can know how stiff you want your forward flex. (This might even change from day to day as the temperature fluctuates, or from run to run as you change styles from skiing bumps to racing gates. It's nice to have a soft flex for absorbing the vertical changes in the moguls, while you want a firm, powerful flex for the hard turns in a race course.) Firm snow and stiff flex? Soft snow, soft ankles? Or maybe for you it's the opposite. The only way to find out is to experiment.

Strong women skiers, as I mentioned earlier, sometimes have trouble solving the fit and performance problem. So-called *women's boots* may fit, but they generally don't have the guts to handle high speeds and big turn forces. Not a single woman on the top race tours skis in a woman's boot. They all end up modifying a man's model to fit their feet. And then they sometimes have to modify them further to soften a too-stiff flex. There is a real need for a lasted woman's boot with the lateral and fore/aft stiffness an expert skier must have.

Among the men's models that have worked for women: the Raichle Flexon, a soft and relatively narrow race boot; Technica's TNT series; and Nordica's classic 980 series. All are overlap, front-entry boots.

Bindings

Expert skiers utilize still higher DIN numbers than do intermediates. Where a 145-pound intermediate might warrant a DIN of 4 or 5, that same skier, if he were an expert, would need a DIN of 7 or 8, simply because of the higher forces generated in his turns.

Bindings for experts (in the neighborhood of $250) have higher DIN ranges (anywhere from 5-

15) and more elasticity. Elasticity is important at this level. Say the skier nearly falls but recovers. The binding gives a few millimeters, laterally or vertically or both, then returns to normal as the force returns to normal. If the system were rigid, the skier would be out of his ski and perhaps on his head. All top end bindings have some elasticity. Look has the most with 40 mm lateral at the toe, 15 mm vertical at the toe, and 30 mm vertical at the heel.

Vertical release at the toe is relatively new. Look, Geze, and Marker have it. Most, if not all of the others should follow. Vertical release allows you to come out of the binding in a straight backward or a backward twisting fall. These were the falls that led to the plethora of knee injuries, replacing broken legs (more or less solved by binding improvements in the 1970s) as the scourge of the 1980s. Time will tell if vertical release really does reduce the numbers of knee problems.

The other hot binding topic among expert skiers is whether or not your binding creates a flat spot on your ski. Some bindings, most notably step-in heel units with long, rigid mounting bases (Salomon, Marker, any rental binding with a long track), do impede the natural flex of a ski. Not everyone can feel it on snow in a turn. But some claim they can and that the flat spot interferes with the ideal carving action. Enter Tyrolia and Atomic/ESS with "floating" heel units which actually move on a piece of spring steel as the ski flexes. Turntable heels, like Look's and Marker's, because of their much smaller mounting plates, apparently don't cause the problem.

The higher price of top-end bindings comes from the casting and machining of aluminum housings. There are quite a few more steps involved. Aluminum isn't any safer than plastic. But it probably is more durable and the increased torsional rigidity probably translates to more precise boot-ski contact.

Poles

You can spend $100 on a pair of poles, or you can spend $15. The $15 pole will be made from 6000-series aluminum, which is quite strong, very ductile (it'll bend in half before breaking), and takes a lot of punishment. The $100 pole will be made from 7000-series aluminum which is much stiffer, can be made thinner and therefore lighter,

and (the only negative) can shatter on breaking. The 7000-series pole has a lighter swing weight, which some experts prize. It's very nice to handle, but you pay the price. Reflex and Allsop are two companies that make the 7000-series pole.

Allsop distinguishes itself further as the only manufacturer of shock-absorber grips. Pole plants over time can be jarring enough to cause tendinitis in some elbows and wrists. The Allsop grip is spring loaded and, according to the maker, absorbs 80 percent of the shock.

EXPERT TECHNIQUE

Good skiers love the steeps because the pull of gravity is so strong there, less impeded as it is by intervening planes of earth. The steeper the pitch, the closer they are to an ultimate human fantasy: flight. To the unprepared, however, the steeps feel like the white rug has somehow been pulled out from under them.

How steep is steep? Beginner runs (green on the maps) rarely surpass 10 degrees from the horizontal. Intermediate (blue) runs usually range from 10 to about 25 degrees. Few black diamonds even approach 35 degrees. A handful of iconographic names across the country— Corbet's Couloir at Jackson Hole, Alta's High Nowhere, Crested Butte's Cesspool, Telluride's Spiral Stairs, the West Basin chutes at Taos, sections of Goat and Starr at Stowe—will push 40 degrees. (PR types at Telluride once sent out a release claiming the Front Face runs there averaged 75 degrees for 3,000 vertical feet. What they meant to say was 75 percent, which is 37.5 degrees, and that, I believe is still an exaggeration.) The steepest slopes ever skied, above Chamonix in the French Alps by the likes of Sylvain Saudan (the self-styled "Skier of the Impossible"), the late Patrick Vallençant, the late Jean-Marc Boivin and others, have been about 60 degrees.

There is nothing nearly that steep in bounds at American ski areas. Yes, people do jump off cliffs at Squaw Valley and elsewhere. And the entrance to Corbet's is often an airy drop of 10-15 feet from the cornice. The steepest pitch I've skied was a convex wall at Bear Valley in California's Sierras, a sperm-whale snout of a roll that locals estimate at about 50 degrees. Reaching downhill for the pole plant felt like leaning off the edge of a roof. But by and large steep skiing here means something in the 30-35-degree range.

(It used to be you could define steep in a simple, mechanical way. If the snow cats could maneuver their way down a slope at night in the process of grooming the snow—flattening moguls or packing new snow—then that pitch was not technically "steep." The runs over which the cat drivers feared to tread were truly steep. But now, with the invention and proliferation of sophisticated winch cats which can climb—or rather pull themselves up—much steeper terrain, that form of classification is out the window.)

DYNAMIC SHORT SWING

So how do you learn to become comfortable on steeper slopes? There is no quick course. Sound fundamentals must be combined with miles and miles of experience. Physical skills must develop hand in hand with a cautious confidence; strength and bravado alone won't do it. But that's the beauty of the mountains. Almost all of them start

gently near the base and get steeper and steeper as you climb.

The obvious key ingredient every successful steep skier possesses is speed control. A good skier can ski any run at a walk. And the key to speed control on the steeps is a mastery of the short-swing turn. I talked a bit about this short-radius, rhythmic skiing at the end of the last chapter. These turns are more pivoted than they are carved. Speed control comes from a positive edge set at the end of each turn. And turns are linked together by means of anticipation and a solid pole plant.

Edge Set

Of these three elements (anticipation and pole plant are inextricably linked) the edge set is the least dispensable. The edge set checks your speed with each swing of the skis. (In fact, an edge set was called a "check" not so long ago.) The edge set also creates a platform from which to launch the next turn. In effect, strong, repetitious edge

A powerful edge set is a primary skill for handling steep slopes. *Tom Lippert*

sets create a series of mini-flat spots down the hill. Look at the track a good short-swing skier leaves on the steep and you'll see the platforms, pressed into the snow across the fall line, one after another like stair steps.

The key to powerful edge sets is a commitment to the outside ski. As we know, the inside edge of the outside ski is the one that does the work, the one that turns you, the one that engages the snow and slows you down. The trouble is, it's also the one you lean away from if you are afraid. Therein lies the irony on the steep: Instinct tells you to pull back from perceived danger, when withholding weight (commitment) from the downhill ski is contrary to the control you need to overcome fear.

It's a Catch 22 only if you try to teach yourself this commitment on the steep. Instead, start where the hill is non-threatening. And start with the same garland exercises described in Chapter 3. From a steep traverse near the fall line, steer your skis across the hill to a stop. Whether you carve or skid the arc is not important. Instead pay attention to the end of the arc where you set the edge—BANG—and you're stopped. Be sure that you are not leaning back or into the hill as you do it. Keep your weight balanced over the center of the outside ski. Bend at the hips and turn slightly so that your upper body faces down the hill while your legs steer the skis across the fall line.

Practice so that when you stop you are still in balance, poised, ready to go, like a ready position in tennis. It helps to plant your pole at the precise instant the skis stop. Reach down the hill, set and plant. If you've done it right, there should be a little energy left over, a bit of rebound in the skis and in your coiled body, that pops you up and toward a new turn. More about this later.

Once you get the feeling of a single edge set to a stop, begin to incorporate them into your skiing. Steer to an edge set and near stop on the tops of small moguls or on the crest of a roll. Set the edges without quite stopping, then ease down and into a direction change.

Or play around with strongly edged, dynamic wedge turns. Keep them short, crisp, springy, in the fall line. The point here is not really to *make* turns, but to get the feeling of stepping from foot to foot, from inside edge to inside edge. While there will be skidding at the beginning of each turn, try to end each one with a full edge set; stop the lateral movement altogether. You should be able to look back at your tracks and see the alternating platforms—right foot, left foot, right, and so on, like an elongated herringbone—where the edge was set each time.

This exercise can be effectively expanded in both directions, that is, slowed down and speeded up. On steeper terrain slow it down so that each turn results in an edge set to a stop. Match your skis (bring them parallel) and finish with a pole plant. Speed it up on gentler terrain. Reduce the size of your wedge to near parallel and emphasize the rhythmic back and forth of stepping from one foot to the other.

Initiation

Next, try this experiment (also touched on in the last chapter). Pick a piece of fairly steep, smooth terrain, and make as many turns as you can in a given space. You'll find that a positive conclusion to each turn, in the form of a crisp edge set, helps. But what will really make a difference, and easily double your score, are the active up and down movements that are necessary for truly short-radius turns. It's easy enough to initiate medium and long-radius turns just by changing edges and standing on the new turning ski. Cruising turns have time and space to unfold. But to get the skis around quickly takes a more active approach.

A strong up movement at the beginning of the turn unweights the skis for a quick pivot. A deep flexion finishes the turn, aids in setting the edge, and coils the spring for the next launch. Good fall-line skiers have a lot of jack-in-the-box in their motion.

Try the turn-counting experiment again. It's not necessary to hop the skis around, although that is an extreme variation on the exercise, and one that you'll see racers doing in training. Just initiate each turn with an energetic up movement and finish with an exaggerated folding of the legs, ankles, knees, and hips.

Remember, this is an exercise at the extreme end of the practical. You wouldn't necessarily go out and ski this way for fun. It's a lot of work. But it will teach you. You'll make more complete direction changes than you ever thought possible in such a short space, and you'll inch down the pitch with an extreme (almost an absurd) speed control. This will translate into real control and confidence when the going gets genuinely steep.

Anticipation

To link the parts smoothly and efficiently together, from one edge set (down) through the active initiation (up) to the following edge set (down), and so on down the hill, you need the stabilizer/spring known as anticipation. This is the dynamic independence of upper and lower bodies I touched on in the last chapter. The skier is anticipated when the skis and lower body have completed a turn across the fall line, while the upper body is in opposition, facing more or less down the hill. Anticipation is the catalyst in the short-turn recipe; it improves quickness, balance, and turning power. Add an anticipated upper body to the turn-counting exercise above, and you will likely increase your total by another 50 percent.

It wouldn't be a true short swing without anticipation. Consider for a moment making short-radius turns with your body square to your skis, that is, with head, shoulders, and hands pointing to the ski tips. Consider the effort (and the time) involved in turning everything, from the skis up to the tip of your hat, around 180 degrees and back again. Now picture the same turns but with the upper body trained more or less continuously down the fall line. You only have to turn the lower body and the skis. Anticipation cuts out unnecessary movement. Turning the entire body is counterproductive to quick edge-to-edge skiing. So, anticipation is absolutely key to quickness.

Anticipation also positions the body effortlessly to the inside of every turn. We know that the body's center of mass must ride inside the arc of the skis in order to balance. If you're skiing square, your center (somewhere between and slightly above your hips) must physically pass over your skis from side to side as you make turns. On the other hand, if you are skiing with an anticipated upper body, your center of mass moves very little from side to side; it's the skis that turn back and forth beneath you. Anticipation, then, contributes mightily to short-swing balance.

The final attribute of anticipation (and again, it was touched on briefly in Chapter 3) is its actual turning power. As the legs twist against the upper body at the end of a turn, muscles tense, energy is stored. The moment that twisted-up energy is released (remember the analogy of the twisted paper or the rubber band), there is impetus towards the new turn. The lower body wants to return to neutral underneath the torso. This works providing the upper body is stabilized, or blocked, by the pole plant. Then when the skis are unweighted, the edge hold released, there is an unwinding effect in the direction of the new turn.

Quickness, balance, and turning power. No wonder anticipation is such a key skill for good skiers. How to develop it? Start with some of the classic exercises from earlier lessons: hockey stop, garlands, target skiing. Work on each with a new concentration on upper body/lower body independence.

In the hockey stop, for instance, make sure that only the legs pivot into the skid and that the hands and chest remain pointed down the fall line. Use your knees to set the edge, and plant your pole simultaneously—BOOM. Do it so the edge set and pole plant signal a potential release of your coiled body spring.

Same with the garlands, only instead of a pivoted skid, you are now winding into an anticipated position through a steered turn. (Some people call a hook like this, preparatory to an edge set, a pre-turn.) Drive the skis through the finish of an arc while reaching downhill with the pole as if to start a new turn. Work it to a complete stop at first—BOOM—edge set and pole plant, upper body fully anticipated. Repeat and add an up movement, an extension of the legs following the pole plant. Set and release. You should see the skis begin to unwind with the unweight. Steer up, edge set, release.

Don't worry about launching into a full turn at first. It's enough to do garland sets (pre-turns) to both sides and to feel the potential unwinding. When that feels natural, go ahead and follow through with an edge change and a full turn. It helps to do them atop a small bump where the edge change and the unwinding from anticipation are facilitated on the fallaway.

In fact, small bumps are often the best learning fields for grooving anticipation. You can use the bumps as targets, planting your edge sets on their flat tops and planting your pole straight downhill on the nose. If the moguls are symmetrical and rhythmic so much the better. You can plot a path directly down the slope with your upper body defining the straight line course while your skis pivot from one platform to the next.

Lacking bumps, it helps to pick a target down the hill on which to focus. With this tree or lift

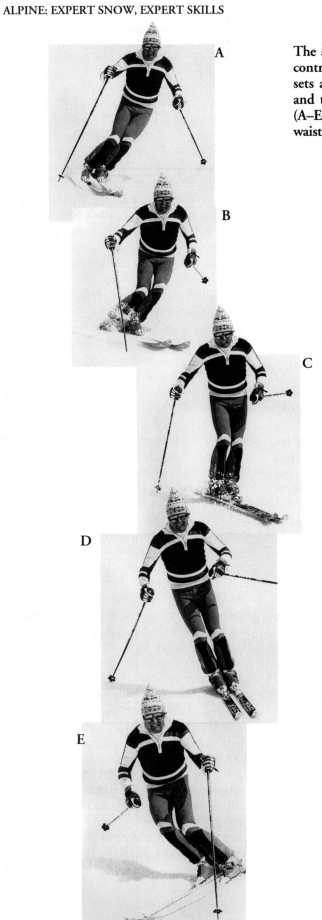

A

B

C

D

E

The short swing is a rhythmic dance for speed control on steeper slopes. Note the crisp edge sets and simultaneous pole plants (B and E), and the continuously anticipated upper body (A–E) All of the steering takes place below the waist. *Tom Lippert*

tower or other skier as a kind of magnet to eyes and shoulders and hands, begin a rhythmic short swing: down, up, down; edge set/pole plant, unwind, edge set/pole plant. Cock your wrist and bring the pole basket forward as soon as you begin the turn, so that it will be ready to plant as soon as the edges engage. Plant the pole downhill (not up by your tips), in line with your target.

Overcoming Fear

And that, in a nutshell, is it. The dynamic short swing, the all-purpose expert tool. Don't expect to take it immediately to the gnarliest *couloir* (French for "hallway through the rocks") on the mountain. Many people do and wonder why their technique scuttles back to a desperate survival stem. They are still afraid. This is natural. You've got to work up to these things.

Things you can do: Practice your short swing on slopes that don't intimidate. Push yourself now and then, but maximize success by choosing terrain carefully. To be effective, the movements of skiing must become ingrained. They must be second nature. You've got to groove the movement patterns over and over, thousands of repetitions, so that the body eventually responds instinctively to stimuli from the skis and feet. Thinking is too slow. To get to the point in that couloir where the body instantly responds by leaning out and down the hill—the only successful pattern for setting an edge—takes a lot of grooving.

It also helps to venture onto steep slopes just to get used to them, to learn that you can survive their pitch. Go out and ski them, slowly, carefully, with whatever technique comes to the fore. Don't insist, in other words, on doing the proper short swing or not doing it at all. I find it helps to undertake this kind of exploration alone. Too often with a group there is pressure (spoken or otherwise) to perform, to keep up, to look good. Alone, you need only work through it, at your own pace, in your own way. Next time, when you come back, you will be one step beyond survival, one step closer to implementing the techniques you are perfecting on gentler terrain.

Assess your skills honestly and balance them against your goals. If you are constantly skiing over your head, you are not skiing well. Your muscles are tight, you are courting bad habits, you are a hazard to yourself and other skiers. Ski instructors always seem to want to drag you back to easier terrain, which is not where you want to be. But they are right. Nobody learns a new motor skill at peak performance conditions. It just doesn't happen. You've got to put in the time —as if you were grooving a tennis stroke against a backstop—until it becomes second nature. Only then can you expect to have it work in the crucible of the steep itself.

MOGULS: The Man-Made Challenge

Moguls are the bane of a huge class of skiers good enough to be on a steep slope but not comfortable with the man-made egg carton that their fellows have thrown up. For many, moguls are the supreme challenge, the all-too-frequent embarrassment, the locked-door to advancement.

For others, the bumps are irresistible. They can't get enough of those pinball rhythms. They bob and weave and pop occasionally into the air like rubber balls bouncing down a stairwell. Bumps are the mountain's obstacle courses, the rough seas allowed to develop and thrive sometimes right along side placid, groomed cruisers.

A student once asked me where the ski area stored the moguls during the summer months. His assumption that bumps resulted from forms beneath the snow was understandable. Moguls don't always ski as if they were the natural result of repeated turns in the same groove. But that is precisely what they are.

It takes only a few days to watch a mogul field form. The first tracks down a pristine powder patch look like strings of curling ribbon. Those strings soon overlap, like strands of DNA, braids of a rope. Soon all but a few puffs of virgin snow are cut up, and skiers begin to repeat the patterns over and over. In the soft snow, skis carve deep grooves, or troughs, varying in length and shape depending on the steepness of the pitch and the skills of the carvers. One after another, skiers cut the troughs deeper; it's much easier to follow the grooves than to ride over the island lumps between them. And in no time—a couple of days to a couple of weeks, depending on the traffic— you have moguls.

Not all moguls are created equal. Good skiers create long, rounded moguls, because that was the shape of their turns. On such hills, the bumps are regular, symmetrical, marching down the slope like lines of buried Volkswagen bugs. Skiing these bumps can be a metronomic pleasure, like riding storm surf or a small-scale roller coaster. Other mogul fields have choppy, inelegant rhythms. Skiers who are moving more slowly to begin with, who pivot their turns more than carve them, and who may be struggling in the soft snow where moguls get their start, leave understandably smaller, less rhythmic, and generally less enjoyable bumps.

Mogul Technique: Smoothing the Ride

Whatever their heritage, moguls provide a special challenge that every good skier must face. With the coming of the winch cat, ski areas are periodically mowing down the moguls on more and more blue and black diamond slopes. But even so, most of the steeper trails retain their coating of bumps from December to April. Whether you love their frenetic exuberance or merely learn to slip through them without jarring, you have to deal with them. To say that you ski the whole mountain is to ski the bumps.

The basic steep-slope short swing is the foundation all successful bumpers start with. You want to be able to ski these things slowly. Then, as confidence grows, you can crank up the speed. A solid edge set, one that can stop you at any moment, or bring your speed down to near zero at the end of any given turn, is your best friend. An anticipated upper body is absolutely essential to linking turns in balance. And an aggressive pole plant, down the hill and quick—quick hands, quick baskets—sets the rhythm for the feet to follow. Basic stuff.

The problem comes from the bumps dictating your choices. The shapes say: turn here, turn here, turn here. The paths of a hundred other skiers have sculpted the grooves and you are more or less required to follow. For proof of this point, take a straight-line traverse across any big mogul field. Skis buck and jolt over mini hill and dale as if they were tracing the imaginary borderline between Tibet and Nepal. The ski wasn't meant to work this way, and neither were you.

Absorption

Watch a good mogul skier blend his body to the terrain. He expands and contracts like a Slinky,

absorbing the vagaries underfoot with his legs while his upper body remains so still you could send cocktails down the hill on his shoulders. It is like breathing, out and in, contraction and extension.

Absorption is the extra ingredient, added to the short swing, that smooths out the bumps. Think of the legs as shock absorbers. When the skis hit a bump, the shock absorbers compress, the body folds, feet and knees come up, soaking up the impact, smoothing the ride. Then when the skis dip into the hollow between bumps, the shocks return to normal, legs extend to fill the gap.

Practice absorption by traversing mogul fields. (Yes, it's an unnatural act, but it's the best way to get the repetitions you need.) Start with shallow, slow-speed traverses and work up to faster lines. Hold a straight line. Suck up the bumps, and extend into the troughs. A French word associated with mogul technique, *avalement,* is descriptive; it means "swallowing." All of the action should take place below the waist. While your skis may be describing a wild sine-wave curve, your head should draw a straight line across the hill. Pretend you're at finishing school walking across the room with a book on your pate.

As always, start out on moderate terrain and work up to steeper slopes and bigger bumps. When straight-line absorption begins to feel like a natural motion (and it should indeed make these wave-tossed crossings much more comfortable), incorporate the movement into your turns. The pattern should go like this. Your contraction, or swallowing of the bump, comes at the same time as your edge set. This should already be a familiar notion: What on smooth, steep slopes was the down movement to set the edge, is now the same action on a mogul. The edge set is simultaneous with the pole plant, as always. But now, instead of extending to unweight the skis, you extend by pushing the skis down, into the trough on the far side of the bump. Steer through the arc of the trough, then absorb the next bump in line and repeat the sequence.

You almost never need to unweight in moguls, because the sharp fallaway on the back side (or down side) of every bump serves as unweighting enough. As you pass over the ridge during initiation, there is no friction to speak of; changing edges and swiveling the feet to match the coming shape is relatively easy. In fact, the challenge is more often to keep from getting

Sound mogul technique means folding at the knees and ankles to absorb the bumps (A and E), extending into the troughs between crests (C), and remaining anticipated throughout. Decisive pole plants, stabbing the tops of the bumps as you absorb them, will help banish hesitation. *Tom Lippert*

airborne in the bumps. A stiff-legged skier will be popped up by the bumps and more often than not, out of rhythm and out of control. It's much better to keep your skis in contact with the snow. Absorption helps accomplish this.

Line

There is more than one way to "see" the moguls, or rather, to see the lines through them. I've described the classic route: from platform to platform (the flat spots at the top of each bump) by way of the troughs. This kind of turning works best when the moguls are regular and well-formed, when you can establish an alpha-wave rhythm where each turn is identical to the one before. But there are at least two other ways to ski the bumps.

In steep bumps, where keeping speed under control is paramount, you can sometimes make two turns per mogul. From the platform at the mogul top, turn sharply across the steep face of the bump, above the trough. Then turn again as you cross over the crest. Two turns between platforms. Because you are skiing on a mini ridge and avoiding the troughs, your turns will more closely resemble a smooth-slope short swing.

The smoothest, and often the most elegant line to take in the bumps is the wide line. In this one, you make your edge sets in the same places, on the platforms, but instead of extending right down into the grooves, you ski wide around

Sometimes even maximum absorption isn't enough to keep you from going airborne in the moguls. *Lori Adamski-Peek*

them, against the side of the next bump over. This gives you a longer line between platforms. It also allows you to bank, or press against the snow in your turn, rather than holding on to the steep, fallaway side of the mogul. In this way the wide line effectively flattens the slope you are skiing on.

Finally, when the bumps are small or misshapen, it is sometimes better to try to ignore them altogether. Good skiers will sometimes carve medium- to long-radius turns down through a welter of bumps as if they weren't there. Of course, they are there, and the skier's legs are working overtime to the absorb the lumpy changes underfoot. Sometimes, given the right speed and a good, upright position from which to scan the coming shapes, it's possible to smoothly link ridges and gullies, in unconventional sequences, through long, round arcs.

Bump Rhythms

Most of the time, you'll want to ski the bumps in line—bump, bump, bump, turn, turn, turn—your rhythm matched to what is given on the slope. But finding that rhythm is not always easy. How many times have you seen someone start into the bumps, link two or three turns, but then get behind, out of balance and bucked off the line. It can happen for a variety of reasons, including poor basic technique, but it also happens to very good skiers who are not in sync.

Skiing a mountain these days requires a lot of gear shifting. Coming into the bumps requires shifting instantly into a more active, more antic mode. A friend once suggested this to me: "Whip two or three turns on that very first mogul, son. Leap and land. Get down! Get ugly! Forget what you look like. Forget the bumps. Ignore 'em." It worked. The overaggressive behavior served to crank my internal metronome up a notch. I was over-frenzied for the conditions, but it was infinitely easier to slow down to match the moguls' natural rhythm than it had been to start slowly and speed up to it. While you wouldn't want to ski this way all the time (who could? it's exhausting), think of it as a trick, a way of increasing your rhythmic range.

Another tip for keeping yourself quick in the bumps: Be fast with your hands. You can only turn as quick as your pole plants. This may seem like putting the cart before the horse, but it isn't. The pole plant is the trigger. If you aren't ready to

pull the trigger at the moment your feet *should* change directions, your feet won't. And you'll be going straight, looking for a place to start the rhythm anew.

Keep your hands well out in front of your body in the bumps, your torso well anticipated. As soon as one hand stabs the bump, the next should be getting ready. Whip the basket forward. It's not enough to have hands in place if the baskets aren't out in front ready to punch in. This is why some very good mogul skiers look a little bit like big bugs, their poles constantly out in front tapping the ground like antennae.

SPEED: Letting Go of the Mountain

Inevitably, speed has to do with seeing, with accepting the world rushing up to meet you. It is an acquired taste. Ask any expert skier, and he or she will tell you, it is superb.

The faster you go the smaller the mountain is. What might be a major dip to a novice plying the slopes at 10 mph is but a tick in the road to a good skier cruising at 35 or 40. The novice is focused down on a relatively small piece of snow. The expert sees a bigger picture. He takes in the larger curves and drops of the mountain. Because he projects well down the hill in front of him, he is able to accept speed in one place knowing the slope will slow him further on. Speed allows him to paint with a freer brushstroke, to bank off sidehills, to lean into the curves, to soar over rough patches, to swoop through short steeps where others, who do not see the larger picture, may be cleaving to the pitch, ski edges like fingernails.

A long-time ski instructor was giving a clinic to a passel of apprentices. The neophytes were mincing their way down a steep, mogully pitch, biting off tiny turns and keeping their speed down, as they thought befitted the terrain. But our teacher became exasperated with us. "Don't you people ever let go of the mountain?" he asked. "You're always holding on, holding on. Do this," he said. And he jumped his skis around straight down the fall line, stood tall as a soldier and schussed the remainder of the pitch. At the bottom, he careened across a flat then disappeared down a road out of sight.

We stood with our collective mouths agape. Surely, one can't simply "let go" of the mountain.

Surely, if one did that, one would end up in a heap before the lodge. Surely, one must have a certain edge grip on the snow, a foot on (or ready to pounce on) the brake at all times. But we did as we were told. One by one we stood straight and bombed the face (which wasn't really very steep for very long). We went fast. But after the initial rush of acceleration, we didn't go any faster. A steady calm replaced the fear in our heads. Yes, you could let go of the mountain and not die. Yes, there is a peace at the core of speed.

The Calm at Terminal Velocity

One must work up slowly to such a calm vision. I can recommend two tried and true methods. One is to pick a long section of novice terrain, one on which you would feel positively haughty at your normal pace, and, when crowds are nonexistent, run it ramrod straight, up tall with chest out like the bowsprit on a wooden boat so that you can lean into the wind. Feel the tiny imperfections in the snow disappear as you're forced to focus on the coming distance. Balance is critical; stay forward, weight centered over your feet. Try to reach terminal velocity for that slope where the resistance from the air and snow matches the pull of gravity. If you do it on the right hill for your skill level, you will expand your speed threshold without scaring yourself. Normal accelerations will seem easier to handle. And speed itself, the wind in your face, the larger view, will become more familiar.

There's a very practical application to this exercise to be found on most mountains. It's the old bugaboo called "the flats." It's the rare mountain that has no aggravating flat spots here and there on its trails. If you know one is coming, or you can see it ahead, try to carry more speed than you ordinarily might off the last steep (let go of the mountain) and sweep past the walkers and pole-pushers who checked their momentum too long.

As a corollary to the terminal velocity exercise, try adding sidecut turns to the formula. At terminal speeds (even at 20 mph on gentle pitches) flat skis tend to wander. Inconsistencies in the snow surface can deflect the tips one way or the other. But, if you are riding ever so slightly on the edge, "riding the rail" in the vernacular, unsteady skis become directionally rock solid. You have something, besides the wind, to push against, to resist. Lightly engaging one inside edge or the other won't slow you down. But it will give you the ability to carve across the slope, to paint a sinuous curving stroke down the hill, and have a steady ski to stand against.

Slow Line Fast

The second technique for learning to go fast is one that racers use a lot in training. The idea is to choose a slow line—either with poles (gates) to ski around, or an imaginary course back and forth across a slope—and ski it fast. Work for speed where it does not come easily. Skate, push, drive for as much speed as you can muster. The goals here are both physical and psychological: First, to become more dynamic, more nimble and aggressive on your feet, and second, to spend time seeking speed as a counterbalance to the normal fear of it.

Like every other exercise, I recommend tackling these using the graduated terrain method: Start where the going is easy, where you can focus on the goals of the work and not on surviving the ski down. Fear is a bad teacher, or rather, makes a poor learner of the would-be student.

Artificial Gravities

Speed changes things. Momentum allows a skier to mess with gravity, to bend it to his needs, to play with it. Consider the following example.

The skier is flying down a large gully, Spar Gulch on Aspen Mountain, for example. The shape is like a giant half pipe, the walls of the gully curving up on either side of the buried creek. Using his speed, the skier charges up one side of the dish, banks into a turn and swoops down, through the transition and up the other side. What's happening up there at the top of his arc, when he may be leaning so far over as to be horizontal with the larger plane of the earth? Why doesn't he just fall off? He doesn't tip over because of his speed. Centrifugal force presses him against the wall, holds him there as long as his momentum is sufficient. He has created an artificial gravity.

This is one of the most playful and inventive things you can do on skis. You can do it on big shapes or small. For example, in the moguls when you ski a wide line and press your skis against the spoon-shaped side of a neighboring mogul, you are creating a mini-artificial gravity. Judging your speed is all-important. Bring too much to the task for a certain turn radius, and you may not be able to hold to the banked shape. Carry too little and you may be forced to cut the turn short or risk tipping over.

Practice on smooth slopes first, preferably ones with character: rolls, dips, sidehills, and gullies. (One of the sad side effects of the grooming revolution has been the summer bulldozing of many intermediate runs, smoothing the rocky bones of the land and replacing such character with easy-to-groom, curb-to-curb boulevard skiing.) Read the landscape and play it, using speed to create new routes, new balances within your own artificial gravities.

SKIING ICE: "Little More Soft"

"Ice is the fairest surface; efficiency is rewarded and mistakes are punished immediately. Soft snow is more fun, but ice is a challenge. It forces you to develop good fundamental technique." Billy Kidd said that. He grew up skiing ice at Stowe, Vermont, ice that had been rain the day before and then froze so clear you could see individual blades of grass through it. Kidd won an Olympic silver in the slalom in 1964, and he won a combined (downhill and slalom) gold in the 1970 World Championships, where the courses were watered with fire hoses to make them harder. He skis on softer stuff these days as director of skiing at Steamboat in Colorado, and rattles off commentary from beneath his trademark cowboy hat for CBS Sports.

Ice in its various forms—whether it be the bluish overflow from a Vermont spring or a sun-hardened Sierra glaze or the bulletproof product of snow-making guns and tank-tread grooming machines—is a skiing fact of life. Ski it often enough, and, as Billy Kidd says, it will force you to develop good fundamental technique. What does that mean exactly? It means precise balancing, pure, one-ski edging, smooth weighting, and good equipment.

Ice Balance

Ice is not tolerant of sloppy balancing. Let your weight get a little too far forward or back and the skis will skitter like a kitten across a newly waxed floor. Ditto for weight too far to the inside (leaning in), which takes pressure off the turning edge, causing it to break free and slide helter-skelter across the hard finish.

Tiger Shaw, like Kidd a Vermonter and a long-time member of the U.S. Ski Team, skis it this way. "I ski as if my ski was as long as my boot; as if my ski was *this* long." (Here he holds his hands apart to indicate 12 inches, no more.) The idea is to keep your weight applied directly down on the center of the turning ski. No depending on the front or the back of the ski to bail you out. No leaning allowed.

Ice Edging

Now you must take this precise, centered balance and apply it to a single edge, the inside edge of the outside ski, the turning edge. If even a little bit of this weight slips up to the uphill ski, you will slide. Keep feet slightly apart in order to edge the outside ski independently, free of any influence from the inside leg.

Try to edge the ski before you apply your weight, in the light time (the unweighted second) between turns. That way the ski has a better chance to bite and hold. If you stand on the ski first, then roll it on edge (a slower initiation to start with), there is a greater risk of skidding.

Ice Pressure

When you do weight the turning ski, do it smoothly, so as not to jar the tenuous grip. Go gently into the turn. Sharp, jittery turns don't hold. Smooth, round ones do. But you can't expect the ski to hold a long arc the way it would in soft snow. As Tiger Shaw says, "To make a long arc on hard snow is very difficult."

Tiger can do it and claims it is one of the great thrills in skiing. But most mortals can't. That's why you see a lot of short-radius turns on hard snow, quick on the edge and then off again. On ice you have to take weight off the edge before the turn is complete. Let off on the pressure at the end of the turn. Fold your legs in a swallowing or down-unweighting motion to allow the ski to complete its arc. Otherwise, your weight and centrifugal forces built up in the turn, can overburden the ski's ability to hold to the line.

U.S. team coach George Capaul was overheard at a rock-hard practice course muttering to himself, "Little more soft, little more soft," as he watched his charges skidding through the gates. This is what he meant: On hard, man-made snow you can't stand very long or push very hard on the edge. It won't hold an arc. Instead, apply pressure gently to an already-edged ski; load the ski only briefly; then lighten up ("little more soft") at the end.

Ice Tools

All of which is going to be less than effective if your equipment isn't in ice trim. Nicks and burrs on a ski's edges will prevent it from holding a clean line on ice. Racers have their skis tuned every night. When they go out on an icy course they have rapiers on their feet; their edges are literally razor sharp.

Most recreational skiers can't afford and don't have the inclination for this kind of fanatic preparation. But by the same token most skiers could benefit, and feel an immediate positive difference, in a well-tuned pair of skis. If you know you will be skiing some very hard snow, take your skis to a shop with a stone grinder and a good hand tuner. The grinder will take all of the rock scars out of your edges and flatten the base. The man with the skilled hands will burnish, de-tune and perhaps put a bevel on the edge for easier turn initiation. If you are so armed, the ice underfoot will behave more like packed powder.

If you have a workbench at home and the interest to tune your own skis, see the special section at the end of this chapter on ski tuning and maintenance.

Ice Attitude

Finally, skiing ice successfully takes a certain up-on-your-toes, aggressive attitude. Everything happens so much faster on ice. A well-executed turn pops around under you so quickly. And a slightly out-of-balance attempt results in the skis sliding out from under you equally quickly. Often the difference between having fun and having a hard time is in an alert, offensive rather than defensive, mind-set.

A defensive posture on ice means a holding back, a tentative approach to speed, weight, commitment down the hill. The very things that lead to a loss of control. An offensive approach means projecting forward, down the hill, never sitting back, but instead driving the skis from a hips-forward position of power, mind out in front carving the next turn.

Ice takes some getting used to. Of course it helps if, like Tiger and Billy, you started when you were four. But the rest of us can learn to feel comfortable on the stuff—with sharp edges and a sharply tuned approach.

POWDER: Rainbow's End

Powder is the unabashed star of the movies, the ski magazines, product and resort advertising, and just about every star-struck skier who has been lucky enough to develop a taste for fresh-fallen, untracked snow.

Actually, the term powder covers a huge spectrum of wild, three-dimensional snows, not all of which fit the glamorous ideal. Some are soft and luscious, like whipped cream, but some are closer to mashed potatoes or soft margarine, and some come with wind or sun crusts on top like an unexpectedly breakable eggshell. What you get depends on an ever-changing recipe of temperature, moisture content, and wind (or lack of same).

Wild snow can come down heavy and wet if the weather system coming through is warm and loaded with moisture. This happens most often in the mountain ranges nearest the coasts—the Northwest Cascades, California's Sierra Nevada, the White Mountains of New Hampshire—but it can occur anywhere. Moisture-laden, gloppy powder (new snow with a water content of 10-15 percent or more) carries the generic moniker "Sierra Cement," although the stigma implied about the California mountains isn't particularly fair.

Storms that mix frigid arctic air with Gulf or Pacific or even Great Lakes moisture can leave piles of snow so light you can blow it away like dandelion fuzz. These snows can have as little as 2 percent water content. The rest is air. These crystals fell straight down, without wind, and remained in six-pointed, classic snow-flake form until they were weighed and measured. Then, chances are the sun began melting them or the wind began to blow, tumbling and breaking off the crystal arms, or the snow began settling and consolidating of its own weight. Snow never stays in one form for very long.

On certain days, skiing powder is like floating through crystalline foam. *Bob Chamberlain*

This downy stuff falls most frequently in the mid-continent ranges, the Rocky Mountains of Colorado, New Mexico, Utah, Wyoming, Idaho, Montana, and interior British Columbia. Storms tend to dry out crossing the desert Great Basin. And by the time they are lifted to the high elevations of the Rockies, they have only light, relatively dry snows to give. But they aren't limited to the Rockies. Every winter New England, the upper Midwest, and the West Coast ranges receive a few such dry, cold storms as well, the exceptions that prove the rule.

Most storms drop snow that is somewhere between these consistency extremes, snow with a 6-10 percent water content. This snow will compact into a snowball in your hands, but it will also feel creamy and soft under your skis.

The big variable with all storms is the wind. Violent winds can strip snow from a ridgeline and deposit it in a gully half a mile away. Wind can sand and compact the top layers of snow into an unbreakable crust—a skier cannot break through even with a hard edge set. When this crust is also sculpted into paisley wind whorls, it is called sastrugi. Or the wind might blow just hard enough to lay down a thin crust, one that will support a skier standing still, but collapse under the greater force of his weight plus his momentum. These are called breakable crusts, and they are among the trickiest natural snows to ski.

Powder may arrive as a one-inch dusting, or it might transform the landscape as a forty-inch dump. The latter is rare, although you can expect at least one per season in the Sierras. Most of the time, a two- to three-day storm will leave three to ten inches in its wake. Depending on the consistency, the three inches may ski pretty much like the packed surface underneath. But ten inches is a different ball game. Ten inches or more requires that you change your expectations and your technique.

Slow-Motion Powder

Everything slows down in powder. On packed surfaces you expect your movements to result in certain near-instant responses. But in powder, because of the increased friction of the deep snow —around skis and boots and legs, and even waists and chests on maximum days—everything takes longer to develop. This is both the beauty and the frustration of it.

The deep snow works against the pull of gravity, allowing you to ski closer to the fall line without going any faster. It slows the actions and the perceptions of skiing, the way a baseball player "in the groove" sees the ball slow down or a tennis player, moving well, feels the game slow down in a dreamy, ecstatic way.

But initially anyway, this slo-mo feeling works against most skier's habits. Try to slow your movements down. Give yourself more time for each turn. In fact, in the beginning, don't turn at all. If you can, make your first couple of forays straight through a gentle powder field. Let the skis run. Bounce a little up and down in the snow. Get a feel for the speed, the resistance, the three-dimensional consistency. At the end of your straight runs, steer into a long turn to a stop. Don't force it; don't hurry.

Try a few single-turn garlands. Start right in the fall line so you are really making only half a turn, the final half. Then, when those feel good, try a few complete turns. But don't turn too much, too energetically or too far across the hill. That will only make life harder. Skilled powder skiers never stray too far from the fall line. You don't need to extend the arc around as far as you would on a packed slope.

Neither should you start your turns from a horizontal traverse. Start from closer to the fall line, at least 45 degrees off the horizontal. Powder pioneer Alf Engen invented something called the Alta start, which makes first turns in powder easier. In deep snow, kick your tails, one at a time, into the snow behind you, so that you are facing straight down the slope. There's no more delicious anticipation than the one you get looking down slope between your tips, suspended in the Alta start position, ready to jump in. When you do push off you'll have less of a turn to make and more momentum to make it with.

Momentum is central to good powder turns. If you take the time to find the point where your speed easily overcomes the resistance from the snow, your turns will be much smoother.

Powder Stance

The powder stance is a little different from the normal packed-slope stance. Placing all your weight on one ski—the goal for good skiers on hard snow—will cause it to dive deeper into the soft snow, while your other ski levitates toward the surface. The result, as Alf would say, is a "big to-do." Try to weight your feet equally in powder. Like water skis. With equal weight, even if the snow is "bottomless," you have the feeling of a platform beneath you, of something to stand and turn against. Experiment with your stance on straight runs. See what happens when you weight first one ski then the other. Now weight them equally, bounce, and curve.

Experiment too, with your balance fore and aft. Lean too far forward and the ski tips will dive in deep snow, bogging you down. Sit back and the tips will indeed come up to the surface, but the strength and balance of the position is poor. There is a myth about sitting back in powder, about sitting in "the invisible chair." It's a myth supported by photographs (which purportedly show powder skiers sitting back when in fact they are projecting their feet forward and to the side during the light phase of the turn) and by lingering memory of stiff skis that would indeed submarine with little provocation in deep snow. Modern skis flex and float easily from a neutral, centered stance. Sitting back only serves to produce burning thigh muscles and a loss of control over the skis.

Linking Powder Turns

Basic short-swing technique applies in powder with only a couple of changes. Those languid, slinky powder descents in the movies are really short-swing turns with a softer edge set and a more forceful outside hand. Here's what I mean.

Rather than set an edge (as you would on hard snow), in powder you finish the turn by pressing the skis, particularly the tails, into the snow, down and to the side. The skis, equally weighted, compress the snow and build their own platform under your feet. There is a soft rebound from this compression, and it is enough to launch you into the next turn.

This is where the outside hand comes in. To aid the unweighting, and the steering of the lightened skis toward the fall line, it helps to bring the outside hand up and forward with some energy. This strong up motion helps free your skis at the beginning of a new turn and also readies

the pole for the next pole plant. The heavier or deeper the snow, the stronger the up motion should be until it is almost, in Alf's term, an "uppercut."

The ultimate smoothing of your powder technique comes when you can absorb or swallow the rebound from the compressed finishes of your turns. When you feel strong resistance against your slowing skis, simply relax your legs and allow that resistance to push your feet, skis, and knees upwards. Simple. Like the extension/compression—the breathing—of a mogul turn, you are light when your legs are pushed up under you (initiation phase), and you complete the turn by extending, pushing, and steering the skis down into the snow (control phase).

All of the other aspects of good short-swing technique apply here. The torso should be fully anticipated for smooth linking of turns. Solid, down-the-hill pole plants help to time and position each turn. Rhythm begets success as small imbalances in one turn can be corrected by the one following. Rhythm blurs the line between the finish of one turn and beginning of the next. Energies flow together in a sinuous, uninterrupted set of esses.

More Powder

Beware, powder skiing can be addictive. Its cloudlike feel and its ability to slow down time will get under your skin and into your dreams. Those who develop a passion for powder are rarely satisfied at ski areas. Snow falls too infrequently and is skied out too fast. For these people the next step is outside the area boundaries, either as a backcountry skier or as a client of one of the snowcat or heli-ski operations. As a backcountry skier (see Chapter 8) you are on your own, committed to walking up for the run down and to learning the rules of utterly uncivilized mountain travel. It's serious business with equally dazzling rewards.

Snowcat Powder

Snowcat skiing is growing in popularity as an alternative to being on your own. The snow is wild, but the responsibilities are minimal. For a hundred dollars (more or less), you get lunch, a guide (who often also serves as a wild-snow ski instructor) and transportation via heated snowcat

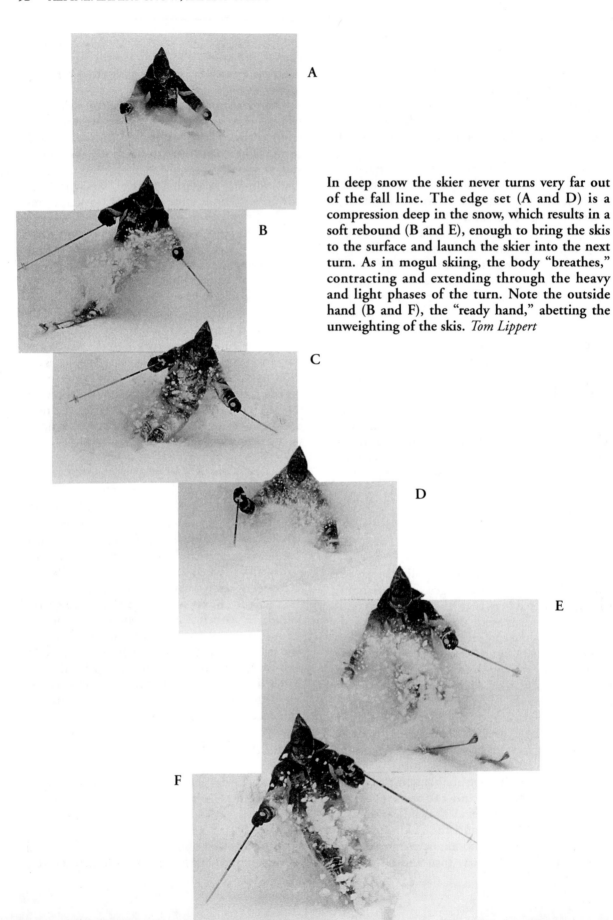

A

B

In deep snow the skier never turns very far out of the fall line. The edge set (A and D) is a compression deep in the snow, which results in a soft rebound (B and E), enough to bring the skis to the surface and launch the skier into the next turn. As in mogul skiing, the body "breathes," contracting and extending through the heavy and light phases of the turn. Note the outside hand (B and F), the "ready hand," abetting the unweighting of the skis. *Tom Lippert*

C

D

E

F

to the top of as many as ten powder runs a day. No hurries. No competition from lift skiers. No chance that the snow will be skied out. Most snowcat operations ply the hills near (or just off the back side of) established ski areas, operations like Powder Adventures at Aspen, Steamboat Powder Cats, and Winter Park's snowcat tours into Parsenne Bowl. A few, like Silvergate at Irwin Lodge (near Crested Butte, Colorado) and Mount Bailey Snowcats (Oregon) are true wilderness outfits.

Heli-Skiing

The ultimate in powder skiing is a week with one of the helicopter skiing companies. Interior British Columbia is the world capital of heli-skiing with at least ten companies sharing four wilderness mountain ranges. Helicopters are all but banned in the high mountains of the European Alps, but there is heli-skiing available in Colorado, Utah, Wyoming, Idaho, and Nevada. Die-hard fanatics also book heli-ski adventures to New Zealand's Alps and even to the Himalayas of Kashmir.

Heli-skiing is extremely expensive, but not unreasonable when you consider that it takes about $1700 in jet fuel (1990 prices) to fly the bird for one hour. The full week at a British Columbia lodge, all meals, and 100,000 vertical feet of skiing is the classic. But you can also arrange for day skiing (for a fee in the hundreds instead of thousands of dollars) at most U.S. heli outfits. The payoff for shelling out all this cash is being able to indulge your powder itch to the limit. The helicopter swoops its belly full of powder hounds to remote and pristine landings, often no bigger than a garage roof atop the peaks, then picks them up again at the valley floor. On a good day a strong-skiing group can wrack up 30,000 feet or more.

Of course, the powder isn't always perfect. Mountain weather is fickle, and sun, wind, and fluctuating temperatures work their transformations on expensive snow just as they do on the snow you take for free out of your car off the pass highway. But when it's good, when there is a blanket of new, crystalline fluff up to your knees, there is no thought of money. Only the soft, partially submerged dance that makes you

Basic ski tuning gear: 10-inch mill bastard file for flattening base and sharpening edges, file card, P-tex candle for filling gouges in base material, metal scraper for removing excess P-tex, plastic scraper for scraping wax, true bar for testing flat base, combination edge sharpening and beveling tool, stone for de-burring edges.

feel like a porpoise at play in an element made for graceful movement.

TIPS & TALES: *Ski Tuning*

A tuned ski does everything better. It goes faster, yes, but it also turns more easily at slow speeds, initiates and finishes turns with less effort on the part of the driver, holds better on hard snow and ice, slips with silky ease through deep snow, and just generally makes skiing more slinky fun.

You can get a decent tune and wax at any specialty ski shop for $15 to $30. Or you can learn to do it yourself for a small investment in tools and a considerable investment in your time and elbow grease. The results will more than pay back your efforts.

You need a workbench long enough to lay the skis out full length. You need a way to hold one ski at a time firmly in place as you work on the base and edges. There are special ski vises for sale for this purpose, or you can fashion something simpler. I use two 2X4 blocks bolted to the workbench to suspend the ski where the binding doesn't interfere. I've glued carpet strips to the top so the ski won't be scratched. And I've cut half-inch-wide by two-inch-deep notches in the blocks so I can hold the ski on edge and work on the sides of the edges.

You'll need a metal paint scraper for shaving down the base material, a diamond stone for taking the case-hardened scratches out of the edges, a ten-inch mill bastard file for sharpening the edges, P-Tex repair candles for filling gouges in the base, ski wax, and an old iron. It also helps to have a guaranteed straight piece of steel, like a tuning bar, to determine if the base is flat, edge to edge.

The biggest problem with skis that haven't been cared for in a long time, or even some skis right out of the box, is they aren't flat. Most skis are tuned at the factory. Some are prepared more carefully than others, and some warp in transit. The worst is "railed" skis. The bottoms are concave, edges higher than bases. Railed skis don't skid easily; they get hung up on their edges. They don't initiate or carve well, so that skiers on railed boards sometimes end up *jumping* their skis into turns. (Convex, base-high skis are less common. They slide very easily but don't hold a proper edge or carve a subtle arc.)

Bring down high edges with alternating applications of the stone and the file. Draw the file (at a 45-degree cutting angle) down the ski with both hands, taking care to keep it flat to the base. (Use heavy rubber bands to secure the ski brakes out of the way.) Sharpen until a fingernail drawn across the edge leaves a bit of epidermis.

Bring down a high base with the sharpened scraper. To sharpen, draw the edge along the side of a file laid flat on the bench. File the sides of the edges at 90 degrees to the base. You may want to buy a special side-filing tool for this job. It holds the file at an unwavering 90 degrees to the base. And some are adjustable so that you can file a slight bevel (.5 to 2.5 degrees) into the bottoms and sides of your edges. Beveling helps skis glide into the turns easier without sacrificing any edge hold. Burnish the edges with a Scotch-Brite kitchen pad.

Once the base is flat, fill in any remaining gouges with the P-Tex candle. Clean the base first with acetone solvent, then light the candle end and drip the plastic into the scratches. When dry, shave off the excess with the scraper.

When everything is smooth, flat, and sharp, it's time for the wax. There are myriad colors and formulas all designed to match temperature and snow texture. The simplest system is made by U.S. Wax: green for very cold (below zero), blue for up to freezing, red for above freezing, gold for a broad middle spectrum. Set the iron for delicate fabrics (cool setting), hold the bar of wax against the iron bottom and drip melted wax onto the ski. Smooth and soak the wax into the base. (Make sure the iron is a cast-off, because it will never again be suitable for any kind of fabric.) When cool and hardened, scrape all of the visible wax off. What remains impregnated in the base will last for days or weeks, depending on the snow.

It takes practice to be a good tuner, as it does to become a good skier. The work is honest. And the rewards are many, including superior performance and that sense of investing in graceful turns to come.

II

CROSS-COUNTRY SKIING

The romance of "crossing country" on skis.

5

The Cross-Country Story

Langlauf. Ski wandern. Ski touring. *Ski de fond.* Nordic skiing. *Langrenn.* They all mean the same: skiing across country.

From those first peat-bog skis (discovered near Hoting, Sweden, and dating from approximately 2500 B.C.) to the most modern foam-core, carbon-fiber, toothpick-thin racing beauties, the point of cross-country skiing has always been to get from here to there over the snow.

At first, it must have been purely practical. Skis were so utilitarian they were called "snow shoes" in Norway and were necessary during the long winters for trading, getting to stands of firewood, stalking reindeer, and just visiting from farm to farm and village to village. A carving on a rune stone from Boksta, Sweden, estimated to be a thousand years old, depicts a bow hunter on skis. He is wearing one long ski (called the "glider" and traditionally about 9 to12 feet long) and one short ski, the "kicker" ski (sometimes equipped with a fur kicker on the bottom). He balances like a tight-rope walker with one long wooden pole. Stories indicate that village hunters were easily identified by their uneven, often quite lopsided gaits.

Norwegian emigrants to the New World brought their skis with them or fashioned new ones from single planks of hickory or oak. They settled in the upper Midwest and in the mining districts of the Rockies and California. One of

the earliest accounts of skiing in California is the story of John "Snowshoe" Thompson. Thompson left his native Norway in 1851 to join the California gold rush.

At that time communications across the Sierra Nevada mountains were cut off each winter due to the 10 to 20 feet of snow blanketing the passes. (The same snow that thwarted the ill-fated Donner party in their efforts to get across in the winter of 1846-47.) Thompson, who was familiar with skiing from his childhood, volunteered to carry the mail on skis. He felled an oak tree, crafted a 25-pound pair of skis, and on January 3, 1856, struck out over the mountains, east from Placerville. He made the 90 miles to Genoa in the Carson Valley on the Nevada side, and returned to Placerville on January 18. The return trip took only three and one-half days, a remarkable feat in any era.

Through the 1860s Snowshoe Thompson was the only winter land link between California and the rest of the nation. Sometimes he'd carry as much as 100 pounds on his back, up the mountains and down, through blizzards and fair weather. Eventually, he was replaced by the railroad and stage, and in 1872 he retired, claiming the U.S. government owed him $5,000 for his years of mail carrying. He never collected.

Meanwhile, the use of Norwegian "snowshoes" spread through the Sierra mining camps.

John A. "Snowshoe" Thompson, a Norwegian immigrant to the gold camps of northern California, carried the mail across the snowbound Sierra Nevada. For several winters in the 1860s he was the sole land link between California and the rest of the country. *Courtesy Western America SkiSport Museum*

Children used them to get to school. Doctors made house calls on skis. Women skied in modest full-length skirts and stood tall in their bindings lest their petticoats fly up about their heads. But it was the miners themselves, largely unemployed during the winter months, who first made the leap from utility to sport. Their informal races quickly developed into multi-day tournaments with cash prizes for men, children, and Chinese laborers. In the 1860s racers at La Porte, California, organized the Alturas Snowshoe Club, probably the world's first ski club.

The courses they ran were straight ahead for speed. Skis were extremely long, up to 14 feet; turning was almost impossible. Special wax formulas, called dope, were brewed up by dopemen on the spot. They carried colorful names like Skedaddle, Greased Lightning, Slip Easy, Catch 'em Quick, Breakneck, and Slip Up. Recipes were closely guarded secrets. One included spermaceti, burgundy pitch, Canada pitch, Barbary tallow, camphor, and castor oil, among other things. The racers developed a low crouch on their skis to cut wind-resistance, a forerunner of the modern tuck position. Calculations show that they went amazingly fast. In 1874, champion Tommy Todd reached speeds of 88 mph.

Typical ski attire for the ladies around the turn of the century included modest skirts and the standard single ski pole. *Courtesy Western America SkiSport Museum*

Sierra miners, among the first to take skiing from pure utility into the realm of sport, raced for high stakes in the gold camps. There were no turns; they raced straight down the mountain. These men practiced their aerodynamic crouches atop 14-foot skis. *Western America SkiSport Museum*

Snowshoe Thompson journeyed 200 miles to compete in the La Porte races in 1869. Already a legend in California, Thompson was an expert at skiing the backcountry, at turning to avoid obstacles and running up and down hills. But he knew nothing about dope or the aerodynamic crouch. Predictably, he lost. But he wasn't converted. He showed nothing but disdain for their straight-running, their dope, and their squat, while the La Porte racers for their part regarded his upright style as effeminate.

Thus was the split between downhill and cross-country skiing symbolically defined. It wasn't until another fifty or sixty years had passed that the split became complete. It took the reinvention of downhill racing in the 1920s by Britain's Sir Arnold Lunn, and the proliferation of ski lifts in the 1930s, for the rift to become formal and irrevocable.

Meanwhile, long before the gold played out and the racing died out in California (the last competition was in 1911), skiing had spread to every other snowy part of the nation. A reverend-cum-mail carrier made his postal and spiritual rounds through the central Colorado mountains on skis. In the upper Midwest, Scandinavian immigrants started an immensely popular ski jumping competition circuit in the 1880s. Homesteaders in Idaho kept up with their neighbors via the ski trails. Denizens of the Northwest were already poking around the glacial lower slopes of Mount Rainier by the turn of the century. A signal event for skiing the Northeast was the formation in 1909 of the Dartmouth Outing Club, which built trails and huts in New Hampshire's White Mountains and promoted skiing and other winter sports.

THE NORDIC/ALPINE SPLIT

In Europe nordic and alpine styles developed separately according to the demands of the terrain. In the gentler, more rolling landscape of Norway and Sweden running and jumping remained the traditional events. Not that people

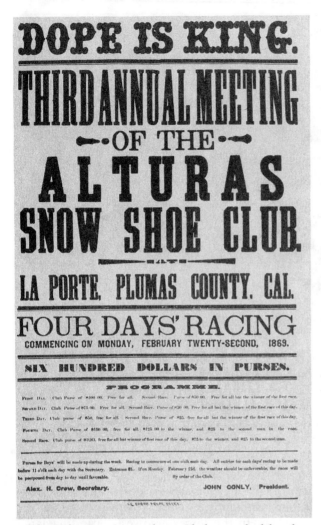

The Alturas Snowshoe Club, probably the world's first ski club, staged multi-day competitions at La Porte, California. Secret speed wax concoctions were known as "dope."
Courtesy Western America SkiSport Museum

weren't winging downhill and even making turns. Sondre Norheim, a native of the Telemark region, invented a striding, feet-apart turn that became the first really effective way of turning skis. Today we know it as the telemark turn. But turning didn't have the urgency in Norway that it did in the Alps. There, skiers like Austria's Mathias Zdarsky needed a way to control their more hair-raising daily descents to town and school, etc. Zdarsky developed a slow-speed stem turn and in 1896 wrote the first book of ski instruction. The alpine age—at least in terms of ski technique—was officially begun.

Ski equipment in Zdarsky's time hadn't yet begun to evolve along the separate lines of cross country and downhill. Skis were long, 7 to 9 feet, and heavy. They were carved from a single plank of wood, steamed, and bent at the tip. Bindings consisted of a leather toe strap which allowed free-heel movement and therefore worked fine walking uphill, but they were less sure on the descent. (Norheim's telemark turn incorporated the free heel, depended on it in fact. Linking telemark turns is very much like walking or striding down the hill.) With the new downhill techniques of Zdarsky and shortly thereafter Hannes Schneider, the free heel was a liability.

ALPINE TAKES OFF

In the 1920s and '30s the evolutionary lines diverged. While cross-country gear and techniques remained largely unchanged, alpine took off with the energy of a real revolution. Sir Arnold Lunn's slalom races, the first to demand a skier make turns around flagged poles, set the stage for the multiple disciplines we know today: slalom, giant slalom, super giant slalom and downhill. Ski inventors added cables and springs to the basic binding to secure the heel in place for better turning control. And then the really huge change: the development of ski lifts. With uphill transportation provided (first with rope tows, then T-bars, then chairlifts), skiing gained mass appeal. You no longer had to be especially hardy to brave the slopes. No one had to walk up any more. And when walking was no longer at least half of the equation, there was no longer any need for free heels. By the 1950s, when alpine skiing boomed exponentially here and in Europe, the tables had almost completely turned: The telemark was all but forgotten; anyone who ventured outside the lift-served area to ski over hill and dale, up and down and cross country, was the eccentric.

The old ways persisted in the nordic countries where ski runners and jumpers were still the national heroes. Free heel was still more practical. The world watched in admiration as Finns on skis and in white camouflage held off the invading Russians. In international competitions, before and after the war, the winners in the nordic events were always Scandinavians, with the Russians coming on in the 1960s and '70s. In this country, nordic skiing commanded a small but loyal

Jump hills proliferated in the upper Midwest beginning in the 1880s. This one is the "Suicide" hill at Ishpeming, Michigan. *National Ski Hall of Fame*

The Ishpeming Ski Club was dominated by names like Saari, Beitila, and Erkkila, names that reflect the Scandinavian influence which brought skiing to North America. *National Ski Hall of Fame.*

**The elegant telemark turn, born in the town of the same name in Norway,
made its comeback in the western American backcountry in the 1970s.**

following, mostly in the upper Midwest, but also at scattered outposts like Sven Wiik's lodge in Colorado and at the von Trapp family lodge in Stowe, Vermont. (The von Trapps are the real-life Austrian family whose story became the basis for *The Sound of Music.*)

The evolution of cross-country equipment lagged behind the changes in alpine. By the early 1970s alpine skis were made of fiberglass and aircraft aluminum, while cross-country skis were still crafted of varnished laminated woods. Alpine boots were then being molded out of high-tech plastics, while nordic boots were leather and laces. Alpine enthusiasts dressed in stretch pants and fashion parkas, while nordic aficionados were still in knickers and reindeer sweaters. Most of cross-country's research and development energy went into waxing. By its up-and-down nature, cross-country waxes had to solve the difficult and dichotomous challenge of providing both grip and glide. Skis had to grip in order for the skier to go uphill without slipping, and they needed to break free and glide on the downhills and flats. Indeed skiers benefited from (and sometimes

suffocated under) a myriad wax combinations and application theories to match every conceivable snow condition.

But well into the decade of the 1970s, cross country was still the poor cousin of alpine, the low-tech, anti-social, anti-fashion, apparently strenuous, odd-ball throwback to skiing's sweatier past. Then, rather quickly, things started to change. Two parallel but separate movements arose.

CROSS-COUNTRY RESURGENCE

On one hand, the very glamour and civility of alpine skiing generated a backlash. A significant number of skiers craved the adventure of the old way of skiing through the backcountry. They craved the wild snow, the camaraderie of the trek and the responsibility of the group to take care of itself. Then too, many people simply couldn't afford downhill skiing any more. All the new lifts and grooming and snow making came with a price. Smaller areas were going under, succumbing to the industry-wide move toward large-scale resort development. It made sense for a lot of people to eschew the lifts altogether, pile the family in the car, drive to the snow and take off on much simpler, much less costly free-heel gear.

In the mid '70s the telemark turn experienced a rebirth. Ski patrolmen at Crested Butte in western Colorado like to take credit for the phoenix-like comeback. More likely the return was simultaneous at a number of ski centers, but theirs is a good story. Patrollers at the Butte had a big chunk of steep terrain just outside the area boundary that was rife with avalanche paths. In order to control the slides, they had to ski the chutes and bowls themselves and hurl an occasional explosive charge into the start zones. The problem was, the bottom of this powder region (now known as the North Face) was below the lowest lift-served point on the mountain. Patrolmen found themselves grunting and sidestepping on their inflexible alpine gear back up to the groomed slopes. The answer was to use cross-country gear. The return was infinitely easier, and the skiers found that the telemark turn worked just fine on the downhill, especially when the snow was deep.

Experienced alpine skiers looking for a new challenge tried the telemark. Others, new to skiing altogether and unwilling or unable to join the alpine set, took to the hills with the new/old gear. It was a soulful revolution, connected to an easily romanticized past, and right in step with the '70s back-to-nature movement. Within a decade, telemarkers were everywhere plying graceful, knee-drop turns on-piste and off.

BOOM ON THE TRACK

The other arm of the revolution took place on the track. In the 1970s alpine ski companies began to branch out and build cross-country skis. Overnight they got lighter and springier and

Track skiing, always a passion in Scandinavia, bloomed world wide with the universal fitness movement of the 1970s and '80s.

much faster. Poles went from bamboo to fiberglass to carbon fiber. Cross-country racers began wearing the slinky, one-piece suits their alpine brethren wore. Coaches began experimenting with various waxless bases, mechanical configurations like fish-scales or "hairy" bases that would serve the function of wax without suffering wax's limitations. The same grooming machines that smoothed the alpine slopes were used to set immaculate, uniform, hard-packed cross-country track, where before skiers or snowmobiles, and even horse-drawn sleighs had done the work.

Then in 1976 America found a cross-country hero. Taciturn Vermonter Bill Koch (pronounced like the soft drink) garnered a silver medal in the 30-kilometer race at the '76 winter games in Innsbruck. Suddenly, cross-country was cool. Touring centers bloomed on the snowy landscape as potentially glamorous as alpine resorts. The boom coincided with the new emphasis on fitness around the country. Sweating was okay again, and cross country was deemed aerobically superior to just about any other activity, better than swimming, bicycling and tennis, and less jarring than running.

But Kochie (as he was known) was to become even more important in the overall scheme of cross country in 1982 when he won four individual races and the year-long World Cup

Touring—inn-to-inn, hut-to-hut, town-to-town, or just out for a day's picnic—is an increasingly popular alternative to alpine skiing.

Solitude, low cost, and adventure have led many skiers to discover cross-country full circle: back to the simple act of crossing the landscape on long, slippery "snow shoes." *Linde Waidhofer*

championship—the first time in history a Scandinavian or a Russian had failed to win it. That an American won was revolutionary enough. *How* he did it was even more radical. Kochie won races by skating on his cross-country skis.

SKATING FEVER

Ski skating was not new. Those Scandinavian hunters are thought to have used skating motions on their skis. More recently, in 1971, East German Gerhard Grimmer won a 50-kilometer race in Oslo using a skating step (one ski in the prepared track while the other ski pushed off outside the track providing the skating propulsion). The weather had changed suddenly, mid-race, and his wax failed. Everyone else's wax

failed too, and they either re-waxed, dropped out, or struggled along in a traditional diagonal stride. Grimmer won the race by several minutes in one of the biggest routs on record.

Somehow, though, no one grasped the importance of what had happened until Kochie appeared in the next decade. Old-liners (primarily Scandinavian) in the FIS (the Federation Internationale du Ski, the sport's ruling body) cried foul and tried to legislate the skate away. "Untraditional," they groused. "Not skiing at all." They tried building snow berms on the tracks to hem skaters in. They set up nets along the trails to snare the tips of offending skaters' skis. One frustrated official actually tackled a skier in an attempt to stop him from skating.

But the racers knew a simple truth: skating was the fastest way to get from point A to point B.

Diagonal striders were left in the (snow)dust. Skating would not go away. Today, in a compromise that recognizes two distinct disciplines (similar to the legislated split between the much faster butterfly and the breaststroke in swimming), Cup and Olympic events are evenly divided between "classic" races, where there is no skating allowed, and "freestyle," where everybody skates. To be competitive on the international circuit, a skier must be good at both techniques.

Citizen racers and recreational cross-country skiers took to the skate like bees to honey. Manufacturers came out with special (and improved) skating gear. Touring centers across the land started grooming a right-hand lane on their trail systems with grooved track for the traditionalists and a left-hand, open lane for the skaters. Skating boosted cross-country skiing into the same recreational arena with alpine skiing, really for the first time since the two split in the early decades of the century.

CROSS COUNTRY BRANCHES

There are other splinter groups or sub-sports to cross country besides the skating and "classic" on-track techniques. There is telemarking, lift-served and in the backcountry; the revival continues with specialized skis, better boots, and new binding systems. There is what is known simply as touring, the snowy version of hiking. Using skis lighter and narrower than telemark gear (but not so toothpick-thin as track skis), tourers strike out on wilderness trails or through virgin, untracked snow for an hour, a day, or a week of snow camping. In Bill Koch's New England, touring from inn to inn and town to town has become a winter equivalent of summer bicycle touring.

Finally, there is an upsurge of interest in this country for alpine touring, or what in Europe is called *randonée* excursioning on skis. Alpine tourers are ski mountaineers, climbing a peak only to turn around and ski its wild shapes back to civilization. The classic alpine tour is the Haute Route, the high route connecting Chamonix, France, with Zermatt, Switzerland. For a week or more skiers stitch together days in the above-timberline alpine snows with nights in judiciously spaced huts. Similar hut-to-hut systems are cropping up in the Colorado Rockies (along the Tenth Mountain Division Trail) and along the Appalachian Trail.

Alpine touring equipment is hybrid stuff. The skis are alpine boards but shorter and more maneuverable. Boots resemble plastic alpine boots but with rubber hiking-boot soles for easier walking and security on rock and ice. The bindings function in two modes, one that allows free heel lift during the ascent and a second to latch the heel down for the downhill run. In the old times skiers affixed seal skins or other animal skin to the bottom of their skis for uphill traction. Today, alpine tourers use "skins" of nylon and polypropylene. The gear has changed dramatically in materials and sophistication of design, but the purpose is unchanged from the earliest days of skiing: to move with ease and as much grace as one can muster up and down over the frozen landscape. In that sense alpine touring has brought the sport full circle.

6

Track Skiing

Out of the aspens come two figures, one in red, the other in blue. At first, at this great distance, it looks like neither is moving very fast, but looks are deceiving. The figure in red is swaying back and forth, first on one leg, then, springing ahead, on the other. Her arms and extra-long poles sweep through each stroke like a canoeist working into the wind. The blue figure is not swaying but rather striding with long, exaggerated arm and leg swings, like a man running in slow motion in sand. As they flash by, bright Lycra suits gleaming in the light, their movements reveal surprising power. They pass in a whoosh of speed, their skis humming over the snow.

They are track skiers, cross-country skiing's version of sleek middle-distance runners. The lady in red is skating on skis, a sight more and more common on cross-country tracks. Born of a revolution on the World Cup racing circuit, the technique has quickly filtered down to recreational skiers and citizen racers. Skating is simple, graceful, and fast, up to twenty percent faster than traditional techniques like the diagonal stride.

That's the technique used by the man in blue. Diagonal or "classic" technique is the oldest movement on skis, the same movement as walking or running. Only with skis on, on snow, there is the added beauty (and speed) of gliding between the steps.

If Snowshoe Thompson had had a set track he probably would have made the Genoa to Placerville trans-Sierra route in a day and a half. This is a relatively new branch on the skiing tree, brought on by advances in trail grooming technology and corresponding leaps in the efficacy of ski gear. It's a very civilized branch. Tracks are now set in big city parks in Minneapolis, Chicago, almost every northern city and town. Most alpine ski areas also provide set track as an alternative for their downhill customers and as an attractive amenity on its own. Tracks range from loops of just a kilometer or two to long, wandering paths of 30 and even 50 kilometers. Most are graded beginner-through-expert just like alpine trails.

People take a spin around the track on their lunch hour the way they might jog in the summer. Or plan whole winter vacations around the track skiing at mega resorts like Royal Gorge in California's Sierra (not far from Thomson's historic route), Giant's Ridge in northern Minnesota, Devil's Thumb Ranch in Colorado, Bretton Woods in New Hampshire, and the Trapp Family Lodge in Stowe, Vermont.

Cross-country resorts typically groom 30 to 150 kilometers of track with parallel grooves for diagonal striders and open lanes for skaters. Warming huts along the trails provide rest stops, shelter from the weather (track skiers can dress

Skating is the newest and fastest technique for sliding around a cross-country track. *Mount Bachelor*

lightly; exercise keeps them warm), sometimes food and hot drink and a waxing bench. At the end of a session, skiers tumble into the base lodge before the fire.

Tracks provide a pleasant, non-wilderness setting in which to experience the freedom of skiing: the graceful movement, the winter air and frosty landscape. And there is no possibility of becoming lost. No need for packs or food, maps or emergency gear. Track skiers are the aerobic dancers of the ski world, out for pure, unencumbered exercise, a swift, elegant passage over the snow without "going" anywhere.

Track skiing fees are typically a quarter (or less) the ticket price for downhill skiing. Track gear, while becoming more sophisticated all the time, is still much less costly than alpine equipment. All of which makes track skiing a viable option for skiing families or anyone stunned by the high price of alpine skiing.

TRACK EQUIPMENT

The first question when it comes to equipment for the track is, what technique will you be using, diagonal or skate? The gear is different for the two skiing styles, and while a beginner may not need to invest in specialized skis, boots and bindings, it is most helpful to have a look at the demands of the two styles and the different solutions the equipment manufacturers have evolved.

Most beginners start with the diagonal stride—although some gifted athletes and any number of children start right in skating. They take to it as they would to a pair of roller skates.

Diagonal takes its name from the action of the arms and legs in a natural walking or running gait—that is, when the right foot strides ahead, the left arm swings forward and vice versa. The arms and legs are opposed, or diagonal. The boot, like a lightweight running shoe, is attached to the ski only at the toe; the heel is completely free to simulate the walking movement.

There are two phases to the diagonal stride, the *kick* and the *glide*. (In fact, diagonal technique is sometimes referred to as kick-and-glide skiing.) In the kick phase, you press the ski's mid-section down onto the snow where the kick wax (or waxless pattern machined into the base) grips the snow and allows you to propel yourself forward.

You kick off one foot and glide on the other, like that slow-motion runner. When the glide slows, you kick again: right, left, right. And so on.

The diagonal-technique ski, therefore, is built with a wax pocket under the foot and a good deal of camber, the built-in arch you see when you put two skis together, base to base. Camber allows the ski to glide smoothly on the tip and tail, which are waxed for speed, while the wax pocket, with its stickier kick wax, skims just above the snow surface. Until, that is, you press down (kick phase), engaging the kick wax.

A diagonal ski is designed to move straight ahead in the grooves. A skate ski, on the other hand, functions outside the grooves on the smooth packed lane to the side. A skater propels himself forward by pushing off an edged ski and striding off at an angle on the other foot, back and forth the way an ice skater does. Skate skis have no wax pocket. They are prepared strictly for glide. They don't need the camber "arch" that diagonal skis have.

Skaters edge sharply with every push and glide, so skate boots need to provide more lateral and torsional stiffness than diagonal boots do. They are still free at the heel, but the boots are usually higher around the ankle and stiffer overall. Skaters generally use shorter skis (so as not to step on their own tails) and longer poles (as long as head height for greater pushing leverage) than do striders.

So you can see that equipment selection, based on technique, is important. As I said in the alpine section, I heartily recommend renting gear for the first few times out. All touring centers have serviceable beginner setups for rent. Then, whether you develop a fondness for one technique or the other, or both, you will know better what you want.

Manufacturers are now making combination gear that works well with both techniques. The skis are a little softer flexing than a pure skate ski but with enough camber to perform the kick-and-glide. Boots are designed to allow the greater foot flex demanded by striding, while at the same time providing enough lateral stiffness to support the motions of skating. Most devoted tracks skiers sport a quiver of skis: the right tool for the job at hand. But for skiers just starting out, the combi gear is a good option.

With that in mind, let's look at the specifics of each equipment category.

DIAGONAL SKIS

Your goal is the pursuit of unencumbered speed, the frictionless slide over the snow. Since speed and friction are mortal enemies, diagonal track skis are designed to slice like javelins through the resistance. Some are, in fact, shaped like javelins, a kind of radical teardrop as little as 42 millimeters wide under the foot, for minimal drag. Others are built straight from tip to tail. Still others are given sidecut, as alpine skis have, with wider tips and tails and a narrower waist. Sidecut improves straight-line tracking and makes turning easier.

Most in-track, diagonal skis are either straight or javelin-shaped. They can weigh as little as 500 grams, or not much more than a pound apiece— so ethereal at times they seem to vanish completely, leaving only a pleasant edgy-slippery feeling at the ends of your feet. All this technology costs money, of course. Thoroughbreds start at about $300-$350, not quite in the same realm as top-of-the-line alpine gear, but getting close. Most manufacturers make slightly detuned (and less expensive) versions for citizen racers and recreation-minded track fans.

The range of ski manufacturers is boggling. There are the traditional Scandinavian ski makers, most of whom started in the wood-ski era and have now switched nearly completely to foam and fiberglass. These include: Äsnes, Bonna, Jarvinen, Karhu, Landsem, and Peltonen. Then there are the alpine ski companies, who joined the fray, most of them, in the 1980s when it became clear that their technologies could compete and even best the slow-changing traditionalists. These include: Atomic, Blizzard, Fischer, Kastle, Kneissl (all Austrian), the French giant Rossignol, and the West German Volkl.

Ski Fit

No matter what ski brand or model you buy, the essential consideration must be fit. Length is only part of the equation. Far more crucial is choosing a ski with the right flex for your weight and skill level. A ski with too stiff a flex (or too much camber) for you will glide like soap, but you will have a difficult time pressing its midsection down for grip. Conversely, too little camber (or too soft flex) will result in good grip but poor glide. Enlist the help of a knowledgeable shop fitter.

Relative shapes of alpine and cross-country skis. The telemark is a slightly narrower version of an alpine ski with a wide shovel and sidecut for downhill turning ease. The touring ski is narrower still with just a little sidecut. And the track ski is straight-sided or even javelin-shaped for frictionless straight running in the grooves.
Lito Tejada-Flores

A simple ski-shop test will go a long way toward preventing a costly mistake. On a carpetless floor, stand on a pair of skis, full weight on one, then on the other. If you can't bend the ski flat, it's too stiff. A second test, somewhat more mystical but equally effective, involves standing the skis up and squeezing them, base-to-base, at their midpoint. If you can easily squeeze them flat with one hand, they may be too soft. One hand with difficulty is about right. Two hands with difficulty, they're probably too stiff.

As for length, a good rule of thumb is head height minus 10 cm for beginners, head height for intermediates, and plus 10 cm for frequent skiers. The longer the ski the more stable it will be. Shorter skis are easier to maneuver at slower speeds.

The Waxless Option

One final consideration—do you want waxable or waxless skis? Wax, and other grippy substances (pine pitch, tar, mohair), go back centuries. The essential problem of climbing hills and pushing across flats without the skis slipping backward required something grabby under the foot. In 1967 a New Englander named William Bennett came up with an entirely new solution. He cut tiny fish-scales in the base, like shingles slanting backwards. It turned out the fish-scales "caught" the snow and kept the skis from sliding backward while still allowing them to slip forward. Bennett's idea eventually became the Trak fish-scale ski, which appealed to a whole generation of new skiers, skiers intrigued with the idea of an easy, fitness-oriented approach to skiing, a group that had no interest in the mysteries of waxing.

How good are waxless skis? They continue to get better, but the fact remains, a well-waxed ski will almost always out-perform a waxless ski. The exception is when temperatures are right at the freezing mark—at or near 32° F. Then waxless skis shine. If you ski in the far West or the Pacific Northwest where warm, marine snow often falls in this near-freezing zone, waxless skis are a good option. In the Rockies, the Midwest, and most winters in the Northeast, where snowfalls are colder and air temperatures remain well below freezing, then waxable skis are probably the better option. (For a complete look at the "mystique" of waxing, see the waxing section later in this chapter.)

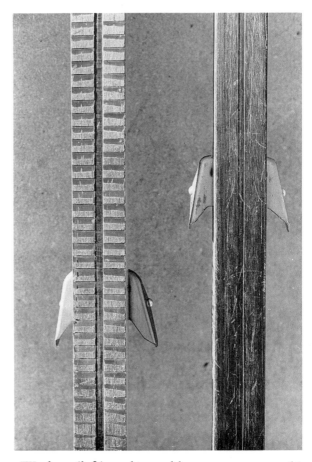

Waxless (left) and waxable cross–country ski bases. The waxless step pattern, like overlapping shingles, allows forward glide but grips the snow to prevent backsliding. The art of waxing for different snow conditions is easier than myth would have it and ultimately provides a better grip and glide. Skiers who get out only occasionally usually prefer waxless, while devotees usually learn (and learn to enjoy) the waxing process.

RECREATIONAL SKIS

"Recreational" is the industry pseudonym for beginning skiers or skiers who get out but once or twice a year. No one, it seems, enjoys being called a beginner. And with rapid progress the rule rather than the exception on the track, few remain beginners for very long. Thus, the "recreational" category makes sense.

Recreational skis are the least expensive in a

given manufacturer's line. Some find their way into the skis/boots/poles packages offered by the big catalog stores like REI and L.L. Bean. (These are often quite a bargain, lopping $100 or more off the total price.) Most have simple constructions: a light foam core with a fiberglass box built around it and a P-tex or other polyethylene plastic base. There are still a few laminated wood skis in production. Norwegian companies Bonna and Äsnes still make inexpensive hickory woodies, but for the most part the lighter weight and maintenance-free nature of fiberglass has erased the wooden ski from sight.

These skis are broader than race skis—anywhere from 45 to 50 mm wide under the foot—for stability. They are also slightly heavier—700 to 900 grams per ski—and softer flexing to tilt performance characteristics toward a good grip as opposed to a slippery glide. These are all things that can help a novice or occasional skier enjoy an outing right off the bat and progress quickly.

Waxless Skis

A high percentage of skis in this category are waxless, on the assumption that eliminating wax makes getting started that much simpler. It's also true that recreational skiers don't demand or need the kind of high performance more serious skiers require. Waxless skis are usually quite reliable on hill climbs, but they are notoriously slow on the glide.

Trak's entire line is waxless, utilizing evolved forms of their original fish-scale pattern. Fischer's larger, rounded scale is called the "Crown" pattern. Kastle calls theirs the "Vario." Kneissl's is the "Pentron." Atomic calls theirs the "Tricone" pattern. And so on. At least two companies, Blizzard and Rossignol, have experimented with viscoelastic materials in the kick zone which act like wax but aren't. Reactions have been mixed. So far pattern bases outperform the space-age experiments, but who knows? Some day the chem labs may come up with a material that does both grip and glide with equal aplomb in all snow conditions.

The length of the pattern tells you for whom the ski was designed. For example, Trak may offer two similar skis, one with a 50-cm-long pattern, the other with a 75-cm pattern. The longer pattern would be more appropriate for beginners and lighter skiers; the shorter one will work best for skiers with more advanced skills.

Waxable Skis

The Scandinavian companies tend to have more waxable skis in recreational models than do the European ski makers. Two exceptions are Fischer and Rossignol, which both offer very good beginners' skis at the higher end of the price spectrum. A pair of Fischer Superlights, for example, will set you back about as much as the full package cost featuring the very good ski Karhu builds for L.L. Bean.

HIGH-PERFORMANCE DIAGONAL

Here again, the terminology requires a little explaining. High performance is the mid-range gear, between recreational and racing. So, even though racers are looking for high performance skis, et al, they would not look in this category. This stuff is for athletic beginners, advancing intermediates or skiers with advanced-level skills who simply don't want a high-strung race ski.

High-performance diagonal skis are almost all waxable, because, as I said before, a properly waxed ski is nearly always faster than a waxless one. The waxless exceptions include the Fischer Superlight Crown, the Atomic Arc Classic Tricone, and the Alpina Touring 1000.

High-performance skis are generally narrower than recreational skis—in the 43 to 47-mm range. They are lighter by around 100 grams per ski, and the more expensive materials that go into that weight shaving (carbon fibers, kevlar) tend to drive the price toward the $300 range.

By the time you are ready to buy in the high-performance category, you probably will want to add your local snow condition into the selection equation. Manufacturers build multiple versions of their race skis (sometimes three or four), for soft-snow or hard-snow tracks. Softer flexing skis work better in soft tracks, firmer skis in hard-snow conditions. Some of this specificity has filtered down to high-performance skis. For example, the Jarvinen RSS Synchron Mix is a soft-track ski, where its sibling, the RSS Synchron Mix Electra, is best suited to very hard snows.

Among the proven classics in the high-performance category are the Karhu SCX, the Fischer SCS Universal, and (despite the seeming misnomer) the Blizzard Racer.

DIAGONAL RACERS

Racers *means* racers. Top-of-the-line performance and price. But you don't have to be a racer to appreciate them. Many expert non-racers simply enjoy the subtle beauties of top-end skis. Be aware though, racing skis do demand a higher level of expertise. Most intermediates would find them too stiff for good grip, and very swift— probably too swift and skittish on the downhills.

Racing skis are the narrowest of their kind (they're sometimes referred to as "toothpick skis") —generally between 43 and 44 mm under the foot, as little as 39 mm at the shovel (tip). They are also the lightest—between 540 and 590 grams per ski. Some have superlight air-channel cores (Fischer). Rossignol uses a carbon honeycomb. High-density urethane foams have all but banished heavier woods as a core material. Most racers choose a ski in the 195-205 cm length depending on the skier's size and the relative stability of the ski model.

Four model lines stand out as having been particularly successful during the 1980s and into the 1990s: the Karhu Matrix series, the Fischer RCS series, the Kneissl White Star series, and the Rossignol Delta series. They are series because each ski comes in versions for differing track and snow conditions. The Karhu Matrix (about $350) is typical. The company makes three editions of the diagonal racing ski (not to mention the skating versions): the Matrix Green, Blue, and Red. The colors refer to wax colors, which in turn indicate suitability for very cold, cold, and warm conditions. The differences are manifested in different flex patterns and different base materials.

Once again, more important than a particular brand name or association (it's only natural to want to put yourself on the same ski that Gunde Svan, the dominant skier of the '80s, skis on—it's Kneissl), more important than expense or the current vogue, is getting a proper fit. The best way to ensure that is to find a ski shop, and a ski fitter, you can trust and to demo as many skis as you can. Nothing beats on-snow experience for deciding what fits your body and your style.

HIGH-PERFORMANCE SKATING SKIS

There are fewer skating skis to choose from than there are diagonal models, and there are virtually none in the recreational category. The assumption is that first-time skaters will already have had some experience track skiing and so will naturally bypass the "recreational" level. Also, skating by nature means more stress on the equipment and so building an inexpensive skating ski doesn't make sense. Thus the base level for skating gear is the high-performance or "training" ski.

Skating has been around for such a short time, that what constitutes a good skate ski is just coming into focus. It is clear that a skate ski must have a powerful midsection and edge, for pushing off the edge is the sole means of propulsion. It must track well on its own, because skaters are not riding in the grooves as are diagonal skiers. They must be fast gliders, because gliding is the name of the game in skating; there is no kick wax, no wax pocket built into the ski's camber, nothing but pure gliding speed to keep the skater going, even up hills.

There are few hard and fast rules for achieving these goals. Some manufacturers (Landsem, Morotto, Rossignol) build a little sidecut into the forebodies of their skating skis to give them straight-line stability and better handling in the turns. Others have stuck with the traditional javelin or straight-side shapes. Some have built-in metal or hard plastic edges, the better to cut through and push off very hard snows. Most track skis have no edges. Some skate skis have multiple grooves cut in their bases to improve tracking, others have just one. Some manufacturers have taken to wrapping the P-tex base material all the way up and around the sidewalls of the skis. This way the sidewalls can be waxed as well as the base. Theoretically at least, since skaters are on edge so much of the time, this should make them faster.

And so on. A few things are agreed upon. Skate skis should be shorter than diagonal models, somewhere between 180 and 200 cm. Longer skis are cumbersome in the side-to-side skating movement. You can trip on your own tails.

Skate skis have a lower tip profile than diagonal skis. They don't need a high tip to aid in steering through the grooves.

Last and most important is the need for different flex patterns for different snow conditions. Skis with relatively soft flex and soft torque resistance glide faster in soft snow. But they will be difficult to handle on a hard track. Similarly, a stiff, high-torque ski will track straight and true on a hard course but will bog down and glide poorly in soft snow. So, where you ski is critical to which ski you choose.

For some reason Finnish skis excel in soft snow, the kind of snow typically found in the Rockies and in the Far West. Peltonen, Jarvinen, and Karhu all make excellent soft-snow skating skis in the $200-$300 range.

It's not surprising that some of the best hard-snow skis come from the alpine manufacturers who have turned their attention to the track: Fischer and Kneissl, Elan (Yugoslavia), Rossignol, and Volkl. The Fischer LS Skating GR, the Rossignol Carbon, and the Volkl Greyhound 400 Skate all excel in the high-performance zone. The Kneissl WM Skate Graphite has become a classic of the genre in just a few years.

Skate Racers

The WM's big brother is Kneissl's full-on skate racer, the White Star Ultra Skate Graphite. It's 120 grams lighter per ski at 554 grams each, a little sliver of lightning on the feet. The Ultra costs about $100 more as well.

The difference between the true racers and the high-performance models one step below is this high-tech shaving of weight and the sacrifice of easy-handling characteristics (tracking ability, stability) for pure glide speed. You have to be a good skier to stay with them. But in races of 15 or 30 kilometers that are won by seconds or even hundredths of seconds, weight and speed are everything.

On the World Cup circuit, track skiing's major leagues, a few companies stand out as dominant. They are the ones pushing the limits of ski-making technologies. Fischer has been a consistent winner with its RCS series, the first skis with superlight honeycomb cores. Karhu's Matrix series skis were among the first with waxable sidewalls and different bases for warm and cold snows. Kneissl has been among the first to experiment with double sintered bases, two kinds of polyethylene in a melded patchwork that may widen the ski's temperature range.

When choosing a race ski, remember: an innovative ski may not be particularly fast on the wrong feet. Fit is even more crucial here than it is at the recreational level. Get some professional advice. Ski on as many different skis as you can through rental and demo programs. If your boot/binding systems are compatible, swap skis with your friends. The investigative work will pay off in the long run.

COMBI SKIS

Recognizing that a good many skiers would probably do both, stride and skate, if they had a ski that could handle both techniques, many manufacturers have come up with combi skis. The combis have a flex pattern that will accommodate kick waxing, but are more powerful on edge than a straight-ahead diagonal ski. They're stiffer torsionally than diagonal models, yet they are more forgiving in the grooves than pure skating skis would be. They're built to be skied in skating lengths (10 to 20 cm shorter than diagonal skis).

Rossignol, Fischer, Landsem, Blizzard, and Peltonen all have combi models in the mid-range, $100-$200 below race ski prices.

BOOTS AND BINDINGS

When you talk boots and bindings for track skis, you are talking boot/binding *systems*. It used to be that just about any boot fit in just about any ski binding. Everything matched the so-called Nordic Norm. All boots had 75-mm-wide toes, and all bindings had 75-mm-wide metal flanges to accept them. Boot soles came with three holes in the toe area, and the bindings had three corresponding pins to hold the boot firmly in place. Whole generations of cross-country skiers were known as "three-pin skiers" or with tongue-in-cheek, "pin heads."

Then in the late 1970s and early 1980s, as cross-country was beginning to boom as an alternative to alpine skiing, manufacturers began fiddling with the standard setup. Adidas, the German running-shoe giant, was the first to introduce a lightweight, step-in, non-universal boot/binding. Their boot (which looked very much like a low-cut running shoe) wouldn't mate with any other binding, and you couldn't use any other shoe in their minimalist, plastic binding.

It became all the rage. Salomon came out with its own boot/binding in 1980. Others followed. The Nordic Norm, with its clunky bails and wide "wings" that bumped the sides of the grooves, all but vanished from the track. (Three-pin bindings are still very much a part of the off-track scene. See Chapter 7.) In its place were a myriad incompatibles. Slowly, "the systems," as they were called, shook out, until now there are only three: the Salomon SNS (Salomon Nordic System), the NNN (New Nordic Norm) system developed by the Norwegian company Rottefella, and Tyrolia's TXC. Each company licenses boot makers who use the system's binding-compatible soles. Salomon's licensees include Hartjes, Jalas, Karhu, Heirling, Trak and Merrell. Hartjes, Rossignol and Alpina build boots to match the NNN binding.

Like the old three-pin, the systems attach only the boot toe to the ski while leaving the heel free to move up and down. But unlike the old norm, the boot/ski connection is much improved when the heel is down. This is due to a channel-and-ridge system underfoot. A channel is molded into the hard plastic of the boot sole to precisely match a ski-top ridge. Resistance to lateral slippage and the twisting forces in turning—forces that eventually ripped apart the toes of three-pin boots—are excellent.

In-track boots should fit like a running shoe

and stabilize the foot in much the same way so you can ride a flat—not a wobbly—ski. Diagonal technique boots are more flexible at the ball of the foot to allow for the bending of the forefoot in a long stride. Skate boots must provide more support for the ankles, the better to edge the ski with. Skate boots are generally higher and stiffer. Some, like the Salomon Profil Equipe Skate and the Karhu Profil Skate (at the top of the range at about $200 a pair) even sport plastic cuffs to firm up the support. Skate boots don't hinge at the forefoot. The action of full-extension skating is accommodated by the hinged binding.

There are also combi boots which work acceptably in both striding and skating. They are higher and stiffer-soled than pure striding boots, but not so rigid as skate boots. Alpina, Salomon, and Tyrolia all make combis in the mid-price range, $50-$75 below top race-boot prices.

POLES

As simple as they may seem, poles have not escaped the equipment revolution. High-tech carbon fibers, while they are too brittle for everyday use, have shaved precious grams from racer models. And while they don't cost nearly what their carbon-fiber fly rod cousins do, they can exceed $200 per pair. Fiberglass and aluminum models, while slightly heavier, are much stronger and much more practical for most

A boot/binding system for track skiing, specifically for skating. As light as a running shoe, the boot clicks into the toe piece providing free-heel movement. Plastic ridge on the the ski fits a corresponding groove in the boot sole to assure lateral stability. The "systems," like this one, are not universal the way 75-mm "nordic norm" bindings are. That is, the binding interface works only with certain boots soles.

skiers. And they command only a quarter the price.

Grips too have changed since the days of leather-wrapped bamboo. Plastic grips may be straight, angled to the shaft or even perpendicular to it, like the head of a walking cane. Swix's Power Thruster handle is one, and is said to give a more powerful push-off. Other companies with off-angle grips include Exel, Reflex, and Leki.

More important than grip shape is length. In-track classical-technique poles should reach about to your shoulder. Skate poles should be longer, up to your mouth or nose.

IN-TRACK CLOTHING

Clothing for the track needn't be fancy. But it must be functional. You're not going off on an expedition; a 10-km loop will likely take less than an hour to circumnavigate. So, you aren't exposing yourself to the kind of extremes that backcountry skiers do. Also, track skiing generates a lot of body heat and perspiration, so heavy clothing isn't necessary. In fact, it is this heat in combination with the colder, wetter environment outside that provides the dressing challenge for track skiers.

Underwear

Exercising in the cold generates a conundrum: Your clothes must keep you both warm enough and cool enough. The key is in layering, and layering with the right fabrics. You'll need underwear, a mid-layer of insulation, and protective outerwear. Start with an underwear layer of snug-fitting polypropylene or other polyester-based fiber such as DuPont's Thermax or Patagonia's Capilene. You need something that is hydrophobic, or water-hating. These fibers wick moisture away from your skin and into the middle and outer layers. The inner layer stays dry, and you feel warm. The opposite of hydrophobic is hydrophilic, or water-loving. Cotton is hydrophilic. It absorbs moisture and locks wetness against your skin. Cotton long johns and T-shirts are ill-suited, even dangerous, for cross-country skiing. (Dangerous because cold, wet skin can lead to a loss of core temperature, known as hypothermia. More on this in Chapter 8, Backcountry Skills.)

Middle Layer

The middle layer is the insulating layer, trapping warm air to keep you toasty. In very cold weather you may wear more than one insulating garment. On warm days out on the track you may not need any.

Wool is the classic choice, because even when wet it continues to insulate. Wool fibers won't compact, which would eliminate the dead-air pockets that slow heat loss. Generally, the thicker the loft, or pile, the more space there is for trapping warm insulating air.

Fleece is a relatively new synthetic insulator that has become popular because it provides the warmth of wool at half the weight. (It is also somewhat more expensive.) Fleece wicks away moisture and dries quickly. Garments made of PolarFleece, PolarPlus, and Polarlite—all manufactured by Malden Mills—are available from many skiwear companies. Patagonia's excellent synthetic fleece is called Synchilla.

Outerwear

Outer garments should be wind- and waterproof (or at least water-repellent) and breathable. They need to protect you from the elements: snow, sleet, rain, wind. And, ideally, they should let your own moisture—in the form of water vapor—out so you aren't a captive inside a fabric sauna. This is important. Old-style waterproof fabrics, like rubber-coated stormwear, is impermeable; water can't get in, but neither can your perspiration get out. And in the snow, wet often leads to cold. Once again, modern science has come to the rescue with the proliferation in the late 20th century of waterproof/breathable fabrics.

Some achieve this by incorporating a waterproof/breathable membrane in a multi-layered fabric. Gore-Tex, the most visible name in the field, does this. A microporous mid layer has holes too small to allow penetration by liquid water, but still large enough to let water vapor pass through to the outside. Other companies use fabric treatments to achieve similar results. Helly-Hansen applies Helly-Tech, a microporous polyurethane treatment to garments made of nylon. Burlington Mills's version is called Ultrex. Still others achieve water repellency and breathability through the ultra dense weave of their fabrics. These include garments made by Entrant, Unitika, and Teijin.

Extremities

Ideally, hats, gloves, and socks should create a similar warm/dry microclimate by incorporating the same three layers. But practically, it's not always necessary. A good wool or fleece hat, for instance, is all you need for your head, except in extreme cold, when a face mask or neck gaiter can be added.

Polypropylene or silk glove and sock liners may be added if hands or feet are cold. But be sure your sock liners don't make your boots fit too tight; you'll decrease the flow of blood to your feet and restrict warming. Boots are usually designed to be skied with just a single, thin pair of socks.

Boots are obviously waterproof (leather or one of the waterproof/breathable fabrics like Gore-Tex); gloves should be too. Be aware that it is possible to over insulate the hands and feet. Studies show that this can result in an overall lowering of the core body temperature.

The Layering Rule

The first rule of layering is to change layers as your comfort level demands. Take off layers as you and/or the day warms up. Add layers as the weather cools, the wind picks up, or you slow your internal engines.

Most racers and regular tracksters ski in Lycra tights or one-piece suits. The colors are wild, they cut the wind beautifully, and they give a slinky, stretchy, near-naked fee. On cold days you can layer under or over them. When the sun is out, you may need nothing else.

Beyond fashion, the point is to regulate your temperature so that you are neither stung by the cold and wind nor overheated and sweaty. The new fabrics and layering systems make the job easier than it has ever been.

WAX AND WAXING

There are two kinds of waxes to do two different jobs: glide wax fine tunes the friction between ski and snow to provide the slickest possible glide; kick wax does just the opposite. It grips the snow just enough to allow the skier to push off and climb hills. Skating skis are waxed strictly for glide, no kick wax at all. Diagonal striders use both, glide wax at the tip and tail of the ski, and kick wax underfoot in the "wax pocket."

Actually, the wax doesn't grip the snow, it's the other way around. Snow, all snow, is composed of tiny particles, whether new star-shaped snowflakes, metamorphosed shrunken crystals, or just tiny lumps of ice (more on the nature of snow in Chapter 8). By waxing skis correctly, the cross-country skier creates a surface just soft enough for these particles to penetrate and grip—when the ski is stationary and the skier is pressing down for his "kick"—but not so soft that a moving, sliding ski will be gripped by the snow.

The key is in the relative sharpness of the snow crystals and the hardness of the wax. The colder the temperature, the harder the wax you'll need. A wax that is too hard for the conditions will result in slipping on the uphills–not enough grip in the kick. A too-soft wax will be deeply penetrated by the snow crystals, creating too much friction and sometimes a complete loss of glide.

Grip Wax

Grip waxes for new and fine-grained snows come in little cans and are color coded for the temperature: greens for the coldest temps, then blues, violets, red, and finally yellow. The temperature range and snow conditions for each wax are clearly written on each can. These are the so-called "crayon" waxes; you rub them on the ski base like a crayon. When you're uncertain of the color, it's best to choose the harder wax to start. If it's too hard, you can apply a softer wax on top. But if you start out too soft, you'll have to remove the wax in order to apply something harder.

Apply grip wax to a dry base, either wiped dry or dried in the sun. Rub on a thin even coat extending a few inches forward of the binding and likewise behind the heel. If the ski still slips on the uphills, use the same wax and lengthen the kick zone. If that still doesn't work, go to a softer wax.

Old snow that has melted and refrozen and new, wet snow require a different tact. In these conditions you use klisters, stickier substances that come in tubes and have the consistency of cold honey. Many a skier has cursed the mess klister makes if it gets loose on clothing, fingers or inside your pack. For safety sake, carry your klisters in separate plastic bags. Despite klister's gooey reputation, it works, especially in warmer temperatures, on spring corn snow, and on tracks chopped up into "sugar" snow by previous skiers. You apply it out of the tube, like toothpaste, and spread it thin with the plastic paddle provided. Klisters also come in a range of temperature-coordinated colors from green to yellow.

Glide Wax

With the advent of skating, skiers could wax entirely for glide, tip to tail. Diagonal skiers glide-wax just the glide zones, on either side of the kick wax. The purpose, obviously, is to make the ski slide better.

The theory goes like this: Glide wax allows just enough crystal-into-wax penetration to produce a controlled amount of friction. This friction causes microscopic melting of the snow crystals, so that the ski glides on tiny droplets of water. If the droplets are too large (too much friction), the ski will be slow. On the other hand, if the wax is too hard, there will be no penetration and not enough friction to cause melting, and therefore poor glide.

Glide waxes work over wider temperature ranges than do kick waxes, so choosing the right one is not so critical. Like grip waxes, they are color and temperature coded. You have but to check a thermometer and read the labels.

Apply glide waxes with an old iron. (Once used for ski waxing, it can never go back to cottons and rayons.) Touch the wax to the warm iron and drip a bead down the length of the glide zone or along the entire base if you're waxing a skating ski. Then iron the wax in. (If the iron is smoking, it's too hot.) Modern bases are very porous. They will absorb much of the liquid wax. The more you iron in, the better the penetration, the longer the wax will last.

The final phase is to scrape off the excess wax. Use a plastic scraper found in any ski shop, and scrape thoroughly from tip to tail until it appears all the wax has been removed. But don't worry, it hasn't. There's still plenty of wax in the pores, and that's what you glide on. Don't forget to scrape the groove or grooves, because these give directional stability to the ski.

Waxing gets a bad rap as a mysterious alchemy in cross-country skiing. Fear of waxing is what drives the robust waxless ski market. But it needn't be so. Beginners can get by with a simple two-wax system, one for cold snow and another for warmer, wetter snow. Jack Rabbit and Toko sell good ones. Nobody, except perhaps the most serious racer, needs the full rainbow spectrum depicted on the wax charts. For most diagonal striders a representative sample of three or four hard waxes—green, blue, violet, and red—plus a klister or two should be sufficient. And, if you've fallen in love with skating, as I have, a couple of different glide formulas—one for early winter cold and one for sunny, spring days—plus a can of Swix Cera F (a lightning fast powdered additive applied over glide wax) will keep you humming along the track, "running," in writer Eric Evans' marvelous phrase, "on the juices of flight."

DIAGONAL STRIDE TECHNIQUE

The diagonal stride is not only the basic movement on the track, akin to walking and running, it is also the foundation for all off-track touring and mountaineering—all traveling across snow. Properly done the movement translates into economy, fluidity, and speed.

An accomplished skier using the stride looks like a slow-motion runner who is somehow swallowing large chunks of real estate with each step. It is very much like running, with two important additions: skis that glide at the end of each stroke, and poles that help to maintain that glide. As in running, the arms and legs work diagonally. That is, the left arm and right leg swing forward as the right arm and left leg swing back and vice versa. This part is completely natural and can be practiced on the track by jogging lightly on skis without poles. The balance of the right/left rhythm should soon establish itself.

Beginnings

But first, you'll want to establish an even more basic relationship with your gear. The old adage says: "If you can walk, you can cross-country ski." It's true, and that's the way you should start out. Take a tour around the flat out in front of the touring center. Step, shuffle, turn (you'll find you must make many small steps in order to complete a 180-degree turn-around), slide a little. Make friends with the lithe, slippery appendages on your feet. Use your poles if you must for balance, but try as much as possible to stand and step without them. Use the poles as an insect would a feeler; touch, tap, "feel" your way with them, but try not to lean on them.

In-track Jogging

Most touring centers have multiple sets of grooved track, short sections, like lines across a football field, reserved for beginners. Before you can really stretch out and run, you must jog. So, try jogging up and back in the grooves. The idea is to add some glide to your basic walking stride.

You get glide by leaning forward as if into a wind. A stiff, upright position will only result in a shuffling stride. Project your weight out over the lead foot, and glide with each step.

In the beginning, it's often easier to jog without your poles. You've got two fewer pieces of equipment to worry about, and you are freer to let the natural arm and leg swing happen. Some people use their poles as balance crutches. Leaving them behind for this exercise also forces the issue of balancing on your feet, just as you must do in alpine skiing, running, any sport.

Begin with small movements, short moments of glide, and work gradually to extend them. If you are taking a lesson, follow closely behind your teacher. Imitate his or her rhythm. Absorb. Be a sponge. Be a shadow. Learn by osmosis.

The diagonal stride: Jogging in-track without poles is a good first step. Project your weight out over the lead foot to generate some glide with each step. Start with small movements, short moments of glide, and gradually extend arm and leg swings. *Linde Waidhofer*

A

B

C

D

Kick and Glide, Kick Phase

The kick or kick/drive is your main thrusting force down the track. It happens when the feet pass each other, when one foot stops to push off and the other shoots forward to begin the glide. In order to generate an effective kick, you have to press the center of the ski with its kick wax (or grippy, nonslip pattern, in the case of waxless skis) onto the snow. The right wax will allow some penetration by the snow crystals, giving you the traction you need to drive forward. I sometimes feel the kick is ill-named. When I think kick, I see a mule lashing out at some irritation behind. The skiing kick is more of a direct downward pressing in preparation for launch. As ski writer John Dostal puts it, "more like springing across a stream than stepping off a curb."

If your kick feels ineffectual it is probably one of three things. You may be improperly waxed; you may need a softer wax for the conditions. Or you might have a ski with too much camber for your weight; you can not bend it flat to the snow to engage the kick wax. (This is unlikely if the ski shop paid attention fitting you with skis.) Or, most likely, your kick is too much like the mule's, firing back instead of pressing down and launching forward.

Glide Phase

The kick phase ends when you shift weight to the gliding foot. Thus begins the free-glide phase. The key here obviously is balancing on one gliding foot. Again, start small and gradually try to extend your glide. If the track has a gentle downhill in one direction, try this exercise. On the downhill, where gravity provides the sliding, play the weight shift game. Pick up one ski and glide for a while on the other. Put it down and pick up the other foot. Efficient nordic skiing, like alpine, is largely a matter of developing one-legged balance on a moving platform.

Back on the flat track, lengthen your movements, and extend your glide. The important thing here is to limit deceleration. Good skiers ride very quietly atop the gliding ski; a break in balance is an interruption of the cherished momentum, and a ski that wobbles against the sidewalls of the track is slowing down more than it has to.

Most racers and good skiers do their gliding on

The classic technique: In kick phase (B and D) the skier presses grip wax (or waxless pattern) down into the snow in preparation for launching forward into glide phase (A, C, E). Note full extension of arms and legs (like running) during glide, weight centered over gliding ski. Poles are planted opposite gliding foot (in the natural rhythm of running) and push through powerfully to extend glide and maintain momentum down the track. *Linde Waidhofer*

A   B

a rather straight leg, the better to transmit momentum to the ski. I've tried it both ways; gliding on a bent forward leg and on a straight one, and I think the racers are right. The bent leg is easier to balance at first, but the straighter leg is more efficient, if only for the fact that it helps to project one's body forward down the track. You hear this kind of talk all the time on the track: "projecting your momentum," "maintaining velocity." It is more than mere jargon. It takes less energy to maintain speed than to generate same. Momentum carries over from stride to stride. Stride length—how far you go with each glide—is more important than a fast tempo. Practice stretching it out by skiing a flat section of track without poles, trying to cross the distance with as few kicks as possible. This is also a good exercise for improving one-legged balance.

Poling

The third and final phase of the diagonal stride is the poling (while gliding) phase. The pole push is a significant power source to keep you moving down the track between kicks.

Correct use of the pole strap is important. Slip your hand through the strap loop from below. Then grip the handle with the strap in the crook of your hand, between your thumb and forefinger. Tighten the strap around the back of your wrist. This way the strap acts as a kind of cradle for the hand and actually contributes to the power of the poling.

In the natural rhythm of running, your arms should swing like pendulums from the shoulders. Reach well forward with the poling hand, careful to keep the pole itself angled back. (If you plant the pole basket forward of your hand, you have no leverage with which to propel yourself along.) With the pole angled back, push down and past your hip, relaxing the arm and hand at the end of the swing. Try to plant as early as you can in the glide phase to maintain that kick-generated speed. A late pole push does nothing to help sustain precious momentum.

To work well, each of the phases must coordinate with the others until they meld into a continuum, like the smooth opening and closing of scissors. Practice in your living room using slow-motion, large-scale movements. Stride

C   D   E

ahead, balance on the gliding foot, pull through the poling arm, and stride again.

Double Pole

When the track is fast and your skis are gliding well, vary the pace by double poling. This is strictly an upper-body movement; the skis coast parallel in the track.

As the name implies, it's a double, or simultaneous pole push. Reach well forward with both arms, plant your poles about even with your feet, break at the waist and lunge into the pole push. It's important that you use the weight of your upper body to augment the arm swing. Arms alone won't generate much power. But arms and the mass of your upper body "falling" through the pole push is a potent generator. Keep your legs straight through the push to transmit

Use the double pole technique across flats and slight down grades when skis are gliding well. Reach well forward (B), plant and lunge into the pole push (C). Break at the waist to add upper body mass to the arm push. Keep legs straight (D) to transmit power directly to the skis. *Linde Waidhofer*

A

B

C

D

power directly to the skis and to avoid "sitting" at the end of the stroke.

Use the double pole on gentle downhills, across flats—anywhere your glide speed is high and you want to break from the diagonal motion.

Uphills

Hills require you to step up the tempo and shorten your stride. Weight distribution is important. If you get back (hips behind your feet) it's tough to maintain momentum and even harder to make the kick wax grip. So, keep your hips forward, and jog up on your toes. Pole plants should be crisp and short; keep leverage on the pole by planting the point well back, that is, behind your feet.

Most tracks have a hill or two that are too steep to diagonal-stride; the wax simply won't hold. Here you must step out of the grooves and herringbone on your edges, tips out, tails together in the characteristic, offset V that leaves a tweedy pattern on the snow. Good skiers can sometimes get a little glide out of their herringbone (for skaters that's the name of the game), but most are content to survive such hills at a walk and resume gliding at the top.

SKATING TECHNIQUES

Skating is a universal movement. On cross-country skis it is nearly identical to ice skating, roller skating, and the skate movements alpine skiers do on their way to the lift line. The technique goes way back into Scandinavian pre-history. Ski hunters used to skate with one long gliding ski and one short pushing ski. (Scandinavian coaches who fought the introduction of skating into World Cup racing in the 1980s, used to cite these very hunters as reason enough. One was quoted as saying, "You can tell the hunters in our villages, because they walk herky-jerky. They had one shorter ski for skating, and now, after pushing off with only that one leg, they have thrown their body out of line and they have a limp." But that "body alignment" argument ultimately made no sense as racers had no problem skating to both sides with skis of the same length.)

Credit for the modern skating revolution is generally given to American Bill Koch, who used the marathon skate to win the overall World Cup in 1982. Racers discovered that skating was the fastest way to get from point A to point B, up to 30 percent faster than striding. Fastest of all was the V skate, with both skis out of the grooves and going hard, back and forth like a speed skater on ice, the skis waxed slick for glide.

Track skiers of all abilities tried it and found skating to be natural, rhythmic, and FAST. The only problem was, skaters wrecked the twin grooves for the striders. So, touring centers began to pack out skating lanes beside the set track using their ever-bigger and better grooming machines (the same snowcats the alpine areas use to buff their slopes to a corduroy finish). Now tracks are like freeways with one lane for striders and one, the fast lane, for skaters.

Since skaters won all the races, the sport's governing bodies decided to split the techniques, the same way swimming made a separate event out of the butterfly, which evolved out of the slower breast stroke. Now races are designated as "classical" (diagonal technique only) or "freestyle" (anything goes, which always means skating).

You don't even have to have a track to skate. One of my most delightful skiing experiences took place on a high Rocky Mountain pass in May. The morning snow was frozen hard into a knubbly surface known as corn. I skated for miles over this white sea, across meadows and through the trees, down creeks and over roller-coaster hills. The skis were like a magic carpet, floating over the shapes. The skating movement itself matched the unbounded quality of the land.

V Skate

The V skate is a herringbone with glide: a lot of glide on downhills and flats, a little glide with each step on the uphills. In fact, glide is king when skating, even more than with the diagonal technique. There is no grip wax. Thrust comes from edging the ski and pushing off perpendicular to the edge.

Begin as you would for diagonal stride, without poles, on a level, groomed practice field. Start with small movements and work your way toward longer and longer extensions. You'll notice a couple of things right away. First, you must push side-to-side between your skis, not back. Second, the step to the gliding ski feels almost like catching yourself from falling. In fact, you should try for this feeling. As you push off your edged ski, your whole body should be aimed, committed, falling in the new direction. The gliding ski/leg catches your fall. You should have full weight transfer to the new side. Then you roll that ski on edge and "fall" back across the center line to repeat the sequence.

Skate Angle

The angle of your skis (the degree of opening of the V) should change with the terrain. On the flat, the angle should be closed; ski tips pointed more nearly down the track. Balance is easier, and you make more distance with each stroke. As the hill steepens, your skate angle should open up, until it becomes, at some point, the wide-mouthed herringbone for waddling up the steepest inclines.

A skate angle that's too wide for the slope (especially in the learning stages on the flat) will be hard to handle. Your feet will be shooting out to the sides, and your center of mass will have a hard time keeping up. Complete weight shift to the gliding ski will be difficult, and your glide time will be commensurately shortened. Too wide a skate angle could also send your tips into the soft snow at the sides of the skate lane.

Edge Angle

To generate power from the skating push, you must drive off a platform created by an edged ski. Edge too little and the ski will wash out, neutralizing your thrust. Edge too much and the ski will dig into the snow creating more friction than need be. Both extremes are really more a case of improper balance. If your ski is too lightly edged you are standing too upright over your skis, not committing your weight, not "falling" in the direction of the glide. If you are overedging, you are perhaps too aggressively committing to the new direction.

Edge angle is paramount on the glide. A flat ski yields the longest glide. A ski that wobbles, or is rolled over early for the next push, causes more drag than a flat ski. (Even skis with waxable sidewalls suffer more friction on edge than if they were riding flat on their bases.) Riding a flat ski is perhaps the single most important skating skill. A flat ski means more glide, more distance per

stride, and less energy expended, which ultimately translates into speed around the course.

Develop one-legged balance the same way you would for diagonal stride. In the furrows of a set track, glide a gentle downhill on one foot only. You may feel like an awkward flamingo at first, but the balance for flat-ski glide will soon improve.

Another exercise is the leaning skier drill. Skating on a flat section of track (still without poles) hold your feet quite close together in the starting position. Tilt towards the skating direction, shoulder first, then torso. As your upper body begins to lean, let your skating ski swing out and land on the snow. Your weight will naturally (and completely) shift to the glide side. Bring the unweighted foot in close again and hold until you are ready to lean back in the other direction. This exercise is improved if you point with your opposing arm. For example: You are gliding on your right ski. You begin to roll the right ski on edge in preparation for push-off. Your body starts to lean to the left. In order to line up body and ski, point in the new direction with your right arm. Point out beyond the ski and the track with good extension, and your head, shoulders, and torso will align themselves over the left, or gliding, foot. In other words, face the direction of glide. Pointing also serves to "pull" your weight forward over the foot, for a long, stable glide.

Extension

The final piece of the puzzle is the full extension of all skating movements. Just as a thrown ball or a tennis ground stroke needs full follow-through and extension of the swing to enjoy full power and accuracy, so you need to extend the motions of the V skate. Push off not just with the leg but with the ankle and foot as well, right down to pointing your toes. Reach out in the direction of the glide with your arms as if stretching for the brass ring. Bring your unweighted foot in close so that you can really fall into the next direction change. Make everything bigger than you think you have to. Exaggerate. Project. We rarely move as boldly as, inside, we think we are doing.

In sum: Start on flat terrain, and without poles (V-1 and V-2 poling cadences, described upcoming, will only detract from concentration on the feet and skis). Begin with small movements, mini-gliding steps from side to side, and gradually work toward longer and longer extensions, longer glides. Glide on a flat ski. Roll to an edge, while simultaneously "falling" toward the new direction. Face the new direction and commit your weight 100 percent to the gliding ski. In the beginning, skating takes a little more energy than does striding, but as Swedish coach Kjell Kratz has said, "Once you learn how to skate the right way and develop the proper rhythm, it becomes the easiest, most natural motion. You feel you can skate forever."

USING POLES

Pole use in skating serves the same purpose as it does for the diagonal stride: to extend the glide and maintain momentum. The different tempos and cadences are myriad, and have led to innumerable skating variations. In the short span since skating's discovery, or rediscovery, the number of designations for offshoots and variations has become about as confusing as the ever-changing model numbers on the skis. I will stick to the two most useful, the V-1, or single-pole skate, and the V-2, or double-pole skate.

V-2

I'll start with the V-2. The name means there are two skating steps for each pole push; you pole with every other stride. It's a double pole action, both arms at once, like the double pole described for diagonal (in the grooves) technique. This is a good technique for flats and downhills (and slight uphills) when the snow is fast.

It works like this: Start by moving your poles and one ski ahead together (preparatory to "falling forward" on that ski). As you pole, lunge out onto the forward ski. Follow through with the pole push (full arm extension to the rear), and glide out over your ski. As you glide, collect yourself for the next skating move. Without poling, skate back onto your other foot. Glide. Collect yourself for another skate/double pole. Begin the sequence again.

Because you are only poling with every other stride, the V-2 has a waltzy, syncopated feel. It's a great way to conserve energy, but after a while, you may feel a lopsided fatigue. Switch and pole on the opposite skate step. Terrain may affect

which side you pole on. If you're skiing on a sidehill with your left ski lower than your right, for example, you will find it more comfortable and efficient to double pole as you skate up onto your right foot (pushing off the left ski, gliding on the right), the poling action adding power to the uphill part of your V skate.

Remember that poling is a way to help maintain velocity, not necessarily to generate it. Overdependence on the arms is exhausting. Use the legs to propel you down the track; use the poles for rhythm, balance, and for extending your glide.

V-1

In the V-1, you pole once with each skate step, and the poling is done one arm at a time, opposite the feet, as in the classical stride. This is a smaller scale movement than the grand sweeps of the V-2. The V-1 is primarily an uphill tool when tempo is quicker and each glide is commensurately shorter.

It works like this. Do a short glide on the left accompanied by a push on the right pole. Skate right and push on the left pole. And so on. The rhythm should be choppy but balanced, as if you were jogging up a long stairway.

Skating Uphill

Skating uphill is a matter of adding glide to the old familiar herringbone. Many people think you have to be moving fast to skate. You don't. You can skate—and glide with each step—at very slow speeds, too. Even if you only glide forward six inches with each step, you are still skating, and moving faster than you would at a plain walk.

Momentum is the key word. It's very much like switching gears on a bicycle in order to maintain momentum over a hill. As you approach a climb, stick with the V-2 until you feel your momentum is suffering. Switch to the V-1 and a more rapid tempo. As the grade steepens open the angle of your V to accommodate it. Try to eke a little glide out of each stroke by keeping your hips up and over your feet. (If you sit back, behind your feet, glide will soon vanish.)

Of course, there are hills too steep and too long to glide up. It's okay. Settle into a cadenced herringbone, using your edges (remember, there is no grip wax) to propel you forward. As the gradient moderates near the top, slide into your

The V-2 skate. Note that there is a full left/right skating movement (two skates) between each double-pole push. Skier skates onto right foot (B and C) and begins simultaneous pole push. As arms follow through to the rear, he skates back left (E and A) and collects himself for next cycle. Note full transfer of weight from foot to foot for balance and longer glide. *Linde Waidhofer*

Use the V-1 skate (one pole push per skating step) when climbing. The cadence is quicker and the glide is shorter than with the waltz-like V-2. The V-1 is a herringbone with glide. The arms work opposite the legs, right pole reaching and pushing opposite the left leg (A and B), left arm assisting the right leg glide (C and D), and so on. *Linde Waidhofer*

V-1 until velocity and terrain allow you to shift once more into the V-2, high gear as it were.

MARATHON SKATE

This is a hybrid, half in the track and half out. The marathon skate was the first skating technique used in modern World Cup racing and is still a viable (and fast) movement, especially on a trail with set-track grooves that is not wide enough to V skate.

In doing the marathon, one ski remains in the groove while the other angles outside the track to provide the skating propulsion. (Like all track techniques, the ability to glide on one foot is crucial.) Angle the skating ski out to the side, forming a lopsided X with the feet close together and the tails of the skis crossed behind. (Because the gliding ski is in the groove several inches below surface snow level, there is no contact.) Now set the skate ski down, edge it into the snow for bite, and push off until you are upright and balanced over the gliding foot. It's like pushing a scooter or pushing off to propel a skateboard.

For greatest power out of the skate stroke, lean out over the skating ski, commit your weight to it, and then spring back to the glide side. Push off to the side and not to the rear. It is this power stroke that gives skating (marathon or V skate) its phenomenal speed. Power is applied over time, up to a full second during the skate—a crescendo of applied force—while in the diagonal stride, power can only be applied for two- or three-tenths of a second, a quick explosion. The difference between the two techniques (speedwise) is this: With the diagonal stride, the pushing ski must stop briefly—as the foot stops during running—so that the kick wax underfoot can grip the snow and provide a platform for the next stride. Nothing stops during skating; there is a continuous, fluid movement down the track.

Finally, add a double pole plant to the marathon skate. Coordinate the pole push with the skating push. As you lean forward into the skate, simultaneously bring the hands forward and begin the double pole. Push back against the poles as you edge and weight the skate ski. Finish the full extension arm swing at the same time you shift off the fully extended skate leg onto the glide ski. During the glide, bring the skate foot in close to the gliding ankle and swing the arms forward

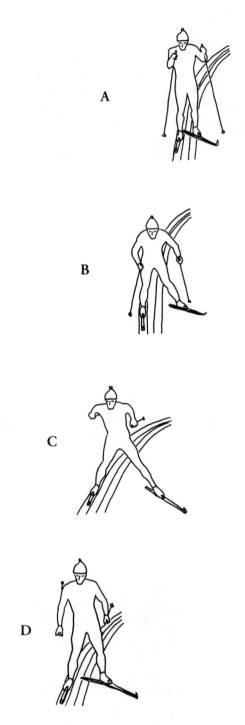

The marathon skate is a one-ski skate; one leg skates while the other glides along in the groove. Begin by reaching forward for the double pole plant (A) and angling the skate ski out to the side. Edge the skating ski and push off (B), both the ski and the pole plant. For maximum power from the stroke, fully extend the skate leg and the arms behind. Recover to a neutral position (D) while gliding on the non-skating foot.

ready to begin the next skate/double pole.

Learn to marathon skate off either side. On sidehills especially, wherever one ski is higher than the other, it's more relaxing to skate off the downhill foot.

Adjust your speed of movement to your speed of travel. When going slowly or uphill, skate more frequently. When going fast, skate less frequently but more powerfully.

IN-TRACK DOWNHILL

Many downhill sections of track require no special technique at all: You just let the skis find their own way down the furrows of set track and ride 'em, happy for the rest and the pleasant, gravity-assisted scudding of skis on snow. On gently-tilted downhills you may want to help gravity out with your own double poling or marathon or even V skating. At borderline speeds—where your poling or skating might or might not increase momentum—you may want to borrow the alpine downhiller's wind-piercing tuck position: body rolled into a tight egg, hands in front of your face, poles tucked back along your hips. But what happens when downhills are steep enough to demand some turning and braking on your part?

One-ski Wedge

The simplest way to scrub off speed is the one-ski wedge. While riding downhill in the grooves, pick up one ski, set it down to the side in the classic A, or snowplow configuration, and use its edging power to brake your speed. If you're in a turn, brake with the ski on the outside of the turn. That way, as centrifugal force presses you to the outside of the curve, the wedged ski will be weighted and controlling.

Wedge and Wedge Turns

If there are no grooves (a purely skating track) or if the grooves have been obliterated on a downhill stretch, use a full wedge, borrowed more or less straight from the alpine book. From a balanced "ready" position—upright, collected, knees flexed, hands in front and weight centered—press your heels out to form the wedge, or snowplow. Skis

Handling the downhills on a track. The skier in the middle is employing the one-ski wedge, one foot in the groove, the other outside applying the brakes. The skier in the back is looking for more speed; he has assumed the aerodynamic tuck used by alpine downhillers.

should be slightly on edge (both inside edges), but knees should remain apart and ski tips should not be crossing. The wedge is an apt metaphor. Not only do the skis describe two sides of a triangle, but the friction created in the snow is a powerful slowing force.

A wedge turn on skinny track skis is not as easy to perform as the same maneuver on alpine gear. Not only are the skis narrower and without metal edges, but most of them have little or no sidecut, the curved shape in the plan view of a ski that aids in turning. Put an alpine ski (with sidecut) on edge and it will scribe a curved arc on the snow. Put most track skis on edge and they simply keep going straight.

So a wedge turn on toothpick skis is slightly

A step turn on skinny skis. Many times the best way to alter your course is not to make a turn at all, but simply pick up your ski and step to a new line.

more problematical. The skier has to provide the turning force, more steering through heel push and pointing the toe in the direction of the turn. The same rules apply here and on the alpine piste; you just need to exaggerate them. Weight the outside, or turning, ski. Brush the snow with the ski edge. Stay in balance between your feet. And keep your upper body quiet; no unnecessary torquing and twisting. Do the turning with your feet and legs, leave the upper body, head and hands facing more or less down the hill, anticipating the big picture.

Step Turn

Some times you don't want to slow down in a turn. Perhaps it's a long sweeper leading to an uphill, and you want to carry as much speed as possible through the curve. Or maybe there's a short, tight jog in the trail where a wedge would be awkward. Many situations, perhaps the majority on most tracks, call for step turns.

A step turn is like a skating step. Sometimes that's all it is, one step out of the previous line onto a new one. Sometimes the turn calls for several steps in the same direction to get around the corner. In every case, it's a gliding movement (no braking) involving the angled displacement of one ski, stepping to it, and following with the other ski.

Try it first on a very gentle plain. Commence gliding in the fall line, then make a series of very small steps to the side. Bite off only a few compass degrees with each step. But keep stepping until you've turned far enough out of the fall line for the slant of the hill to slow and stop you. Beginners sometimes must fight the instinct to cross over with the following foot. When instinct wins, ski tips cross and the skier goes down in a tangle. Keep the steps small, incremental, and balanced.

Move to steeper slopes and higher speeds. Keep your hands out in front of you (to prevent your weight slipping back), and center your weight laterally between your feet. At higher speeds edge your skis, as if you were pushing off on a skate, to prevent washout (or sideways slippage) in a turn.

At higher speeds there is the temptation to lean in the direction you want to go, as if riding a bicycle into a turn. Track skiers, like their alpine brethren, must fight this tendency with angulation, flexing at the waist and centering the upper body mass over the feet. Monitor the correct stance with hands low and forward and shoulders turned slightly to the outside of the curve. Only then will the edges hold and your steps succeed in carrying you around the bend.

Some track skis, skating skis in particular, do have a little sidecut built in, and these will enter more naturally into a turn than will straight-sided or javelin-shaped skis.

TIPS & TALES: Wooden Skis

Leather hiking boots. Bamboo fly rods, Wooden skis. Some classics are eclipsed but never replaced.

My first cross-country skis were all wood, and in some ways they were the best skis I've ever had. They had a light spruce core, hickory sole and top, and birch sidewalls with rock-hard

Some of the best cross-country tracks are springing up adjacent to the alpine lifts. This one is at Mount Bachelor near Bend, Oregon.

lignostone (compressed beech) edges. They were the product of twenty-five separate laminations, each five millimeters thin, sawed and glued and pressed into curves, the grain of each piece carefully coordinated by craftsmen working closer to art than science.

I still have one of those skis. The tip of the other is nailed above my shop door, the victim of a hidden stump. I'd pay handsomely to find a new mate, but the Norwegian company that made the skis now manufacturers wooden door and window frames.

It is a fact that the fiberglass revolution has largely eclipsed the wooden ski, and there is good reason for this: Fiberglass skis are lighter, faster, stronger, cheaper, and more maintenance-free. Serious racers and backcountry skiers can't get along without them. But there are days, on the track (striding not skating) and on the trail, when it's still hard to beat a well-made wooden ski. No one has been able to reproduce wood's stable, quiet ride, or replace our natural affection for the living thing.

Wooden skis perform, especially for beginning skiers. They climb better than glass skis for a couple of reasons: Hickory is more porous than polyethylene, so wooden skis can hold their wax longer than P-tex bases. And because they are generally built with a soft, single camber (no wax pocket), it's easier to depress the ski's full length onto the snow where the wax can do its job.

On snow, wood has a solid, quiet touch. Foam cores transmit a light but hollow, boxy feel; there is a corresponding jumpy resonance. Wooden skis bend softly with the memory of branches in the wind, swallowing the noise of an icy track and dampening vibrations. They lie in the snow like a dog on a favorite rug before the fire. Lively? Not particularly. Dependable, predictable, and true? Most assuredly.

For me, the maintenance that wooden skis require is part and parcel of the magic. The preseason recipe goes like this: Heat Dixie pine tar until it flows like molasses. Apply in long strokes with a rag to waterproof the wood. Cook it down into the wood itself, torch flame hissing, tiny pine tar bubbles dancing on hickory. Wipe smooth. Melt on sticky base wax until it's like silk from tip to tail, rubbing as you go with that ever-present, pine-sweet rag. Set ski outside to cool in the brisk air. Bring in again and apply coats of hard wax—green, special green, or blue. Buff to a high sheen.

It should be noted that my wooden ski splintered because of pilot error and an ignorance of proper care. Wood, I learned too late, gets brittle when stored over the summer in a sunbaked shed. Treated right, all-wood skis are decidedly tough. The Norwegian army lashes wooden skis together to make sleds and then drags them over gravel roads. Every fiberglass ski they've tried has blown up.

A few Scandinavian companies still make and export wooden cross-country skis. Lansem is one. Their Tur-Langrenn is a classic all-around ski. Bonna and Äsnes still build wooden beauties in the $150-$250 range.

It used to be everybody who skied cross-country skied on wood. Now you have to seek out a pair. They're not for everybody. But well cared for they have a special magic. Bent into a turn, you can feel the hands of the man who made them. You can feel that they are alive.

7

Off-Track Skiing

The equipment may be plastic and aluminum instead of wood, but the act of splashing through feathery snow in a pristine setting is as old as skiing itself. They are four, a family perhaps, Mom and Dad and the kids. Dad breaks trail through the woods and out into a sparkling meadow. Their movements are unhurried, graceful. The skis slice through the snow and buoy the skiers along as if they were floating atop a white sea. The skiers are encumbered only by light day packs.

Touring off-track is skiing in its oldest and purest form. Skiing cross country. Skiing as travel. Off-track skiing is skiing come full circle, around from pure utility, to skiing as sport, through the split with alpine skiing, and back—back to skiing as simple, self-powered movement, from here to there and home again on long, flexy "snowshoes."

Touring can take a variety of forms, from simple half-day tours out from the car and back, to following long, well-marked paths through the woods surrounding a touring center, to multiple-day tours from inn-to-inn in New England or hut-to-hut in the heart of the Colorado wilderness. You can tour in town or you can tour around the base of Mount Everest as Jan Reynolds and Ned Gillette did in 1982. My children learned to ski by touring around the backyard. You can stick to the flats touring the beach fronts along Lake Superior or the Massachusetts coast,

or you can tour with a serious vertical component, going out with the express purpose of climbing a mountain just to ski down its slinky flanks. Off-track skiers in search of the downhill rush often learn the ancient and eminently serviceable telemark turn and become modern telemark skiers.

The range of styles and equipment choices is huge, and the definitions may overlap, but the mode of transportation is the same in each case: free-heel skiing off the track, on your own in the snow.

OFF-TRACK EQUIPMENT

Equipment varies with the kind of terrain and snow you will encounter, the distance from civilization, and the length of your trip. We'll look at three broad categories: touring, telemarking, and alpine touring.

Touring most often means skiing close to home, or at least close to the car or lodge. It might be on a preset trail, an old logging road or a summer hiking trail, or it might involve breaking trail through unskied snow. But in general, when I think of touring, I think of terrain that is flat or rolling rather than steep and demanding. Touring gear is designed to handle trail skiing and some downhills but not the kinds of precipitous ascents and descents favored by telemarkers and

Touring off-track is skiing in its oldest and purest form. *Bob Chamberlain*

Backyard touring, one of cross-country's myriad variations.

backcountry devotees. Much of the new touring gear is svelt enough to make an occasional appearance on the track.

Telemarking skis, boots and bindings, on the other hand, are designed specifically for downhill skiing, for making carved turns whether at a lift-served area or in the backcountry. The gear is much sturdier than touring equipment, commensurately wider and heavier and less gainly on a track.

Alpine touring has been popular for decades in Europe, though this clever adaptation of alpine gear for cross-country skiing is just beginning to catch on in North America. The key ingredient is a binding with dual capabilities, or modes: one for walking free-heel (the touring mode), and the other for skiing downhill in the alpine style, with the heel locked down on the ski. Alpine touring is a good option for died-in-the-wool alpine skiers who haven't learned the telemark turn but who nevertheless want to get out into wild snows beyond the boundaries of the ski areas.

Touring Skis

There is a boggling diversity under the broad banner of "the touring ski." You'll find models designated "light touring," "general touring," "backcountry touring," "in-and-off-track combinations," and on and on. The categories don't have to be confusing if you know what you want to do, and especially if you have a reliable ski fitter to assist you.

(Once again, I encourage first-time skiers to rent first. All touring centers and most alpine-area rental shops have basic gear for rent by the hour or the day. Then when you know what type of ski you want to buy, try as many as you can, either by borrowing or through demo plans at ski shops.)

Thankfully, touring skis are not in the same price range as thoroughbred race skis. You can spend under $100 for a pair of inexpensive Bonna wood skis, or as much as $250 for Trak's most costly waxless backcountry models. Package deals are common at the big sporting goods chains and through mail order at places like L.L. Bean and REI (Recreation Equipment, Inc.). A complete package including skis, boots, bindings, and poles will often net you a savings of $100 or more off the cost of the separates.

Because you tour in wild snow, touring skis are wider underfoot than in-track models, anywhere from 45 mm to about 55 mm. Most are in the 48-52 mm range. Your choice should be guided by the kind of snow you most often ski. A wider platform performs better in deep snows. A narrower ski will be faster (less friction) on harder snow and trails that are regularly packed out, either by track setter, snowmobile, or other skiers.

Touring skis are tougher than their in-track brethren, with beefier core materials (wood for instance) that push their weight into the 750-900 grams-per-ski realm. Still light compared to the days of solid hickory, but not so ethereal as in-track toothpicks.

Most touring skis are designed with sidecut, that is a narrower waist than shovel and tail. As Sondre Norheim, the father of modern skiing, discovered in the late 1800s, the resulting (plan view) curve helps the skis track straight ahead, and, when tilted on edge, makes turning a much more natural affair. Some touring skis, especially those billed for both in- and off-track use, are nearly straight from tip to tail. Whereas the classic off-track Fischer Europa 99 sports a 16 mm difference between shovel and waist measurements from 63 mm down to 47 mm. The Europa is a turning machine.

A majority of touring skis these days come with waxless bases in deference to the entry-level and occasional skier. The perception is most cross-country skiers would rather not deal with wax and suffer the (relatively) slight decrease in performance that comes with the waxless compromise. For no-compromise tourers (or for those who enjoy the waxing's challenge and reward), there are these options: classic wooden skis from Asnes and Bonna, the previously mentioned Fischer Europa 99, Karhu's Fuzion Sintered, and the Rossignol LTS 49—all reasonably priced.

Most waxless skis come with pattern bases—fishscales, shingles, steps—machined into the base material. The idea is to allow forward glide while at the same time "gripping" the snow to prevent backsliding. Fischer's Crown series, Atomic's Tricone pattern, Karhu's Bearclaw, and Trak's Omnitrak, an update of their pioneering fishscale pattern, are successful examples. Blizzard and Rossignol, among others, have gone beyond pattern theory and experimented with viscoelastic base materials. These feel smooth to the touch but behave something like wax. The reviews have been mixed. So far the patterns are more consistent over a wider range of snow types and weather conditions.

As with track skis, getting a proper fit is in part a function of where you ski, what the snow and temperature ranges are likely to be. No skis do it all. Every manufacturer builds one ski to shine in the hard snow of the Midwest and East and another best suited to the powdery or slushy snows of the Rockies and Pacific Northwest. For example, Karhu makes two similar-looking waxless skis, the Quest Kinetic and the SP5350 Kinetic (both in the mid-price range under $200). Different flex patterns make the Quest a better hard-snow ski, while the SP5350 is a better bet in soft snow.

In general, the softer the ski, the better its soft-snow performance, while firmer flex indicates a hard-snow glider. All other factors being equal, softer flex also spells better grip relative to glide, which is important for learning skiers. There is nothing more frustrating than slipping backwards when you don't want to. The belly of a soft ski may create a little more drag on the downhills, but the compromise is worth it. Stiffer skis require more skill to make them hold (grip) on the uphills. The payoff is a better glide coming back down.

Touring Boots and Bindings

You can still find some of the old Nordic Norm 75-mm three-pin touring bindings around. They are not particularly easy to get in and out of. Snow clogs the three holes in the boot soles. The wire bails holding the boot toe down in the binding tend to break at inopportune times, and their wide metal flanges bump the snow when the ski is tilted up in a turn, but they have the great advantage of being universal: no matter what boot you wear, you can step into virtually any pair of skis, and off you go.

But now the old norm is quickly being replaced by the "systems." Salomon's SNS system has been on the market since 1980, and keeps changing and improving yearly. The other newcomer is Rottefella's NNN, or New Nordic Norm, which has been licensing bootmakers since 1989. The systems are lighter, simpler, and sleeker than pins. Both systems offer step-in convenience, with spring-loaded clamps that secure the toe and release with a touch of the pole. They provide much better boot-to-ski control than their predecessors. A length-of-the-foot channel in the boot sole mates to a mirror-image guide ridge on the ski. It's almost impossible to twist your heel off the ski.

The only drawback to the systems is they're not interchangable. You have to buy a matched set, boots and bindings, and you may not be able to switch skis with your friends quite so readily. The problem is ameliorated, however, by the licensing network. Salomon makes its own boots, and licenses bootmakers Karhu and Jalas to use Salomon soles. The NNN system licensees include Jartjes, Rossignol, Alpina, Alfa, Asolo,

A typical touring/light telemarking setup. This is a three-pin binding, the old 75-mm "nordic norm," compatible with any three-pin boot sole. While the nordic norm still predominates, the new "incompatibles," boots that only work with certain bindings and vice versa, have made strong inroads.

Artex and Nortur. So, the choices are good.

All bootmakers have a lighter weight shoe for touring and occasional telemarking. The upper may be all leather or some combination of leather and waterproof fabric, such as Gore-Tex. Rossignol, Alpina, Salomon, and Nortur build especially good ones, in the $200 range.

Somewhat heavier boots, for wild snow and more frequent telemarking include, the Asolo 660 with its higher, thicker leather upper, the Salomon 711, the Karhu Control, and the Alpina 3000 with its plastic exterior cuff borrowed from skate-boot technology. Expect to pay $25-$50 more for these sturdier touring boots.

The off-track versions of Salomon's and Rottefella's bindings feature beefier components than their on-track models. Salomon's is called the SR Profil Automatic. Rottefella's is the NNN-BC (for backcountry).

Touring Poles

Poles for touring need not be the high-tech proposition they are for serious track skiers. On-track, long, light poles can make a real difference in your glide. Off-track, because the movements are more pedestrian and the snow is unpredictable (glide is only an occasional surprise bonus), it's more practical to use alpine-length poles with traditional, vertical grips. Nose-height track poles just make for awkward arm movements in deep snow.

Almost any (reasonable length) pole will do for light touring. I still use 15-year-old, $15 tonkin (bamboo) poles when I'm not worried about breaking them on a difficult downhill. If my tour involves a good bit of downhill skiing, I'll take a pair of aluminum alpine poles. They're about elbow height from the floor. Used alpine poles from autumn ski swaps are one of life's last great bargains. I've picked them up like new for $3.

If you become seriously involved in telemark and/or backcountry skiing, you will want to consider backcountry poles from Leki, Ramer, or Life-Link. Some are length-adjustable for traversing, skiing downhill, and stowing in a suitcase. Others convert to become avalanche probe poles. More on them in Chapter 8, Backcountry Skills.

Telemark Skis

Modern telemarkers practice an ancient turn on sophisticated gear. How much more difficult it must have been when skis were all wood, had no edges, weighed 5 pounds apiece, and bent as readily as a 2X4!

Telemark skis behave very much like narrow alpine skis. And that, really, is what they are. They are built with alpine wet-wrap or sandwich constructions out of the same materials as alpine skis, they have full-length metal edges for holding an arc, and they have an alpine, single-camber flex. Very few telemark skis are built with a wax pocket; the emphasis is on downhill turn characteristics rather than cross-country travel.

Tele-boards are significantly wider than touring models (up to 62 mm underfoot) and a good deal heavier, too (1200 to 1500 grams per ski). The width gives flotation in deep snow, and the heavier materials mean a smoother ride at downhill speeds. Some are designed to handle the demands of "yo-yo" skiing (up and down and up and . . .), riding the lifts at an alpine area. (In recent years telemarking has come out from its lair in the backwoods and developed a splinter sport on the groomed pistes. There are even telemark

Skins make climbing steep terrain easy. Once made of seal skin, today they are nylon or wool mohair. These are glue-on skins. They stick to the ski bases then peel off without affecting wax or leaving any residue. *Linde Waidhofer*

slalom races. The gear is pretty much the same as that used in the wild, although regular in-area telemarkers prefer the strongest skis, the beefiest bindings and the highest, most rigid boots.) All telemark skis come with plenty of sidecut for ease of turning.

Two classics of the genre (backcountry division) are the soft-flexing Tua Tele Sauvage and the Karhu XCD Extreme ($300 and up). Karhu also makes a superb tele ski for lift-served terrain, the wood-core Ultimate. Rossignol has always been near the top of the heap for groomed-piste tele-

boards. Their Haute Route Tele is a perennial. At the extreme end of hard-snow performance (not recommended for backcountry powder) are the stiff, race-bred tele-skis like the Atomic ARC Telemark Racing and the Asnes Telemark Comp.

Because the emphasis is heavily weighted toward downhill performance, few telemark skis come with waxless bases. Three that do are the Chouinard Valmonte X, the Karhu XCD GT Kinetic, and the Rossignol TMS AR, all slightly less expensive than the thoroughbreds.

Skins

Obviously if telemarkers are riding the lifts, they don't need uphill grip. When they're in the backcountry, many rely on climbing skis instead of wax. Modern skins are synthetic descendants of the seal skins skiers used up until the turn of the 20th century. The new skins are made of nylon or mohair. Mohair has the better glide, but nylon grips better and is more durable. All skins climb well, far better than wax on the steep. The little backward-facing hairs grip the snow while still allowing for some glide on the downhill stretches. They come in two forms, glue-ons and strap-ons.

Glue-ons from Black Diamond Equipment or Ascension Enterprises are expensive (up to $100 a set) but they work beautifully. The glue sticks the skins to the ski bases even in the coldest temperatures, but remains tractable and peels off leaving no sticky residue. Magic stuff. The glue does provide some handling challenges: It must be kept dry, and so cannot be applied to a wet ski bottom; and like a sticky fly strip, must be folded with care when not in use. Depending on how well you protect the glue from contamination, it will keep sticking a full season or more before it needs refreshing. Skins usually come with an extra tube of glue.

The alternative to glue is a strap-on skin from Ascension Enterprises or Wasatch Mountaineering. Strap-ons hook over the ends of the skis and secure with various straps and cleats. Ascension's three-quarter length skins are particularly versatile and easy to take on and off. You do have to screw a tiny cleat onto the top back of your ski. The rap on glueless skins is that snow can work in between the ski and the skin adding weight and reducing the ski's efficacy on steep traverses where you need a clean edge.

Telemark Boots and Bindings

Although Rottefella has been targeting casual telemarkers with its beefed up NNN-BC boots and bindings, serious teleboarders remain the last stronghold loyal to the venerable three-pin Nordic Norm and the sturdy, welted leather boot. Occasional telemarkers certainly should check out the NNN-BC setups. And no doubt these will improve with the years. But for now, nothing beats the ruggedness of a three-pin or cable metal binding.

Telemark turns put incredible stress on boots and bindings. The twisting forces can rip the toes out of a pair of molded-sole boots, snap a bail, or break the wings of the binding itself. That's why experienced telemarkers wear thick, welted-sole boots, carry extra bails (or cables) and even, if they're on a trip far from the nearest road, carry spare bindings and screws.

Rottefella, Alpina and Black Diamond make three-pin bindings for telemarking ($30-$60 depending on the relative thickness and strength of the metals). Black Diamond Equipment makes the most popular cable bindings, two versions for about $55 and $70. The cable snugs around the heel of the boot, and a spring-loaded throw pulls it forward into the toe irons in exactly the same way that alpine bindings of the 1930s did.

Telemark boots look like throwbacks too. Some are ringers for the heavy, lace-up leather boots of alpine skiing's formative decades. Inside though, they are considerably more high-tech. Most are insulated with 2 mm or more of closed-cell foam or 3M's Thinsulate material. They are lined with nylon or Cambrelle, a tough, quick-drying synthetic. All feature wedged plastic midsoles for torsional stiffness, and most have some sort of lugged outer sole, like the popular Vibram, for hiking over snow and rock. All use the strong Norwegian welt construction stitching the upper to the midsole.

There are two categories of telemark boot, the so-called touring/telemark compromise, and the full-on, "heavy metal," downhill- only monster boots. The lighter boots are designed with enough fore/aft flexibility to make touring pleasant and with enough torsional rigidity to generate powerful telemark turning forces. Downhill-only boots sacrifice the walking comfort for pure torsional strength, which translates into power in the turns.

Long-time compromise favorites include the

A telemark setup utilizing a heavy, double boot and cable binding. The cable allows free-heel motion but snugs the boot into the toe iron and provides good transmission of turning forces to the ski.

Alfa Rocky Mountain, the Asolo Snowpine, the Chouinard Expresso, the Fabiano Telemark I, and the Merrell Legend (not quite in the same price bracket as alpine boots but pushing it at around $300/pair). The Asolo, the Fabiano, and the Chouinard are all made in the same small valley of Asolo in northern Italy.

Heavy-duty boots, suitable for racing at downhill areas or for maximum control on backcountry descents, include Chouinard's Sauvage double boot (extra lateral support and more warmth), the two-buckle Asolo Extreme Pro, and the four-buckle Merrell Super Comp, which some have accused of reinventing the alpine boot all over again. These guys are in the alpine price realm of $400 and up.

Telemark Accessories

Skiers who prefer the softer touring/tele-boots but still want maximum turn control can add a binding plate called the Voile (under $50 from Black Diamond Equipment). A quarter-inch-thick polyethylene plate mounts under the three-pin binding and when fastened to the boot heel stiffens the lateral and torsional effect of the boot without overly restricting the fore/aft, free-heel hinging.

Telemark skiers use alpine-length poles. Anything longer just gets in the way when you assume the low telemark position. (The dated image of a telemark skier mid-turn with his hands and poles held high like a matador approaching the bull, was a result of over-long touring poles dictating the skier's stance. Modern telemarkers, with alpine-length poles, hold their hands low and forward for balance in the turn.) Adjustable poles, like those offered by Leki and Ramer, are a flexible (though more expensive) alternative. Use them long for touring, shorter for downhill and fully retracted for stowing and travel.

Long-time telemarkers swear by their knee pads, both for in-area skiing and for the backcountry when rocks, stumps, or hidden ice may be encountered. The trailing knee sometimes dips as low as the boot top, and can catch on unforeseen obstacles.

Alpine-Touring Skis

This is hybrid stuff, born of pure alpine gear and modified for the demands of ski mountaineering, climbing up and skiing down. The skis are made to be skied short, anywhere from 10 to 20 cm shorter than a normal alpine ski. For most men this means an alpine touring ski of 180 or 190 cm, and for most women, a 170 cm or a 180 cm. Short skis are lighter, easier to maneuver on the climbs, easier to carry on a backpack (for walking where there is no snow), and easier to handle in the varied wild snow conditions on the peaks.

AT skis are short and they are wide, 70 mm or so at the waist. This helps them "float" in deep snow, and gives them stability to offset the shorter length. Many AT skis also have an extended, longer/higher tip profile, which helps in steering through sloppy and crusty snow that might entomb a lower-profile tip.

Almost all European alpine ski manufacturers make a short, fat alpine-touring model. But unfortunately, few of these skis reach the small U.S. market. Among those that are imported on a regular basis are the Italian Tua Excaliber, the Fischer Alpin Tour, and the Rossignol Heli Guide. In the U.S. three manufacturers produce skis that, while they are not called alpine-touring models, still function beautifully in that capacity in the shorter lengths. These are the PRE Extreme Powder, the Miller Soft, and the RD (Research Dynamics) Helidog. Shorter does not mean cheaper, however. Expect to pay top-of-the-line prices, $400 and up.

Alpine-Touring Bindings

The good news is you don't have to have a special ski to enjoy this kind of skiing. Almost any alpine ski will suffice if you put an alpine touring binding on it. The binding is the thing which by itself defines this kind of skiing. A straight alpine binding doesn't allow the free-heel function that is so necessary for walking and climbing comfortably. And a standard three-pin or cable telemark binding can't provide the solid security and release functions that alpine skiers require for their downhill runs. Alpine touring bindings are marvels of engineering that do both.

The simplest way to convert to an alpine touring setup is with the Swiss-made Secura-Fix. This is not a binding per se, it is a binding insert used in conjunction with a standard alpine toe-and-heel binding. The adjustable-length base of the Secura-Fix mimics the sole of your alpine boot. On top, there is a hinged contraption that

A typical alpine touring setup. The boot is flexible enough for walking and has a lug sole for climbing on rock or ice. When the buckles are secured, the boot has adequate downhill stiffness. Top, the binding is in free-heel mode; the climbing plug is in place for ascending steep pitches. Below, the heel is locked in place for downhill mode.

holds your boot in the walking mode. When the unit is inserted into your bindings it functions as a free-heel binding. With climbing skins on, you can ascend anywhere a skier on special alpine touring gear can go. When you are ready to ski downhill, you pop the inserts out of your bindings, stow them in your pack, and step in to ski as always.

The Secura-Fix has the advantage of versatility and the security of skiing downhill on your alpine bindings. (Despite improvements in recent years, alpine touring bindings still are not as reliable for retention and release functions as are alpine bindings.) The disadvantage of the Secura-Fix has to do with the weight and rigidity of alpine gear. Alpine skis are usually longer and heavier than their AT counterparts. Boots and bindings are also heavier (the old saw goes: a pound on your feet is equal to five pounds on your back), and the boots are not well adapted to walking (too stiff) or to scrambling on rock and ice (no cleated rubber soles as AT boots have). If your aim is to ski in the backcountry only occasionally and perhaps take off on the spur of the moment from the lift-served terrain for an out-of-area powder run, then the Secura-Fix is a great tool to carry. If, on the other hand, alpine touring becomes a passion, then you will probably want the lightest, most job-specific gear you can get.

Alpine-touring bindings include the perennial German-made favorite Silvretta (at about $225 at the lower end of the price spectrum), the more expensive French Emery binding, the increasingly popular Petzl, and the only American-made binding, the Ramer Universal. Colorado's Paul Ramer has been a tireless inventor, promoter, and manufacturer of alpine-touring equipment. A lover and admirer of the French-Swiss Haute Route, a week-long connecting of high-elevation huts from Chamonix to Zermatt, he has pioneered a Colorado high route, called the Grand Tour, which connects the ski resorts of Eldora, Winter Park, Loveland, Arapahoe Basin, Breckenridge, Copper Mountain, and Vail.

Alpine-Touring Boots

AT boots are also hybrids, in this case a cross between a high, plastic alpine ski boot and the trimmer, lighter, lug-soled mountaineering or ice-climbing boot. Alpine-touring boots use the latter's rubber soles for traction on rock and ice. They have a hinged cuff for ankle freedom while walking, but you can lock it in place for added control on the descent. They have removable inner boots for easy drying and for lounging around a camp or hut.

Almost all of the AT boots we see in this country come from three Austrian bootmakers: Dachstein, Koflach, and Dynafit. The Dynafit Tourlite (about $300) has gobbled a big share of the market because of its Gore-Tex bootie and its extremely light weight.

Alpine-Touring Necessities

I'll talk more about safety and avalanche rescue gear in the next chapter on the backcountry. For now, let's consider the minimum an alpine tourer should carry. Skins, naturally. Skins for alpine touring come wider than for telemark skis, up to 62 mm wide. You can get them from Coll-tex (imported by Alpine Crafts Co. in San Francisco), Chouinard, and Ascension Enterprises. Glue-ons are more reliable provided you fold them properly, base to base, sticky bottoms thoroughly protected from contamination by dirt or snow.

If you aren't wearing ski pants with built in boot cuffs, you'll need a good pair of gaiters. Gaiters are made of waterproofed nylon and usually zip around the lower leg to provide a tight seal over the boot top. Snow in the boot is not a happy situation. Insulated gaiters that cover the whole boot are also available for extreme cold weather or for people with chronically cold toes. Manufacturers include Outdoor Research of Seattle and Wild Country in Center Conway, New Hampshire.

And you'll need a pack to carry skins, lunch, Secura-Fix, sun screen, extra sweater, what have you. External frame packs are out—too stiff and clunky. Small frameless rucksacks are fine for day trips. If you are going longer or need to carry more gear, internal frame packs of 3,000 cubic inches or less are the ticket. A good internal frame pack distributes weight between shoulders and hips, conforms to the shape of your body, and rides close to the back for minimal load shifting while skiing. REI makes excellent packs for reasonable prices. Lowe and Gregory make more technically sophisticated and more expensive packs.

Two well-dressed tourers in pile insulating sweaters, waterproof/breathable outerwear, gaiters to keep snow out of boots, good hand and eye protection. If they were going very far, they would also carry day packs with food and water, first aid, and storm gear. *Linde Waidhofer*

OFF-TRACK TECHNIQUE

As a tourer, my aim is to get off-track. I want to get away, if only for an hour or two, into the silence beyond the trailhead, to sample the untracked snows, to wander, to choose a destination and find my own way there and back. There might be a trail or an old logging road to follow, or there might not. I must be more self-sufficient than my track-skier persona, and my technique will have to be more versatile as well.

A lot of this technique has been covered already in the on-track and alpine instruction sections. The diagonal stride is the basic mode of transportation off the track as well as on. (Off-track skiers rely on the stride even more heavily, because the surface underfoot rarely allows for more exotic techniques like skating.) And the basic tenants of downhill technique apply away from the lifts as well as on the pistes.

But if the movements are essentially the same, tourers nevertheless have a very different set of problems to solve with them. Like breaking trail. And ascending that steep hillside without slipping backward. And coming back down with decorum intact. Tourers need a sense of touch that track skiing rarely taps. They need to develop the art of uphill edge control. And they need new technical skills for coming down on free-heel gear, namely the telemark turn.

Uphill Skiing

Say you want to climb a steep hill and there is no trail. You could try bolting straight up it, but most likely your wax won't hold and you will slip backwards. Even skins will not hold on many a pitch.

If a direct attack doesn't work (and herringboning is exhausting on a long haul, especially through unbroken snow), try modifying the angle. Sailboats can't sail directly into the wind; they must tack. So must skiers traverse back and forth when the going gets steep. Finding the optimal climbing angle is a matter of touch, of subtle decision-making, depending on the steepness of the pitch, the depth and consistency of the snow. No two situations will ever be identical.

Hill climbing has to do with edge control as well as touch. Herringboning substitutes the holding power of the entire ski (with an edge dug in against the snow) for the grip of the wax or skins. The edged ski creates a snow platform against which the skier can push and advance. This is especially true for side-stepping, a ponderous but useful technique when the snow surface is steep. Moving sideways up the hill, crablike, you cut a bench with the lead ski, pull up to it, balance, and reach up to cut another. Obviously, if the skis are not well edged—angled into the hill—they will slip off into the pull of gravity. You can side-step straight up the fall line, or, more practically, side-step at an ascending angle, moving forward as well as up with each platform. This is less tiring, and even very steep pitches can be climbed by linking such traverses—tacking up a mountain side.

Kick Turn

Perhaps the single most important technique for hill climbing (and for certain tricky descents as well) is the oft-maligned kick turn. True, it is somewhat awkward at first, but mastering it makes getting around in wild snow so much easier.

Suppose you are zigzagging up a hill, tacking. How do you move from one traverse to the next? A step turn up the hill is risky and exhausting. A downhill turn loses much of the vertical you have just gained. The only practical way to connect your traverses is with a kick turn. Start by establishing a good platform, one on which you can balance confidently. Kick one ski up and around to where it faces the new direction. (You can kick either the uphill or the downhill ski. Start by mastering the downhill kick turn, then try the other.) You are now turned out in what would be called fourth position in ballet: one foot pointing across the hill in one direction, the other just the opposite. Take time to feel secure on the new-direction ski before weighting it and swinging the other one around. Failure to establish sure platforms is the most common cause of debilitating, midturn tangles. Good platforms are a result of your sense of slope, touch, and edge control.

Alpine-Touring Hint

Most AT bindings come equipped with heel plugs or heel risers for steep climbing above 15 or 20

The kick turn is indispensable when you need to turn around and you can't (or you don't want to) make a downhill turn. Start by establishing a solid platform (A), kick the downhill ski up and around (B and C), establish new platform (D), and swing around to finish. *Linde Waidhofer*

Breaking trail can be hard work. Take turns, and you will have a happier and evenly rested crew.

degrees. The plugs click up or down into place beneath the heel of your boot, giving you, in effect, high heels. Risers "flatten out" the slope. It feels like you're walking up stairs, and it reduces the strain on the calves and Achilles tendon over the long haul. Kick turns with the risers in place can be even trickier than without, but the comfort level on the straight-ahead climb more than makes up for it.

A couple of points about breaking trail through untracked snow. Depending on how deep this snow is, the lead person on a tour is doing a lot more work than those who follow. Take turns

breaking trail, and you will have a happier and more evenly rested crew.

When it's your turn to lead, try to streamline your actions as much as possible. Slide your feet forward through the unbroken snow wherever you can instead of lifting your skis up (with the weight of all that snow on top of them) and plopping them down and forward. Skis glide under the snow with surprisingly little effort.

Plant your poles in a diagonal rhythm as you lead, but don't depend on them for balance and forward power. Overdependence on the arms and shoulders is exhausting. Instead, use your poles as feelers, additional light balance points, while the much stronger muscles in your legs do the work of ascending.

Summit Suggestions

So, you've made it to the top. Or just to the point on your tour where you're turning around. Stretching out before you is a field of sparkling, virgin powder. Gravity is now an ally. The downhill run will be the icing on the day's cake, the chance to answer the uphill effort with some graceful human etchings on the snow. But first, the well-deserved picnic. A few practical hints. Carry some kind of foam pad with you to sit on. Or find a fallen log. Or stomp out a place for your feet and sit on your skis. The point of this being to stay dry. And consequently warm.

When you stop, unless the sun is really warm, put on another insulating layer and/or a wind shell. Again, this is to prevent the loss of body heat. Hypothermia, a drop in the body's core temperature, can come on quickly when you're sitting inactive in the snow. When it happens, it will make you listless and uncoordinated. What's worse, you won't care. It's an insidious hazard, definitely to be guarded against. Stay warm. Drink plenty of liquids; you lost more on the way up than you imagine. (Beer and wine are diuretics; they result in a net loss of fluids in the system. The effects of alcohol at high altitudes are magnified.) And refuel the body's engine with high-energy foods like fruits, nuts, and complex carbohydrates: bagels are the most portable bread imaginable; they don't crumble and they're full of goodness.

Take care to protect skin and eyes from the sun. Wear good quality sunglasses or goggles with 100% ultraviolet protection. Snow blindness is a painful, though rarely permanent, condition caused by staring at the the sun's reflected light on the snow. That same reflective quality causes sunburn on exposed skin even more quickly than on a beach. And even in cloudy or hazy weather. So use an SP 15 or higher number sunblock.

DOWNHILL TECHNIQUES

Downhill is so addictive for some skiers that it becomes *the* reason to go out. It's the challenge, the adrenaline, the reward. It's a chance for artistry. Certainly, it's the yin to the uphill yang. And with a few downhill skills in your quiver, it needn't ever be the daunting part of a tour.

Telemark Position

First, let's consider balance. Rapid acceleration and deceleration are the destabilizing devils of downhill. Drop-offs and reduced friction from harder snow cause the former; terrain upturns and deeper, softer snow, the latter. How to handle the fore/aft balance problems? Spread your feet, front and back, in the classic telemark position, the same one ski jumpers use when landing. Forget turning for the moment. This sturdy, flexible triangle, with you centered somewhere in the

The telemark position is a stable triangle: one foot forward and one foot back with your center of mass securely in the middle. Changes in terrain and snow texture are easily absorbed by the fore/aft flexibility and the inherent balance of the stance. *Lito Teiada-Flores*

middle, is the essential tool for handling changes in terrain and snow consistency. A solid telemark traverse coupled with a steady kick turn will get you down anything—guaranteed. Also use the tele-position in-track anytime the terrain threatens to buck you off-balance. The telemark turn is naturally more complex than the straight-running tele-position, but it derives its versatility in the outback from the stability of this same fore/aft spread.

First Turns

Before diving into the telemark, however, there are two turns you should learn first, the step turn and the wedge turn. (Both were covered in the chapter on track skiing but bear a quick refresher here.)

To do the step turn, learn to "walk" around a turn using small, divergent steps. The Professional Ski Instructors of America used to call this turn the Thousand Steps. With patience and enough steps, you will come around to a stop. You will develop balance, and you will have a turn, one that will serve you well time and again no matter how proficient you become at more sophisticated turns. Especially in difficult, grabby,

A

B

C

D

A wedge turn on skinny skis requires more exaggerated steering than it would on alpine gear. The softer boot/ski connection and the narrower, straighter skis mean the skier must edge strongly (B-D) with his left knee, and actively direct the ski with foot steering. Note how he keeps his body centered over the wedge platform (D), though his weight is clearly pressing on the outside ski. *Linde Waidhofer*

or crusty snows, where nothing else seems to work, this one is the ultimate safety valve.

The snowplow or wedge turn is the ideal platform for developing steering skills, on packed snow or out touring. A steered ski is one that is weighted, edged, and directed, using the twisting power of the leg and foot. Try this on packed snow first: in a gliding wedge position—tips converging, tails spread out behind, weight centered between the feet, both inside edges scraping the snow as you go—begin a straight run. From here it's easy to feel the effects of the three elements. Pressure (weight) the right ski and it wants to turn you to the left, the direction in which it is pointing. Edge the ski sharply, and the resistance of the snow will make it "hold" in the new direction. (Conversely, flatten the ski to the snow surface, and it will skid across the resistance.) Add some twisting, some pivoting of the ski underfoot, and you can further encourage the turning action. Experiment. The wedge is a rich learning center as well as a handy brake when you need to slow down but don't have the room to make a turn.

THE TELEMARK TURN

The telemark turn is the *pièce de résistance* for touring skiers, an elegant combination of grace and free-heel downhill control. It was the first effective ski turn, developed when boots were soft and bindings were floppy at best. Snow was ungroomed, often wild and deep. A steered parallel turn, in the sense we talk about it today, was just about impossible on the old gear. Instead, the first telemarkers, in effect, turned two balky skis into one long, more manageable one. By striding into the tele-position and varying the angle of their skis one to the other (like a hinge; a wide open, nearly parallel, angle resulted in a long-radius curve, while a sharper, more acute, angle provided a snappier direction change), they found they could carve arcs in just about any snow condition. Today, an accomplished telemarker—whose deep knee bends remind me of a knight genuflecting before his queen—can carve arcs as precise and quick as an alpine skier using parallel techniques. And there is a fluid continuity of motion to good telemarking, like stepping down a mountain on wide stairs, that even alpine skiers can't match.

When learning any turn, first attempts are best made on smooth, packed slopes. Deep snow adds a third dimension that takes a lot of getting used to.

In a slow-speed straight run, skis parallel, practice dropping into the tele position and coming back up. No need to advance the skis too far apart; six to twelve inches is plenty. Flex at the ankles and the knees. Keep your weight centered between your front and back feet, that is, the ball of your flexed back foot and the whole of your flat front foot. Glide forward with alternate feet to get the feeling of striding into the tele position.

Wedge Telemarks

The next step is to use the wedge to initiate a telemark turn. In a gliding wedge on a gentle pitch, steer the right ski into a turn and tuck the left leg in behind as in the telemark position. Begin the turn in a wedge; finish it in the tele position. Begin the turn in a tall, upright stance, then sink into the weighting of the outside ski while simultaneously tucking the rear leg behind, flexing both ankles and knees.

Try linking wedge teles down a shallow slope. Combine the two movements of wedging and sinking into one smooth motion. Sink into the telemark position at the same time you wedge your outside ski. You should feel as though you were walking pigeon-toed from one tele to the next.

Where the hill is gentlest, minimize the displacement of the wedging ski and concentrate instead on edging both skis into the turn. Press in on the big-toe side of the lead foot and on the little-toe side of the trailing foot.

Where the hill is steeper, use more wedge to brake your speed and to create a sharper angle between the skis. Think of them as one long, hinged ski instead of two. The sharper the angle created between the two skis the faster you'll get around the corner. Remember that the lead ski initiates the direction change; it's the one you steer. The trailing ski is not actively steered, but it should be edged and weighted as well; it is the keel, the solid soul of the arc. With beginning telemarkers the temptation is to focus too completely on the lead ski, with the result that the turns "wash out." They lack the stability that a well-weighted rear ski brings to the arc.

A

B

C

D

E

The telemark turn: At the completion of one turn (A) the skier strides ahead, slides his new lead ski foreward and to the side (B and C), edging and steering into the turn. Sinking into the turn (deeply flexed at knees and ankles), he edges and weights the trailing ski as well (D), finishing in the classic tele position (E, A). Note how his upper body remains angulated, tilted out over the turning ski for balance and pressure on the edge. *Linde Waidhofer*

Step Telemark

Now instead of wedging to initiate the turn, begin with a more dynamic step. From a traverse step the uphill ski (soon to become the lead or steering ski) forward and angle the tip downhill. Edge and press on that ski. As both skis turn and point downhill, continue to guide the front foot in the direction of the turn while at the same time sinking into the telemark position. Tuck your rear leg under you where you can effectively weight that foot. Don't let it straggle too far behind; the stance then becomes too spread out, awkward of balance and can result in the trailing ski crossing behind the lead foot, a debilitating tangle that requires some real gymnastics to repair. Again, once the turn is begun, concentrate on weighting and edging both skis to experience the telemark's long single-ski effect.

Simultaneous Edge Change

Both the wedge and step initiations are sequential in nature. That is, the skis are edged in sequence, first the lead ski then the trailing ski. There's nothing wrong with this. It offers real security on steep slopes, in moguls, in unpredictable snow—any time, in telemark guru Paul Parker's words, you need "to feel your way along" the pitch. But there is a more elegant, smoother way to telemark, and that is with a simultaneous edge change.

It's the same concept as the simultaneous edge change (erroneously referred to as "parallel" technique) in alpine skiing. It takes some time to master, but the resulting turns will be more precise, closer to the carved ideal than the more common sideways skid.

To back up slightly, telemark skis, like their alpine cousins, come with strong turning tendencies built in. They have a side geometry known as sidecut that, when placed on snow (tilted on edge), will result in a curved path, not a straight one. Do nothing else but stand on an edged ski (you do need a little help from gravity) and you will scribe a turn that mirrors the radius of the ski's own side shape.

The skis want to turn. But that built-in arc is too long for most mountain situations. To tighten the arc, you have to bend the ski. Bend them throug your combined weight and momentum in a turn, and the sidecut arc

becomes even more pronounced. Out of the careful modulation of these ingredients, edging and weighting, comes the carved turn. No one makes pure carved turns 100% of the time. It's just not possible or practical. Skidding the skis sideways is the flip side of the coin, and an equally valuable skill. But carving is the precision tool for handling speed and terrain. It opens up the world of advanced skiing, and it should be your primary learning goal.

That said, back to simultaneous edge changes. Two-step initiations are less likely to result in carved turns. A ski displaced to the side is apt to keep moving that way, skidding as it arcs ahead. This is good when you want to make a short-radius, quick direction change. But if you want to carve a longer arc, a simultaneous movement is more efficient. As you rise between turns, keep both skis flat during the lead change. Once the correct foot is forward for the next turn, sink and edge both skis at once, both knees shifting to the inside of the turn. Pressure the skis at the same time. Bend them into one long bow, and they will cut a clean line in the snow. Stand up, change leads, and repeat.

Advanced Tele Tips

Advanced telemarking shares a lot with advanced alpine skiing. In fact, the better you become at both techniques, the more closely they are related. There's carving, and there's body position, anticipation. Both styles utilize an independence between upper and lower bodies.

In both, the skier's feet and skis finish a turn out of the fall line across the hill, while the upper body, shoulders, head and hands, continue to face down the hill, in the direction of—anticipating—the coming turn. Anticipation helps you to balance your weight over your feet, sets you up for your pole plant, and acts to "coil" your body like a spring for release into the new turn. (See Chapter 3, Alpine: A Basic Progression.) The difference is, in alpine skiing your uphill ski is slightly ahead of your downhill ski; your pelvis faces down the hill. The tele skier, however, leads with his downhill ski; the hips rotate with the turn rather than facing downhill. So for a telemark skier to achieve anticipation, he has to twist his torso opposite his hips.

The resulting wind-up is a powerful torquing

of stomach and back muscles. In fact, tele-anticipation can be an even more effective spring than alpine anticipation. As Paul Parker says, "If you feel that your abdomen is really getting a workout, then you are probably doing it right."

Deep Snow Telemark

The problem posed by powder snow is the added dimension: your skis can now move up and down in the snow as well as forward and across the plane. The trick in skiing it well is to keep both skis on the same level at the same time: both skis deep in the new-snow layer, both floating somewhere in the middle of the soup, or both skimming the surface together.

To do this, you have to weight your skis equally. Packed-snow technique dictates that you weight the outside, or downhill, ski more than the inside ski, or in the case of the telemark, you weight the lead ski more than the tailing ski. But if you do that in powder, the weighted ski will dive while the unweighted one will climb to the surface, resulting in a mess of conflicting resistances and a likely cartwheel.

Practice equal weight first on straight runs over gentle powder slopes. (These will be much easier to find in the backcountry than at the ski areas, where new snow quickly vanishes under the tracks of both grooming machines and powder-hungry skiers.) Run straight, and shift your weight from one foot to the other. Note the result. Now do it with your weight evenly distributed fore and aft between your feet. Bounce up and down as you

The telemark is an excellent technique for three-dimensional snows: powder, crud, in this case, spring slush. The thing to remember is to keep weight on the trailing foot—equal weight on both skis. Otherwise the heavy ski (almost always the lead foot) will dive while the light ski sails to the surface.

After the climb up comes the reward on the downhill run.

during the heaviest part of the turn, at the end, and extend completely during the light phase of the turn, as you are changing leads and tilting the skis into the new turn. Good powder skiing is always a matter of this breathing, of extending and contracting through the light and heavy phases of every turn.

One more tip. When you bounce up to unweight and change leads, raise your outside arm and pole with some vigor to encourage the unweighting, and free the skis temporarily from the snow's embrace. Alta, Utah, powder master Alf Engen calls this move the "ready hand." It not only generates power (unweighting and twisting forces) for the beginning of the turn, but it readies the pole and arm for the next pole plant. The deeper or more difficult the snow, the more vigorous the "ready hand," until, as Alf says, "it becomes like an uppercut."

ALPINE TOURING DOWNHILL

The "ready hand" works for making parallel turns on AT gear as well. In fact, all of the key ingredients in advanced alpine technique apply here as well: anticipation, setting a solid edge, reaching downhill with the pole plant, initiating with unweighting and the "ready hand."

There are a few things to emphasize, however, due to differences between AT equipment and standard alpine gear. One of them is the flexibility of the boots. In order to be comfortable climbing up, AT boots give away a certain amount of rigid control coming back down. Unlike alpine boots you may not be able to lean against the tongue of your AT boot and get an immediate response from the ski. The same applies to pressuring the back of the boot and expecting the tail of the ski to hold at the end of a hard turn. An AT boot requires you to stand on your feet, to use an old ski-instructor expression. You won't be able to get away with indiscretions in fore/aft balance; you need to stand flat-footed, centered, and you need to stay there. Because the skis are shorter and often very quick, they will usually respond to subtle "foot steering" movements.

The skis are short, and they are wide. This means that it takes more force to hold that wider ski up on edge. Luckily, alpine touring boots are quite rigid laterally, so achieving and sustaining

glide straight ahead. (Most powder over 4 or 5 inches deep has a springy, bread-dough feel.) Bounce up and unweight as you switch leads. Then sink into your tele position, weight evenly distributed front and back.

Now add the simultaneous edging mentioned above. Do it on the same mellow slope so that turning for speed control is not an issue. Begin with slight changes of direction, quick scoops of the long, bent ski. Quickly unweight, change leads, and edge the other way. Carve a series of shallow crescents down the hill.

Gradually work toward longer, more complete arcs. You'll need to finish your turns, to press your skis across the fall line and down in the deep-snow resistance, in order to maintain control on steep slopes. As your turns come further and further across the hill, remember to keep your upper body anticipated, coiled as it were, toward the turn to come. Avoid stepping into your initiations; displacing and weighting one ski at a time is asking for trouble in deep snow. Try for the smooth, simultaneous edge change.

Exaggerate the flexion and extension you employ in packed-snow telemark turns. Flex low

edge hold is not a problem. Just remember that it may take slightly more active edging on your part to get the same results you would enjoy with a narrower slalom ski.

In deep snow alpine touring gear is a dream. The skis' short lever arm makes them easy to turn even in heavy snows. The wide platform keeps you floating in or near the softer top layers. And the soft-flexing boots allow an ankle freedom that powder skiers cherish: Free hinging at the ankle joints means you can stay balanced through the most expansive extensions and contractions. No matter what terrain changes the mountain throws at you, you don't have to sit back (the result of bent knees and straight ankles) in order to absorb them. Your weight stays forward, ready, come what may.

TIPS & TALES: Teaching Kids

Kids just wanna have fun. And sometimes, putting them in school—ski school, that is—can kill off fledgling enthusiasms. Take your children skiing yourself, and remember that they may not share your athletic/aesthetic love of the sport.

Make it easy. Do everything you can to guarantee the fun. Pick nice days—cold weather can rob the strength and joy from little bodies in a twinkling. Dress them well, against cold (or overheating if the sun is blazing), for freedom of movement and water repellency; kids spend as much time in the snow as on it. Jeans and other cotton fabrics are quickly soaked. Wool is better. Synthetic pile is better yet. Best of all is a wool or pile insulating layer covered with waterproof/breathable outerwear. If it all seems too expensive, comfort yourself with the knowledge that ski swaps are everywhere, and that the resale value of kids' gear is extremely high.

Find soft snow if you can; the magic of snow is that it's plastic, flowing, like beach sand, only softer.

Pop for appropriate skis and boots. Rent or buy, but be sure the skis are shorter than the child is tall, waxless, to make climbing a snap. Get them real cross-country shoes—cable, three-pin, or integrated systems. Inexpensive, strap-on bindings and galoshes don't work. Poles are least important; in the beginning, in fact, they can be skipped altogether.

Make it a game. In the beginning, avoid set track. Most track setters lay down veritable

Kids just wanna have fun. On a nice day a cross-country picnic even beats the beach.

canyons, too wide and too deep for little legs. Don't set out to do a couple of kilometers. Pick a spot with varied terrain and make it your playground. Set a course yourself with your skis quite close together. Include plenty of downhill schusses. It's no accident that kids take so easily to downhill skiing; walking is work, gravity is a rush. Pack out a small slope for sidestepping and snowplowing. Build a jump. The young Stein Ericksen loved jumping so much he did it by candlelight in the backyard.

Seek adventure. Follow animal tracks into the woods. See if you can identify the tracks of snowshoe hares, mice, weasels, deer, foxes, elk, or the delicate wing splashes left when a big bird like a jay or an owl swoops down to the snow surface. Ski down a frozen creek. Explore. Ski at night. Ski on the roof if you can. (I've done this with my kids at a high-country cabin where the space between the north roof and the ground disappeared in a prodigious snow winter.)

Along the way you may want to introduce the notions of kick and glide, kick turns, skating, herringboning, and so on. The kids, in turn, will teach you a lot about pure, unadulterated fun.

Backcountry skiers find camaraderie and responsibility along with
unhurried, untrammeled, untracked snows.

8

Backcountry Skills

After crossing Greenland on skis in 1888, Norwegian polar explorer Fritjof Nansen wrote: "I know of no form of sport which renders the body so strong and elastic, which teaches so well the qualities of dexterity and resourcefulness, which in equal degree calls for decision and resolution, and which gives the same vigor and exhilaration to mind and body alike . . ."

Backcountry skiing differs from other branches of the sport in two ways: the reward and the responsibility.

Getting there is its own reward. Traveling through untracked snow to reach a wilderness hut or climbing a peak in the pink dawn are ends in themselves. But oftentimes when you get there, there is more: personal satisfaction at having done it; deep quiet like a drink of mountain water; and a giddy feeling that you've had a peek at absolute harmony in the natural world. Then too, there is the reward of skiing back down. For many backcountry skiers, this is the frosting on the cake, the untouched, uncontested, unhurried, unbelievable powder snow.

Or more accurately, wild snow. The backcountry skier comes to appreciate the variety and complexity of natural snow from pancake-batter glop to ice nubbles, from wind-drifted porcelain snow to perfect crystalline foam. Skiing in the backcountry is an altogether more sensuous experience than skiing the pack and the track.

Backcountry skiing is practically synonymous with exploration. It's the flip side of the track loop, that amusement park ride laid out for your pleasure and challenge, but on which you cannot possibly get lost. In the backcountry you face the blank page of infinite possibility. The payoff is discovery, geographic and personal.

But if the rewards are potent, the responsibilities are equally formidable. Getting everybody back safely is not an option; it is required. The backcountry is beautiful and uncaring, inhuman. Self-sufficiency is mandatory. Wilderness demands more of its visitors than does ski-area skiing. Then again it is more engrossing; it requires (and makes easy I should say) a clarity of attention. There are no other distractions, no snowcats, no safety nets, no ski patrol, no first aid room at the bottom of the hill. What do you do if equipment breaks down, if somebody gets too tired, if you think you might be lost, if the weather changes suddenly for the worse? The questions and the answers are integral to the backcountry experience.

PAY YOUR DUES

Before you take off for the wild snows take reasonable stock of your preparedness. This doesn't mean that you have to be an expert skier to have fun and be safe in the backcountry. Far from it. It does mean you need to be realistic about matching your skill level against the contemplated adventure. Any number of safe and easy day tours can be found in virtually any of the skiing provinces of the country. But even they take a minimum grounding in the skiing skills discussed so far. And they require a bit of extra gear and the knowledge to go with it. The point is, don't make the mistake of falling in love with the notion of backcountry skiing and then just set off for the hills. You must pay your dues first.

I once took off on a three-day hut trek into the San Juan Mountains with a secret novice in the group. He was the new doctor in town, young, spirited, and suited up in all the latest gear. But atop the first pass, we discovered to our horror that the good doctor couldn't make a turn, any kind of turn. It was a potentially dangerous situation, and we did spend one night out in a storm because of our slowed pace. Sound bivouac skills and some luck—storm temperatures remained relatively warm—got us through the night.

Whether you choose to explore the outback on telemark or alpine-touring gear, or even lightweight off-track (general) touring gear, work on your packed-snow technique first. Practice your kick-and-glide on the tracks and trails. Work on downhill balance and turns. Take lessons. Find a mentor. Learn by osmosis, by imitation. Put in some miles. *Then* you can start thinking about taking off beyond the trails, about laying down fresh tracks in an otherwise untouched landscape.

SAFETY FIRST

Every decision you make on a backcountry trip should be grounded first in the safety of skiers. This is not to say that you can or should eliminate all risk. In the first place it's not possible, and secondly, risk is an essential spice in the skiing recipe, one of the reasons we are transported by it, enriched and enlivened by it. The object here is to reduce the risks to manageable levels.

Selecting a Tour

Choose an appropriate tour for the members of the group. If skill levels vary, consider the pace of the slowest member. Many easy tours have challenging side trips—ridges to climb, powder glades to ski down—extra explorations for the

more advanced skiers. But if you take a weak skier where he is seriously in over his head, you've got trouble, and the whole group must work to get him back out.

Watch the Weather

A simple day tour in calm, sunny weather is an altogether different story in a storm. While no one can predict the weather, satellite images and computer forecasting make guessing a lot more informed. It's still a good idea to choose gentle days for beginning backcountry skiers and children. Children, because of their greater surface-area-to-mass ratio, become colder faster than adults. *Extreme cold* can rob you of your joy and even your good judgment, if your body's core temperature slips a few degrees into hypothermia. (More on prevention and treatment of hypothermia later in this chapter.)

Cold is not the only weather consideration. You could get wet. Snow and rain sometimes travel together, especially in the Pacific Northwest and in maritime New England. You can even get wet in the "dry-snow" Rockies if your stormwear melts through, or you sit too long in the snow, or if you are overdressed for the day and your exertion level. As long as you're moving, generating lots of body heat, being wet is more uncomfortable than it is serious. But once you stop moving vigorously, moisture on the skin can quickly lead to chills and worse.

Visibility is another consideration. Fog and whiteout conditions can disorient even the best skiers. You could lose the trail, lose your way, or lose your balance to a condition called vertigo. When clouds close in so close that you can't distinguish snow from sky, it's hard sometimes to tell up from down, or even whether you're moving or standing still. Skiers have been known to drop off cliffs when they thought they were well stopped. And other times I've seen skiers still making turning motions long after they have ceased to move down the hill. It's disorienting, spooky, and occasionally dangerous.

Weather is particularly critical above timberline in the high alpine zone. There conditions can change quickly. Wind at the ridgetops is often many times stronger than it is in the valleys. New snow can pile up in avalanche start zones. Your own return tracks can fill in, vanish. And a skier who is blinded by a whiteout might easily wander

Some of the best ski days are stormy days. So long as you are prepared. *Bob Chamberlain*

into someplace he doesn't want to be, fall off a ledge or move unwittingly onto slide-prone terrain.

Stormy weather in the trees is less critical. Visibility is usually much better, as the woods give definition to the snow underfoot. The wind is broken by the canopy, and avalanches in general are far less likely. But even in the trees and on gentler terrain, an unexpected storm can lead to slowed travel, cold, and the possibility, because of the lack of distinguishing landmarks, of becoming lost.

For the prepared, stormy-day skiing can be beautiful. In a storm, winter seems even more elemental, howling and wracking, purifying, wiping away petty worries, replenishing the earth. Some storms are even gentle—snow falling straight down in a silent stillness. On these days you feel a privileged interloper. But only the prepared feel this way. They've got the right clothing and routefinding skills. They're snug inside their nylon cocoons and managing the risk in calm comfort.

Predicting the Weather

How does one predict the weather? Even with satellites, barometers, hygrometers, and computers to help them, weathermen are not always right. You can do almost as well by quoting the rhymes developed by ancient mariners, farmers, and yes, skiers, rhymes that do have sound science behind them.

Red sky at morning, sailor take warning; red sky at night, sailor's delight. Fair weather involves high-pressure areas composed of dry, stagnant air. Low-angle light through dust and haze in high-pressure air refracts red. Thus a brilliant evening sunset indicates high-pressure air lying to the west (the direction of prevailing winds in the northern hemisphere and thus the direction from which our weather approaches). Conversely, a crimson

"Hen's scratchings and mare's tails make tall ships carry low sails." High-altitude cirrus presage a coming low-pressure system and possible bad weather. *Jerry Roberts*

dawn signals that high-pressure air has passed eastward. High pressure is often followed by low pressure, and lousy weather arrives in low-pressure air masses.

Here's another valuable saying: *Hen's scratchings and mare's tails make tall ships carry low sails.* The "hen's scratchings and mare's tails" refer to high-altitude cirrus clouds. These little clusters of wispy clouds, like groups of apostrophes in the sky, are forerunners of a low-pressure air mass and again the probability of poor weather.

If a lower, thicker veil of clouds trails in behind the mare's tails, the likelihood of a storm is even greater. If you are watching the sky the day before a planned tour, this scenario might lead you to postpone until another day. If you are on the trail trying to decide whether or not to take one more downhill run before heading back to the hut, you might be convinced to forgo the play and head back. If you are camping, these indicators might mean you stop early and set up the tents before the snow sets in.

A backing wind says storms are nigh. A veering wind will clear the sky. Wind is an indicator too. Wind direction changes as low pressure areas come and go. Prevailing fair-weather winds tend to blow from the west or north, while bad-weather winds usually growl up from the southwest, south, or east. If you notice the wind backing (shifting counterclockwise, from westerly to southwesterly, for example) expect worsening weather. Likewise, if the weather has been poor and the wind veers (shifts clockwise, say, southwesterly to westerly), you should see improving weather. When trying to decide if the wind is backing or veering, be sure to look beyond the winds at ground level (flags, trees, etc.). Watch the clouds. Their movement will tell you the true wind direction.

One more invaluable (certainly not foolproof; nothing is where the weather is concerned) rhyme: *Ring around the moon, rain by noon. Ring around the sun, rain before night is done.* Or snow, as the case may be. Atmospheric ice crystals scatter the light of the sun or moon, creating rings or halos. The most common culprits are high cirrus clouds; we know that those hen's scratchings indicate possible wet weather on the way. Halos can grow as the cloud level lowers and the depression (low pressure system) draws nearer, giving rise to the saying: "The bigger the ring, the nearer the wet."

Many's the night I've watched a ring glow around the moon and hoped that a storm was indeed approaching. Skiers are that way. There's nothing to refresh the spirit and excite anticipation like a fresh fall of powder. But depending on the length and severity of the storm, I may want to change my ski plans: ski in the lower-elevation forests instead of above treeline; ski at the ski area instead of the backcountry; put it off just until the wind veers, the sky clears and the new snow sparkles under a brilliant sun.

Backcountry's Golden Rule

Always tell someone where you are going and when you expect to be back. This is a courtesy to all the skiers in your group, to those who would worry if you're not back on time, and to those who will go look for you, if necessary.

A Backcountry Attitude

Every member of a backcountry ski group should take care to ski within his limits. You have a responsibility to the group to have your gear together, to ski in such a way that you don't endanger yourself or others. Because the point is, away from the road and the convenient proximity of ski patrols, if you hurt yourself, you are endangering the others. At a ski area you might jump from a rock to the powder below or ski a tempting steep slope that just might slide beneath you. In the backcountry, a tiny governor inside should weigh the consequences more conservatively. A mistake could mean a cold, overnight bivouac for the whole crew. Or the risk of exposing your rescuers to avalanche danger. Or the physical and emotional rigors of a difficult evacuation. Everybody owes the same consideration to everybody else.

Skiing Alone

How many is a safe number to take into the backcountry? Two is safer than one, obviously; you have some help if one of you gets stuck. But with two, you run the risk of having to leave the injured person alone to get help.

Three is a better number. One can stay with the hurt party while the third skis out for help. Four is even better; then the person skiing out has a buddy. Beyond four, it doesn't much matter until the group reaches an unwieldy mass, a number that varies with the compatibility and skill levels of each party.

Skiing alone has obvious drawbacks. It's like scuba diving alone or cutting firewood in the forest alone; you're not supposed to do it. But I admit that on occasion I do ski into the backcountry by myself. Never for overnights or extended tours, but just for a few hours now and then. All my senses are heightened. The quiet is deeper. The cold tang of the air sharper in my nose. The swish of skis through wild snow is more sensuous, more immediate, more precious when I'm alone. But when I'm alone my governor is on extra alert. There is no room for stupid or even slightly thoughtless mistakes. No one to pick up the pieces. No one to even watch.

Skiing alone is an unmatched private reverie and should be mated to the strongest sort of self-preservation instinct.

DRESSING THE PART

I've already touched on backcountry clothing in the last chapter on off-track skiing. The basic tenets bear repeating, because in the backcountry—especially if you're not just hours but days from civilization—what you wear is of surpassing importance.

The trick is to keep warm enough *and* dry enough. The dry part is the tricky part. You can get wet two ways, from the outside and from the inside. Outside, of course, is snow, sleet, rain, tumbling in a creek, what have you. The new shell fabrics out there do a great job of stopping outside moisture: Gore-Tex and other micro-porous "membrane" fabrics; extra-tight weave nylons; and coated nylons like Patagonia's H2No, Entrant, and Burlington's Ultrex. Casual skiers and day-tourers can get away with just a weatherproof top and some kind of warm and breathable (but not necessarily waterproof) pants—wool knickers, wool or Lycra tights. Skiers going into the alpine zone or on multi-day trips should have weatherproof tops and bottoms.

The inside moisture is of course the perspiration from your working engine. It can just as easily make you cold as moisture from without. The first way to deal with it is to modulate what you wear so you don't get hot in the first place. Thus the emphasis in previous chapters on layering. Take off a layer or two when you're really moving in the sun, when you're climbing. Put them back on when you ski downhill, when you stop for lunch, when the clouds hide the sun.

But you will sweat. Most every trip into the backcountry means *some* sweat. The best way to deal with it is to wear garments that transport the moisture away from your skin. Silk underwear has good "wicking" properties as do Patagonia's capilene and the myriad weaves of polypropylene on the market. Acrylic insulating layers (fleece, pile, etc.) continue the outward transportation of moisture better than do natural fibers like wool or cotton. Finally, the moisture escapes to the outside via the breathable qualities of your outer shell fabric or through venting: through your open collar, through pocket vents in REI's jackets, underarm vents on Patagonia and The North Face gear, and front zippers on most everything.

Even if you sweat a lot before you stop for lunch, you will not feel the chilling effects of evaporation off the skin with the new hydrophobic (water hating) synthetics.

Going for a full day or more into the outback requires that you carry more than the basic three layers. You'll probably want an additional insulating garment for your torso. Down vests are warm and extremely light and compressible; they take up almost no room in a pack. A second pile jacket or a wool sweater will also do. Backcountry snow campers, or anyone who will be standing around for long periods, often include a full down parka in the kit.

You may also want to bring along a spare warm hat (wool or pile), mittens (Austrian boiled-wool Dachsteins are my favorite), a neck gaiter and goggles if the sky starts spitting. You may not need the gear yourself but your being prepared might save somebody else whose hands become cold or who forgets to bring sun glasses.

IN YOUR PACK

The well-prepared tourer is a turtle with a compact, ready-for-anything shell on his back. Even a simple day tour requires a certain safe minimum. Besides your *extra clothing*, you'll need to have room for *food and water*. High-energy foods like bagels, cheeses, chocolates, nuts and dried fruits, are compact and don't squash easily. More elaborate picnics might include flat breads, sardines, peanut butter, carrot and celery sticks, perhaps even some wine. The ultra-prepared day-tripper will carry a camper's bottled-gas stove. (The MSR WhisperLite, about $45 from REI, weighs a mere 13 ounces and nests in its own 1 1/2 liter pot.) Hot soup or tea can be the supreme luxury on a cold day, but even more important is its emergency value. If someone becomes seriously cold (hypothermic), then the stove becomes invaluable first aid.

Water is an undervalued commodity in the frozen cold. You may not think you are perspiring much, but you are, even on a very cold day. Each person should have at least one liter of water for a day tour. If it's a strenuous one, two or more. If the temperature is well below freezing, an insulated plastic bottle will keep your drinking water from freezing. Or you can carry a

shatterproof thermos. Cokes and beers and caffeinated teas and coffees are not recommended because they are diuretics. That is, they result in a net loss of fluids in the body.

Dehydration can contribute to hypothermia and to mild altitude sickness if you are high in the mountains. So keep yourself well hydrated. Sucking snow, while it refreshes, provides very little moisture. Water (or fruit drinks, or non-caffeinated sodas, or whatever you prefer) is heavy. But you've got to carry it. Either that or carry a stove and pot for melting snow.

Carry a *map* of the area you are exploring and a *space blanket* for wrapping up in in case you have to spend the night out. They weigh only a couple of ounces and fold up small.

You should also have a *repair kit*. I have different ones for day tours and long outings. The small one includes: a Swiss Army knife with screwdriver blade; pliers; extra binding screws; extra bail; spare plastic tip in case somebody breaks a ski tip on a hidden stump (this happens much less often now that skis are fiberglass instead of wood, but it does happen); a small coil of wire for repairing bindings, pole baskets; spool of duct tape for repairing almost anything. I keep these things in a small nylon zip bag, which I stow separately from my zip-lock-bagged *wax kit* and my other (draw-string) nylon bag which contains my first-aid kit.

For longer trips, overnights or hut-to-hut, you might add to the basic repair kit: a spare pole basket; nylon cord (for building an emergency sled out of a pair of skis); steel wool (for stuffing in remounted binding holes); needle and thread; spare zipper heads and sliders.

The day-tour *first-aid kit* might include: Ace bandage (for sprains); moleskin (for blisters); sterile bandages; gauze; tape; tweezers; eye drops; sunscreen/lip balm (highest SPF—sun protection factor—rating available; SPF 30 is good); aspirin for mild altitude-induced headache.

The long-tour kit should have added: a portable splint; Lomotil or some other anti-diarrhea drug; codeine or other prescription painkiller.

Additional items that come in very handy: *toilet paper* in a zip-lock bag; a foam pad to sit on (some internal frame packs have removable foam pads just for this purpose); battery-powered *headlamp* (lithium batteries last many times longer than alkaline) for setting up camp in the dark.

A well-equipped day pack might include (counterclockwise from upper left): an emergency tool kit including wire, silver tape, extra binding screws, and tools; shovel; avalanche rescue beacon; skins; water bottle; high-energy foods like dried fruit and nuts; sun block creams; matches in waterproof plastic bottle; map and compass; space blanket; whistle (the human voice carries poorly, especially in the woods); first aid kit; extra mittens, hat, goggles and pile sweater.

If you are going into steep country where avalanches are a consideration each member of your group *must* carry a *shovel* and a *transceiver,* commonly known as a beeper. Shovels are made by Chouinard, Voile, Salewa, and Life-Link, among others. Life-Link offers a lifetime guarantee on its very light and strong plastic blade. Most snow shovels have removable handles for easy stowing in your pack. A shovel is a good idea even if you aren't heading into steep country. A shovel is handy for digging snow for melt water, digging holes for waste, for sitting on, and, most important, for digging a hasty shelter if you are caught out overnight and otherwise unprepared.

Avalanche transceivers are tiny radios, no bigger than a cigarette pack, that fit comfortably inside your ski clothes. They transmit heartbeat-like signals when in the "send" mode, and can home in on those signals when switched to the receive mode. Three or four different models are available in the U.S. (all selling in the $250-350 range): the Skadi, the Ramer Avalert, the Pieps (available through REI or Marmot Mountain Works in Seattle), and the European-made Ortovox. All operate on the same frequency, and the Ortovox operates on the most common European frequency as well.

Beepers have a range of about thirty meters and have saved countless buried avalanche victims, some as deep as four or five meters under the snow. Skilled searchers can find a buried comrade within five to ten minutes. But a beeper will do you absolutely no good if you don't practice using it. Bury one radio in the snow (not the whole person) and practice locating it with another, using the right-angle search pattern described with the transceiver. The units are not directional, but operate instead on the relative strength of the signal; the beeps get louder as you close in. It takes some repetition, to train your ear and to work the pattern.

Naturally, one beeper in a group does no one any good. In a tragic accident near Telluride, Colorado, a few years ago, two of the three skiers in a group had transceivers, but the first onto the avalanche slope was the one without. He was buried and found forty-five minutes later, too late to save his life. This has everything to do with the backcountry attitude, of taking care that each individual is thinking first about the safety of the group. In avalanche country, everybody should be wearing a beeper and know how to use it.

One more word about your pack. While it may seem like we're talking about a lot of gear here, it's really not too much for a skiing turtle. Self-sufficiency is important, and it's satisfying. You may get to the point, as I have, of feeling undressed *without* a pack on your back. It becomes a comfortable part of your skiing self. A final note: a larger backpack loosely filled is ever so much more comfortable than a smaller pack crammed to bursting.

THE OUTBACK TERRAIN

For the backcountry skier, "landscape is like sacrament to be read." Writer Seamus Heaney may not have been thinking specifically of skiers when he said that, but the sentiment couldn't be more perfect. Reading terrain is the key to fun and safety, to finding the best snow, and not getting lost.

Maps

Learning to read a U.S. Geologic Survey (USGS) topographic map will compliment the skill you develop reading the actual landscape. USGS topos are available for virtually every corner of the country. The best are the 7.5 minute series quadrangles with a scale of 1:24,000 or about 2½ inches to the mile.

Topos are so called because they show vertical terrain features (the up and down) as well as standard two-dimensional representations. Concentric lines indicate elevation changes (on the 7.5 minute maps the contour interval is every 40 feet of elevation), in effect providing you a three-dimensional image on the page. Teach yourself to visualize the contours, the highs and lows of the landscape as described by the contour lines. High points and peaks show as concentric circles closing in to a point. Many lines jammed tightly together indicate extremely steep terrain or cliffs. Flats and valley bottoms show relatively few lines widely spread apart. Alpine bowls show as nests of U-shaped lines with the opening pointing downhill. Passes, two sets of U-shaped lines back to back opening away from one another.

There are other clues to the land as well. Green background on the maps indicates forest cover. White is meadowland or above-timber alpine terrain. Lakes and roads and major summer trails are drawn in, and perhaps most important for tourers, creeks show as blue lines. In gentle, forested terrain like the hills of the Midwest and East, stream courses, confluences with other streams or lakes, may be your best orienting clues. In such terrain, without distinguishing high points, a *compass* is invaluable for orienting the map with the four directions.

In somewhat steeper terrain, like the mesas and foothills of the Rockies or the western slope of the Sierra, orienting the map shouldn't be a problem. Simply pick out a couple of major land features, find yourself on the map, and go from there.

In alpine terrain near and above timberline, the map is really not so important, not in terms of getting lost anyway. Up high, there is so much vertical definition to the landscape. Major features soar above or below in clear view.

Routefinding

In the high mountains, routefinding is about finding the best and safest snow. It's important to distinguish the two. Sometimes the best for skiing—the softest, deepest, easiest to glide through—might turn out to be the most dangerous as well. Consider this example:

Your goal for the day is to reach the cirque at the head of a V-shaped valley. The creek in the valley bottom runs east/west. There is no trail; you could choose any route up either side of the creek. The south-facing hillside is devoid of trees; the climbing would be unobstructed, the views magnificent, the sun warming. But the sun has had its way with the snow as well. It has a crunchy crust on top; breaking a trail through the crust would likely make for difficult going.

Routefinding in the backcountry is a learned skill. These skiers are following a low-angle grade next to the trees away from steep faces and obvious avalanche paths. *Tom Lippert*

Whereas on the north-facing side, the sun's rays are oblique, weak. It's colder, and the view not as grand, but the snow is soft in the trees. Just as you are about to go with the north-facing side, you notice what might be avalanche paths cutting clear swaths here and there through the trees. Are they safe to cross? It's been a while since the last snowfall; you judge the snow to be stable, and you vow to cross the paths judiciously, one skier at a time. (More on managing the risks of avalanches in an upcoming section.) All things considered, you choose the shady side.

Up in the bowl at the head of the valley you decide you have plenty of time to climb to the col, or saddle, on the ridge above for your picnic. The view will be splendid, and the wind today is not strong. The direct route to the col would mean zig-zagging up the face of the ridge. It's treeless and steep. A cornice of wind-blow snow arches over the snow field at the top, indicating that prevailing winds have deposited much snow on the face, on the lee side of the ridge. Although it's a good deal farther to go, you opt to stay in the trees until you reach an ancillary ridge line, then follow the ridge top on its windward side to the col. The snow here is crunchy and almost stripped bare by past winds—not the best skiing—but there is no chance it will slide.

Coming back down after lunch this same group will face more decisions. Where is the easiest downhill skiing for the least-proficient members of the group? Where is the softest snow (for linking a few telemark turns) that is also free of avalanche danger? Has the heat of the sun changed the snow they passed through on the way up? Might it now be more fun and just as safe to descend the other side of the valley?

So, routefinding is a complex matter, full of balancing expediency, travel ease, snow quality, downhill temptations, and avalanche concerns. Experience is the best teacher, along with the wisdom of a knowledgeable guide or friend. Here are a few rules of thumb:

- Ridgelines and old forests are generally the safest from avalanches (although slides in the trees when snow is deep and new are not unheard of).
- Avoid gully bottoms where slide danger might lurk unseen above. Down in the gullies you have nowhere to escape, and slide debris, should it come, piles deepest there.
- Watch out for creeks flowing under the snow. You don't want to get wet breaking through a weak snow bridge when crossing from one side to the other.
- Avoid steep wind-loaded lee slopes where fat pillows of snow grow far deeper than surrounding slopes, and where the weight of a skier could be enough to trigger a slide.
- Be very careful walking across the tops of overhanging cornices; the weight of a skier might be enough to crack it off. Never ski directly beneath such cornices.
- Learn to recognize the hour-glass shape of the classic avalanche path. From timberline up to the ridges, the rocky catchment basins fill like bowls with snow; these are the *start zones*. Then come narrow-waisted *tracks* through the timber, down which the accumulated snow pours. The most active tracks are scarred treeless. Less active paths may show two-year, five-year, or ten-year growth, depending on the frequency of major events. (Scarred or branchless trees will sometimes reveal a slide path where more obvious physical characteristics are not present.) Finally, there are the *runout zones*, the hourglass bases, like alluvial fans, where the debris comes to rest.

Many slides, especially smaller ones, don't conform to the classic shape. They may simply be steep snow-covered humps or rolls, hidden cliff bands or open faces tense with overloaded snow and ready to fracture. The big ones are relatively easy to spot and avoid. The smaller, more innocuous ones deserve your special diligence.

- And finally, if you must cross an obvious slide path, do so one skier at a time. Never expose more than one person at a time to the danger.

THE MYSTERY OF SNOW

We take all these precautions because snow is one of the least understood and most volatile substances on earth. To the non-skier it would seem that snow is simple: it falls from the sky as lovely six-sided stars (no two alike according to the common wisdom); it covers the winter landscape; and occasionally, if too much of it falls in one place, it avalanches down to a new state of equilibrium. All true. But only a small fraction of the story. The rest of the story is a good deal more mysterious. As a backcountry skier the depth of your understanding of this basic material will go a long way to increasing your pleasure and safety.

Snow Crystals

Eskimo peoples are said to have a hundred words for snow. Snow scientists have a good many more than that. Most snowflakes are not the delicate six-sided stellar crystals that children learn to cut out of folded paper. That is one kind of crystal, but there are scores of others. Spatial dendrites, which look like jacks in the child's pick-up game, are considerably more common than stellar crystals. Their arms interlock in the snowpack and tend to create a strong, cohesive layer. Other crystals fall as plates, or as columns or tiny, cohesionless needles. Other storms create graupel, which is really a bunching of many crystals together in a kind of soft hail.

Crystals may fall in the classic stellar form and then be dashed and broken as they're bounced along by the wind. Some snow actually arrives as super-cooled water droplets. Known as rime snow, it plasters to any fixed object and transforms timberline trees into a zoo of white gargoyles. Other crystals don't fall out of the sky at all; they grow right on the old snow surface out of water vapor in the air. These are known as hoar frost or surface hoar.

The variety of snow as it falls is remarkable, but the story doesn't stop there. Inside a multi-layered snowpack dramatic transformations are taking place throughout the course of the winter. Some changes make the snow more stable, others weaken the pack, making it more likely to slide. These changes are forms of metamorphism. There are three types: equitemperature (ET) metamorphism, temperature gradient (TG) metamorphism, and melt-freeze (MF) metamorphism.

ET Snow

As soon as snow settles on the ground or on an existing snowpack (assuming a small temperature difference between the bottom of the snow layer and the top), ET metamorphism starts up. The weight of the snow itself causes it to settle and the individual snow grains to bunch closer together. Then a marvelous thing happens, the snow begins to "simplify" its form, to knit together into a tighter, stronger texture. It doesn't need to melt to do this; it happens by sublimation, an only partly understood process. In it, molecules of the solid (ice) turn to water vapor (usually at the points of the crystals) without passing through the liquid stage (this is what mystifies researchers) and then rejoin the solid elsewhere, usually in the concave neck areas. The resulting grains are smaller, rounder, and, if the process is allowed to continue to maturity, bonded together in interlocking structures.

TG Snow

ET snow tends toward stability. TG metamorphism does the opposite; it weakens the snowpack. It works like this: Assume the first storm of the season deposits a foot of snow on a shady north slope. The temperature at the ground is 32 degrees Fahrenheit. This is just about always constant. Twelve inches away at the snow surface, the temperature averages, say, zero degrees for the next two weeks. This intense difference in temperatures (temperature gradient) creates a strong vapor flow within the snow from the warmer ground level up to the colder surface. Water vapor is redeposited (that mysterious sublimation again) on the bodies of the snow grains, not the necks that connect them. Individual crystals grow into assorted prisms, cups, and pyramids; the grains become larger, and the bonds between them weaker.

In its advanced stages, TG snow is completely cohesionless; it falls through your fingers like sugar. In fact, it is sometimes referred to as sugar snow or depth hoar. In the Rockies, early snows and cold temperatures almost guarantee a layer of depth hoar on shady slopes. And almost as surely, when midwinter snows pile up on top, it is these cohesionless layers which collapse, shift, "grease the skids," or otherwise contribute to avalanche activity.

TG metamorphism can occur in mid-pack layers as well—any time there is a sufficient temperature gradient—and these weak strata may also be culprits in snow "failure," namely avalanches.

TG is most common in the continental climate of the Rockies, from Canada all way down to northern New Mexico. These mountains share the common factors of high elevation, cold temperatures and relatively light snowfall, creating perfect conditions for temperature gradients. TG is less prevalent in the maritime climates of New England and the Pacific coast ranges where warm temperatures (and prodigious snowfalls out

Digging a snow pit can help you evaluate the stability of the snowpack, and influence your routefinding and downhill skiing decisions. The snowpack reads like a layer-cake time line, oldest snows on the bottom, newest at the surface. Weak layers or poorly bonded strata could indicate avalanche-prone terrain. On the other hand, a strongly knit snowpack is a good sign for slope stability. *Jerry Roberts*

west) favor snowpack-strengthening ET metamorphism. This is not to say that they don't have avalanches in the Sierra and the Cascades; they have some ferocious cycles. But the cause of the snow letting go is more likely to be poor bonding between layers of heavy, cohesive snows than it is the ball-bearing effect of buried sugar.

MF Metamorphism

Melt-freeze changes generally happen in the spring when air temperatures warm up and the snowpack becomes isothermic—that is, of uniform temperature (32 degrees F from the ground all the way to the surface). In spring the warm days melt the surface layers of the snowpack. Free water dribbles down through the layers. Then everything freezes up again at night. When this cycle has gone on for several days and nights, the snow is no longer made up of crystals but of large polygranular lumps, what skiers call "corn snow."

In mid-morning, when just the very top surface of the corn has begun melting, the skiing is sublime, like sliding over crushed velvet. MF

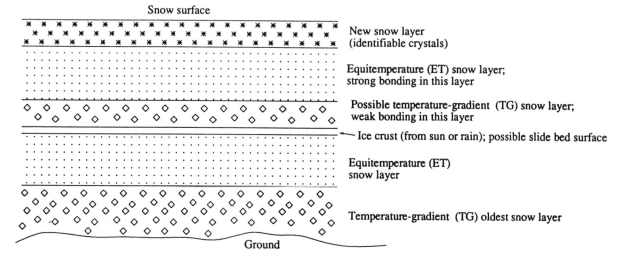

Snow surface

New snow layer
(identifiable crystals)

Equitemperature (ET) snow layer;
strong bonding in this layer

Possible temperature-gradient (TG) snow layer;
weak bonding in this layer

Ice crust (from sun or rain); possible slide bed surface

Equitemperature (ET)
snow layer

Temperature-gradient (TG) oldest snow layer

Ground

Snow strata, as revealed in the vertical wall of a snow pit, might look something like this: The newest snow is on the surface; if it's quite new you'll be able to identify crystal shapes. Is there enough new snow to worry about loose-snow avalanches? Next might come a layer of equitemperature snow which over time has undergone bonding or "sintering." ET snow tends to strengthen the snow pack. Look for mid-pack weak layers like this temperature-gradient layer which might collapse under a skier's weight and trigger a slide. This sugary, TG layer overlies an old ice crust which might serve as a bed surface on which the snow above could slide. Finally, the oldest snow, nearest the ground, is the most likely to show advanced TG properties: cohesionless, large, regrown, cup-shaped crystals. Are the layers above strong enough to keep it from collapsing? A snow pit is only one tool in evaluating the situation. *Lito Tejada-Flores*

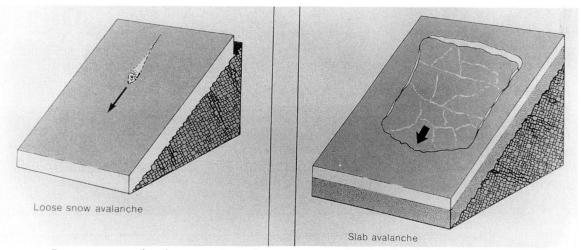

Loose snow avalanche

Slab avalanche

Loose snow avalanches, or point releases, occur, quite simply when new snow exceeds its angle of repose. LIke a sand dune building past its maximum steepness, a small section of snow breaks loose and starts a chain reaction until the slope regains stability. Slab avalanches occur when a layer or layers of snow break free of the slope all at once. Slabs "fracture" along the top and sides and run atop a "bed surface," a harder layer of snow or even the ground. Slabs are more complex, much harder to predict, and therefore more dangerous for skiers than are loose snow slides. *Alexis Kelner*

Seven small point releases have run across this mountain face. *Jerry Roberts*

snow is generally very stable and safe, particularly in the mornings. As the day heats up, however, and the snow begins to melt down the layers, skiers should beware of wet, saturated snowslides. These tend to move slowly, but even the small ones can grind down the hill with powerfully destructive force.

Wet-snow slides usually happen in the afternoon, when melt water has percolated deep into the pack. At this time of day the skiing is lousy, heavy and sloppy, so skiers are not often tempted to be out in the first place.

whenever you go out in avalanche country!

A snow pit reads like a time line, from the bottom up, telling the history of the winter, oldest snows at the ground and newest additions at the top. Learning to read the stratigraphy adds another layer of enjoyment to any tour, and takes on special meaning when you are considering skiing down a suspect slope.

Choose a representative spot near the top of a slope with the same orientation (north, northeast, etc.) as the slope you are thinking of skiing. Dig straight down to the ground, not perpendicular to the slope, but so that you have a vertical wall of snow to look at. Smooth the wall with the shovel tip, and look first for obvious weak layers, layers of depth hoar near the ground, other TG layers in the pack, any layer that is not bonded well to its neighbors and might therefore shear free.

Next use a credit card or other thin straightedge and draw it down through the various layers, feeling the textural differences in the snow cake. At the top, new snow offers little resistance to the slicing card. Scrape a few grains onto the back of your glove and you will likely still see individual crystals, and perhaps the beginnings of some ET sintering.

You will feel more resistance from a layer of densely packed wind-deposited snow, a so-called wind slab. You may find thin layers of buried surface hoar or very hard layers, called crusts, where sun, or even rain, has formed an ice layer. These are potential bed surfaces on which a future avalanche could run.

A snow pit can tell you what's there. It can't tell you what will happen. The stability of the snowpack is a dynamic, ever-changing thing. Snow is elastic, full of stresses. Gravity is constantly trying to pull it down the hill; there are points of tension and compression in every slope. The question for you as a skier is: Are the stresses within the snow great enough to overcome what might be a fragile stability? Might the weight of a skier or skiers be the straw that breaks the camel's back, collapses the weak TG layer or causes a brittle wind slab to let go its hold on the crust below? What makes the snow slide?

AVALANCHE MECHANICS

There are two kinds of avalanches, loose-snow slides and slab avalanches. *Loose-snow slides* usually

Digging a Snow Pit

How do you know what lurks beneath the surface of the snow you're blissfully sliding over? You can't know unless you dig a hole and look at it. Another great reason to carry a snow shovel

This slab avalanche didn't catch any skiers, but it did run across a well-used ascending track. Better route-finding might have meant avoiding such steep, open faces. *Jerry Roberts*

occur during or just after storms when, quite simply, unconsolidated snow piles up and exceeds its angle of repose. Like a sand dune building past its maximum steepness, a small section of snow breaks loose and starts a chain reaction until the slope returns to stability.

Loose-snow slides are also known as point releases, a working term that makes them easy to spot in the wild. The slips begin at a single, identifiable point and draw down into an A-shaped repose. Point releases rarely involve more than the newest surface layer. I have skied in and caused a number of these slides. It's not an uncommon occurrence to be moving along with a soft mass of hissing, airy snow. A big one can bury a skier, but by and large, they aren't as powerful or dangerous as slab avalanches.

Slab avalanches occur when a layer or many layers of snow break free of the slope all at once.

Slabs are said to fracture, and indeed this type of slide leaves a clear fracture line horizontally across the top of the release. The fracture might be 10 feet wide or a quarter mile across. It might be just the surface layer letting go, or it might involve the whole snowpack sandwich down to the ground. These last are known as climax avalanches.

Why do they fracture? It may be one or a combination of many factors.

Steepness. Most slab releases happen on slopes from 30-45 degrees. Steeper than that and the new snow usually sloughs off before it can build to dangerous levels. Pitches gentler than 30 degrees are generally pretty safe, though heavy snow loading can deceive: What looks like a 20-degree slope on the surface may in fact be a 30-degree pitch at ground level.

The sheer weight of the snow. Trees and rocks anchor slabs to the slope. But at some point, the weight of snow loading, after a heavy wind deposit, for example, simply overcomes the effect of the anchors and the slab breaks free.

Failure of a weak layer. Slabs always slide over a bed surface. There is always a weak layer or a poor bond above the bed surface layer which "fails," which allows the slab above to shear away. It could be sugar snow at ground level or a mid-pack weakness above a more cohesive layer. When you dig a snow pit, you're looking for weak layers and possible bed surfaces.

Trigger. Something triggers the failure. It could be cornice snow falling onto a tender start zone. It could be the natural collapse of a TG layer which starts the snow above moving. (In the Soviet Pamirs, earthquakes are known to trigger avalanches.) Or it could be a skier cutting through a zone of stress in the snow; it could be high in the start zone, or along the flanks of ripe slidepath, or even in the compression area at the base of a slide, holding up as it were the snow load above it.

Once a slab get moving, it generates terrific power. Big, soft-slab powder avalanches can freight-train down a track at 100 miles per hour and propel a shock wave of air capable of knocking down 200-year-old trees and bowling over ski lift towers. Whole buildings full of sleeping men were swept away in Colorado's San Juan Mountains during the mining heydays of the 1880s and '90s. Practically the entire town of Alta, Utah, was leveled by a single slide in the winter of 1885.

Most avalanches are much smaller. Hundreds fall every winter unseen and wreaking no damage at all. Mining operations have learned to site their buildings out of harm's way. The people most in danger, miners and mule drivers and mail carriers, no longer ply the high trails in winter. These days it is skiers and snowmobilers who are most likely to encounter the beasts.

America's mountains are relatively uninhabited compared to the Alps. The Swiss have been forced to developed the most extensive avalanche control systems in the world. Miles and miles of retaining walls and snow fences hold snow in start zones high above threatened villages. Earth and concrete deflection structures divert snow either around or over buildings in the path. Snow sheds cover highways where they are exposed to recurring slides. On both sides of the Atlantic, explosives are used by ski areas and highway departments to cause the early release of avalanches before they get large enough to be a danger to roads or structures or in-bounds skiers.

Estimating the Hazard

Out in the backcountry, there are no institutional protections. Estimating the hazard and taking the necessary precautions is the job of every skier. There are things you can do to keep the odds in your favor.

Watch the weather. Be extra conservative when skiing in the most slide-prone times, during and immediately after storms.

Pay attention to the generalized avalanche danger. Most Rocky Mountain states issue daily avalanche reports on the radio, listing avalanche danger over wide areas of the mountains as High, Moderate, or Low. The reports then get more specific by region. For example, the Colorado report might say: "The hazard is rated low overall for the southwest mountains, low below treeline with pockets of moderate hazard above treeline, especially on slopes facing north through southeast in the Red Mountain and Telluride areas." This last might be due to particularly well-developed TG layers in those areas. Plan your days accordingly.

Learn to recognize localized hazards, that is specific slide paths. This is the key to your group's safety. Take a course from one of the very good avalanche schools, such as the American Avalanche Institute in Wilson, Wyoming, the Silverton Avalanche School in Silverton, Colorado, or from the National Ski Patrol headquartered in Palo Alto, California. A number of colleges and universities offer avalanche and snow-related courses, including: the University of Utah in Salt Lake City, the University of British Columbia in Vancouver, and Sierra College in Rocklin, California.

Study the U.S. Agriculture Department's *Avalanche Handbook,* by Ronald Perla and M. Martinelli. It is the bible on the subject, profusely illustrated and written in clear, non-technical language. Whenever possible ski with an experienced backcountry hand. There's no substitute for hands-on learning: Dig snow pits. Study old slides, observe where they let go, how they ran over the landscape, and try to sleuth out why they released using the clues of landscape, recent weather, and the history revealed in the snowpack. Learn how to see and avoid potential danger zones.

Look for tension cracks in the snow. Listen for the unmistakable "whump" of snow settling suddenly (caused by the collapse of a rotten, hollow layer) under the weight of your tour group. Neither sign means that you will positively encounter avalanches, but both are signs to be on your guard.

Bring the basic avalanche rescue gear: a transceiver, shovel, and convertible probe poles for every member of the group.

Trust your intuition. If your gut says don't ski something, don't ski it. Avalanche avoidance is as much art as it is science. As Don Bachman, one of my first snow gurus at the Silverton Avalanche School, said to me, "You learn as much as you can and you pay attention, and you keep learning. But ultimately," he said, "you're gonna have to rely on your intuition. Listen to it."

SKIING AVALANCHE PATHS

Sometimes you can't help it. Sometimes you simply have to cross a known or suspected slide path. Or maybe you just can't resist skiing the enticing steep powder of a possible avalanche path. There are a few rules that will lessen the risk.

1. If you are crossing a slide path, do it as high as possible in the start zone. That way, if it does release, the snow might just slide out from under you; there'd be very little snow above you to knock you down and carry you off.

2. Expose yourself for as short a time as possible. Move deliberately but quickly across the slide to a safe spot—in the trees, on the ridge, etc.—on the other side.

3. Expose only one person at a time. Determine safe havens on both sides of the slide, then everybody else stay put while only one skier at a time moves across.

4. If you're skiing down a suspect slope, the same rule applies—one person exposed at a time. Everybody else watches. If the snow does cut loose, it's important to follow the skier as long as you can to speed up any rescue should it be necessary.

5. Ski the sides of the slide path rather than the middle. If the snow moves, you may be able to ski out of it to the side.

6. Look closely at the runout zone of any potential avalanche/ski slope. If it ends in a sharp V gully, consider skiing someplace else. Far better to be tumbled along in a slide with a long, flat runout than to be buried under twenty feet of snow in a dead-end stream bed.

If You Are Caught

Avalanches start without much warning. There may be no sound at all, or there may be a dull thud as the slab fractures. In any event, the first sign you may have that you're in an avalanche is that the snow under your feet is moving.

The first thing to do is try to ski out of it. This works in a surprising number of cases. Don't give up and just let it take you; fight to keep your balance and ski toward the side. Even if you don't make it all the way to the edge, your chances of being buried are less on the sides than in the middle of the path.

If you have fallen and are being swept along, try to shed as much gear as you can: poles (it's a good idea to ski with pole straps off in avalanche terrain), packs, skis if you can. Then swim. Swim hard. Try to stay on the surface of the slide as if it were an ocean wave. Many slide victims end up on the surface or only partially buried.

When you feel the slide slowing down, thrust a hand toward the surface. Your friends may just see it and your rescue will be fast.

At the last second use your other hand and arm to create a hollow space in front of your face. The snow becomes very hard the instant the slide stops, due to the tremendous kinetic energy of all that motion. You likely won't be able to move a finger. So, push out a little breathing space, and when the snow sets, try your best to relax. There's nothing more you can do. If you've all got beepers, your friends should find you in a few minutes. If you aren't wearing a beeper, gather your thoughts and pray that some part of you is sticking out on the snow surface.

Avalanche Rescue

After thirty minutes a buried victim has only a 50/50 chance of survival. So, if someone in your party is buried, search first, search like crazy, before you even think about sending for help. Chances are, by the time help arrives, it'll be too late.

Even if the victim is wearing a transmitter, do a quick search, known in the parlance as a *hasty search*, first. Mark the last-seen spot with a pole or a pack and proceed rapidly straight down the fall line. You might find a pole or a hand or a ski sticking out of the rubble, saving a lot of search time. If there are enough people in your party, send some of them on a hasty search while the others begin the more methodical transceiver search.

As soon as it is clear that someone is buried, everybody else must switch his radio from transmit to receive; the last thing you need is for the victim's signal to be contaminated, or confused, with another signal above ground.

With radios on receive, searchers should descend from the last-seen point, walking abreast no more than 30 meters apart to cover the full width of the slide. If there is only one searcher he should make a zig-zag descent from one side of the debris to the other. Start with the radios on maximum volume. When you pick up the signal, turn the volume down, and zero in on the location using the right-angle search pattern described on the beacons themselves or on literature accompanying them. (You will have practiced this routine before heading into avalanche country.) Beacons are accurate to within a foot or two, so when you get there start digging and probing at the same time.

If the victim is not wearing a beacon, or if, heaven forbid, the beacon is not turned on (this happened in a tragic case in Utah involving a young couple who were touring with their beepers off and in their packs), and the hasty search fails to turn up anything, you're only choice is to probe. Kick the baskets and grips off your poles, screw the two halves together and do a fast "coarse" probe with as many searchers as you have. Probe first in the most likely places: in a direct line down from the last-seen point; in clumps of trees or rocks where the victim might have fetched up as the rest of the snow wave moved on downhill, on the uphill side of rolls in the terrain, anything that might have caught or slowed your friend.

When you pull your friend from the snow, he may or may not be breathing. He may have injuries suffered in the ride. Your work may just be beginning. But I'll not go into the tenets of basic first aid here as this is a book on skiing, and there are excellent books devoted exclusively to

the subject. When you feel the need to go beyond the Red Cross first aid manual, an excellent, comprehensive treatment is *Medicine for Mountaineering*, published by the Mountaineers, Seattle.

A final note on avalanches. I've been blunt in this section, not to scare anybody away from backcountry skiing, but rather to impress on present and future skiers the magnitude and seriousness of these phenomena. Avalanches deserve all the respect we can muster. At the same time, these are not malevolent forces. They are utterly neutral, like the weather and the mountains themselves. We can learn an awful lot about them, and what we can't know we can mitigate through sound decision-making and common sense. In nearly twenty years of backcountry skiing, I have never had to dig a comrade out of a slide. But I go out every time prepared for that possibility. Avalanches are part of the risk of moving through mountains in winter. But it's a manageable risk, assuming you take the time to learn the rules. Then it becomes an integral part of that feeling backcountry skiers get of being intensely alive, alert, and aware of the power and beauty around them.

There are a couple of backcountry problems that are actually a good deal more dangerous than getting caught in a slide: namely getting cold, and getting caught out for the night.

BIVOUAC

Oops. An unplanned night out on the trail. It happens. Maybe you're lost. Maybe somebody in the group is hurt or sick. Maybe you just underestimated the time to the hut or to your car.

The most important thing here is not to panic. Dozens of people spend unplanned nights out every winter and do just fine. With your snow shovel and a little architectural common sense, you can fashion yourself a shelter that will get you through the night. You may not sleep much, and you may feel cold, but you will be alive.

Snow is a remarkable insulator. The best shelter is a snow cave carved out of a thick bank of snow on the leeward side of a hill. Dig straight in a few feet (keep the entry hole small), then expand the room to the sides to be just big enough for all of the members of your party. A rounded ceiling is the strongest shape to thwart roof collapse. Your snow cave should be no taller or wider than it has to be for sitting, shoulder-to-shoulder, arms wrapped around knees. This is the warmest position, and you don't want to warm up any more cold air volume than you have to.

If you didn't bring a snow shovel (shame on you), you can dig with your skis, though this is considerably more difficult. If you are on flat terrain and can't dig a cave, dig a simple trench instead. Cover the roof with your skis, a tarp or poncho if you have one, or tree branches. If you cannot dig at all, snuggle down in a tree well, that slightly hollow space under the branches surrounding the trunks of snowbound trees.

Try to insulate yourself from the ground. Sit on your closed-cell foam picnic pad, or your pack, or your skis. The snow is a good insulator, but it will also rob you of body heat if you are in direct contact with it. Put on all the clothes you have, eat your high-energy food to keep your metabolism up, and think good thoughts 'til daybreak. Some stranded skiers have even been known to fall asleep in such circumstances. It is definitely not true that if you let yourself fall asleep you will not wake up again. If your shelter is reasonably secure from the wind and the outside air, and you have other bodies to help keep yours warm, everybody should be fine. Miserable, but fine.

COLD

One situation that is definitely not fine is hypothermia, the chilling of the body's core temperature to below 98 degrees F. It doesn't have to be especially cold for this to happen. It's strictly a matter of the body's losing heat and then being unable to regenerate enough to maintain a stable core temperature. Dampness, wind, even dehydration or hunger, can contribute. And it doesn't take much of a drop for hypothermia to become serious.

In its early stages, with a body temperature of 93-95 degrees, the symptoms include fatigue, lack of coordination, stumbling, thickness of speech, intense shivering and muscle tensing, and worst of all, a debilitating lack of judgment; the hypothermia victim can't seem to take the action necessary to make himself warm. He won't stop to take off a wet undershirt, for example, or stop to dig in his pack for a heat-generating candy bar.

His logic is fuzzy, he may not seem to care; everything seems too complicated or simply too hard.

It's the responsibility of other members of the group to spot hypothermia in a buddy and take steps immediately to warm him up. Get him out of the wind. Get his wet clothes off, if he is wet, and get new dry ones back on. Prepare hot drinks to warm him from the inside out, and force him to eat to keep his blood sugar up.

You must act quickly, because advanced hypothermia, where the core temperature drops to 93-90 degrees, is very much more serious. Now the body can't produce enough heat to warm itself up, even in a sleeping bag. Shivering stops. The victim may lose consciousness. Below 90 degrees, coma leads to death by ventricular fibrillation (erratic, ineffective heart beats). An unhappy scene, but one that needn't occur if you are alert and reasonably well-equipped.

Treatment of advanced hypothermia includes warming the victim from the inside and from the outside. Feed him hot fluids and get him in a sleeping bag with one or two other people whose body heat can help warm him from without. Add hot water bottles (this assumes, of course, that you have a camp stove with you) to neck, groin and underarm areas, places where major arteries run close to the surface.

Here again I don't mean to scare anybody. Like avalanches, hypothermia is not some inevitable, or even especially common, demon waiting in the woods to turn a pleasant adventure into tragedy. It's entirely avoidable. With today's advanced clothing systems—hydrophobic-fiber underwear that keeps you dry at skin level, lightweight, efficient insulators that work well even when wet, and nearly bomb-proof, wind- and weather-resistant outer shells—you'd have to try pretty hard to get hypothermic.

Beyond having the right gear, there are several things you can do as insurance against getting too cold.

Most important is to really *use* your layering system. Take layers off when you are working hard and sweating a lot. Put layers back on when you stop, when the wind kicks up, when the sky starts to rain or snow. A great clothing system won't do you much good if it stays in your pack, or always on your back.

Drink plenty of fluids to stay hydrated—at least a couple of liters on a hard day tour—and stop to eat frequently; a run-down engine is more susceptible to cold.

Don't try to do more than you are realistically capable of doing. Don't push for that one extra mile, for instance. Don't try to go too high, too fast. Don't rush to get back. Hurrying in the mountains is never a good idea, and there is some evidence to suggest that people near the end of their psychological rope are more likely to get seriously cold. Better to stop and dig in for the night than to risk exhaustion and hypothermia on a forced march.

Frostbite

The old saying goes, "If your feet are cold, put on another sweater." Frostbite is the body's way of preventing hypothermia. When your core starts to get cold, the body withholds circulation from the extremities, the fingers and toes, to concentrate more blood and therefore warmth, in the central core. Frostbite happens when flesh at the extremities freezes due to this withholding of circulation.

Cross-country skiers rarely have a problem with frostbite because they are so active, arms and hands and feet in nearly constant motion, flexing and gripping, balancing and pushing off. But in intense, midwinter cold, it is something to be on the lookout for.

The first line of prevention is to make sure your torso is well insulated and protected from wind-chill. A happy core should translate to no circulation loss to the extremities. Some people still get cold hands and feet, however. For them, the answer lies in better gear: mittens instead of gloves (the fingers keep each other toasty), double boots instead of single, or insulated "supergaiters" over the boots you have.

On very cold days watch out for early-stage frostbite on exposed noses, cheeks and ears. It's difficult to feel this happening to your own face, so make it a habit to check your companions' faces regularly. If you see a patch of white skin, remove a glove and place your warm palm over the affected area. Don't rub; that could cause tissue damage. The skin should return to pink in just a few seconds. If you're going to be out for long periods in such weather, face masks of silk, polypropylene, or neoprene are a good idea.

When toes or fingers begin to go numb ("frostnip" stage), stop immediately and warm them up. Shake, rub, kick, stamp, twirl your arms like a helicopter. Place your hands in your own warm armpits. I once came upon two friends sitting facing each other in the snow on a bitterly cold peak climb. One had his boots off and had his feet tucked inside the other's jacket in the relative ovens under his friend's arms. It works. Don't wait for your digits to get really frozen. Take care of it at the first sign.

Once they have been frozen for a number of hours, treatment and logistics become more complicated. The ideal treatment is to thaw the affected part in 105-degree water. If it's your feet that freeze, you don't dare ski out after thawing; you risk doing much worse tissue damage. Your only option then is evacuation, either by jerry-rigged sled or by outside help: snowmobile, helicopter, what have you. Fingers are obviously less critical in terms of getting out of the backcountry under your own steam.

The option is to let the fingers or toes remain frozen. Skiing on frozen toes will not damage the tissue further. In either case, you must seek a doctor's care immediately upon returning to civilization. And, depending on the severity of the freeze, you will face a painful and somewhat grisly recovery period.

TIPS & TALES: Skiing Hut-to-Hut

Some people love snow camping: pitching a tent or carving out a snug snow cave, sculpting a kitchen bench and seats out of a snow bank, waddling around in Michelin-man bulky down clothes against the cold, setting up the stove, melting snow for hot brews, cooking everything in one pot, marching away from camp through thigh-high snow for bathroom duty, sweeping snow out of the tent every time somebody comes in, sleeping with a hot water bottle at your feet, waking in the morning in an ice tunnel of frozen condensed breath.

I like it myself on occasion. But in recent years I have discovered an alternative that provides all of the joys of snow camping in the wilderness—the pink snow of reflected sunrises and sunsets, the astonishing quiet, the day-time travel through inspiring wild terrain—with none of the drawbacks, chief among them having to carry your entire complement of civilization on your back.

Skiing from hut to hut is an old story in Europe, where mountain travelers have for hundreds of years depended on remote refuges for a hot meal and a simple bed. In this country, it's a new phenomenon but growing fast. The Appalachian Mountain Club has maintained huts in the Presidential Range of New Hampshire for decades, mostly for summer use. In the Sierra and the Cascades and Rockies, universities and mountain clubs have operated their own huts, scattered here and there, but never in concert. The first real hut system is the 10th Mountain Hut and Trail System in central Colorado in the high country between the ski resorts of Aspen and Vail.

So far the system includes over 300 miles of trail in a rough circle around the Holy Cross Wilderness connecting Aspen with the town of Leadville and on to Vail Pass. Plans call for an eventual link to Vail itself and for link-ups with new trail and hut systems in neighboring regions. Every six or eight miles along the trail (about one day's journey on skis) there is a mountain hut stocked with firewood, wood-burning heat and cook stoves, pots and pans, mattresses, candles, chemical toilets, even (in most of the huts) solar-powered, photovoltaic lights.

So instead of digging in for the night, 10th Mountain skiers can kick their boots off, hang their gaiters up to dry, and settle in inside glowing log walls. You still have to melt snow for drinking water, but the task is made easy by huge kettles provided just for the task. You don't have to carry the world on your back, just your food and a sleeping bag. Every hut has its own trailhead, so you can ski in and out to any one of them. Or you can link several huts on the line, or ski the entire system, a trek that would take more than two weeks.

The cost is minimal (currently $18 per person per night). If you go with a guide company the price jumps to about $40 per night, but the guides carry the food. Or they have stocked the cabins in advance (including wine), and everybody's loads are that much lighter.

The idea for the trail and huts came from architect and 10th Mountain Division veteran Fritz Benedict. The 10th trained at Camp Hale in the early 1940s, just over the Continental Divide from Aspen. Benedict loved the country, returned after the war to settle in Aspen, and thought a trail would be fitting tribute to the most-decorated division of WWII.

Since the first two huts opened in 1985, thousands of skiers have experienced what guide and 10th Mountain Trail Association board member Buck Elliot calls "the bridge." "The huts are the bridge, the comfort and safety that allows people who never would to experience the magic of these mountains."

III

SUPPLEMENTAL PLEASURES

Racing is the crucible from which come virtually all advances in ski equipment and technique. Alpine racing has a seventy-year history in the Alps. This slalom race is in Bormio, Italy. *Lori Adamski-Peek*

9

Competition

Serious competition has always produced the best skiers. Why is that? Why haven't the greatest skiers come from a strictly recreational foundation? After all, skiing, in its purest form, has the ability to free us from the constraints of measurement and comparison. Shouldn't that freedom produce great skiers too?

I suppose the answer lies in human nature, the desire to see how we stack up against our fellows. Once the competitive juices flow, even very noncompetitive people push themselves beyond their norms. This is good. Out of the adrenaline and frenzy of racing come quantifiable achievements (and sometimes less-tangible epiphanies), indelible memories and occasional cause for pride.

I have a friend who has been teaching skiing for over twenty years. He is a sublime powder skier, a master of all terrain and snow conditions. But he told me not too long ago that the one thing that holds his interest from day to day is racing. He is not a great racer, never will be. His challenge is with himself. "You never get there," he told me. Even his best runs in the gates, when his edges flash like rapiers and every pole falls before his onslaught, could have been better. Out of more discipline will come greater freedom.

At the highest levels, competition becomes the crucible from which most equipment and technical revolutions are born. Ski hard goods manufacturers spend hundreds of thousands of

dollars each year on their race teams whether they be amateurs on national teams or pros on one of the professional circuits. They spend even more money on research and development to come up with new skis and boots and waxes to make these racers ever faster. For their part racers and their coaches are forever looking for a biomechanical edge, for a way to ride these newer, faster skis just that much better than the other guys.

All of these advancements eventually filter down to the recreational skier. We slide today on skis that are slicker, quieter, and easier to turn than were the best racing skis of only a generation ago. And because of the racers' example, we drive those skis in a more efficient, more dynamic way than any skiers before us.

So, we benefit without doing a thing ourselves. But we can do more. We can learn from the racers we see on television, on video tape and in person. We can become better skiers by watching. I am not a good racer. But I am a better racer today than I was a couple of years ago or a couple of years before that. Why? Because I watch good racers. I watch them with more than casual interest. I steal from them. I crawl into their tautly muscled skins and see with their eyes. They see differently than we do. Given their speed and precision, the mountain is relatively smaller for them. They look way ahead at the big picture, ignoring the minor terrain changes underfoot for the grander gesture. Put it another way, they paint with a bigger brush. And when I begin to see that way, even with my slower speeds and less-polished technique, I am a better skier.

I study their tracks. Once, in Aspen when the American team was training for a World Cup giant slalom race, I snuck onto their practice course between rounds. The marks their skis left on the snow were like knife cuts; they weren't sliding sideways at all, not one inch. I watched how they balance, how they center their bodies like yogis to resist the centrifugal forces—nothing extraneous, nothing for show. I watched and then I skied like a shadow to soak it in deep beyond explanations into muscle fiber. My free skiing jumped up a notch in precision and daring, and when, later I did get on a race course again I had something to call on, someone to be, which for me is much better motivation than an abstract foe like time.

Anyone can do this. Whether you're interested in alpine or cross-country racing, biathlon, freestyle skiing, speed skiing, or mountaineering racing. The discipline of the set course, the Zen of exact repetition, the alchemy of prescribed turn after turn, will result in better skiing for you.

A BRIEF HISTORY OF COMPETITION

It's difficult to imagine skiers not competing in informal ways from the very beginning. Hunters racing each other home down the final hill. Scandinavian ski scouts in the 13th century challenging to be first to the top of the next rise. Children, as children everywhere do, racing each other on skis as they would barefooted in summer. But for some reason the formal or recorded history of ski competitions is relatively brief. Perhaps the serious nature of skiing as transportation precluded the notion of skiing as sport. Or perhaps it was so taken for granted that organized competition would have been trite or blasphemous. Perhaps there simply wasn't time or energy during the short winter days up north for ski sport.

Things changed in the mid-19th century, in the Scandinavian cradle of skiing and in America and central Europe, where skiing had spread. The first documented ski races were not in Stockholm or Oslo but in the California gold rush towns of La Porte and Onion Valley. Scandinavian immigrant miners lugged their 12-foot-long, solid-wood "snow shoes"—carefully prepared with secret wax formulas called "dope"—to the top of a hill, strapped them to their feet with leather thongs, and schussed straight down to the finish a half-mile below. By the mid-1860s, La Porte had become the capital of the western ski world. The world's first ski club, the Alturas Snow Shoe Club, organized three- and four-day ski meets. There were purses for the winners ranging from $25 to $75 and a Grand Ball on the final night. The racers developed sophisticated crouches to cut the resistance of the air. Many had their own coaches and mysterious "dopemen." Turning on the long boards was difficult if not impossible.

At about this same time organized contests were becoming fashionable in the mother countries. The first Holmenkollen was staged in Oslo in 1866, a combined ski running and jumping competition that is an annual event even today. Ski marathons grew in number and popularity. The Swedish Vasalop marathon, which began in 1922, today draws 10,000 starters.

That initial flourish of ski racing in the Sierran mining camps died out with the gold and silver shortly after the turn of the century. But a new spectator sport was developing in the upper Midwest and New England. Beginning in the 1880s Scandinavian jumpers staged meets that drew huge crowds to watch the men soar hundreds of feet off elaborately constructed ramps. Jumps were built in parks, inside soccer stadiums; one meet saw jumpers perform on crushed ice inside the Los Angeles Coliseum. Professional jumping exhibition/competitions toured the U.S. with great success up until WWII. Since then, jumping has attracted only a small cadre of dedicated amateurs.

Alpine competition in this country got its start with the Dartmouth Outing Club. Formed in 1909 to encourage students at the New Hampshire college to "take advantage of winter," the club was an immediate success. That year Dartmouth held its first "Winter Meet," the forerunner of the now-famous Dartmouth Winter Carnival. In 1913 the Outing Club traveled to McGill University in Montreal for the first intercollegiate ski competition in the Americas.

These first competitions were nordic-only (running and jumping), but in the 1920s Dartmouth took the lead in alpine skiing as well.

They staged the first-ever slalom competition in 1923. Dartmouth's powerful alpine teams of the 1920s and '30s dominated U.S. racing and provided most of the members of the first U.S. alpine Olympic team in 1936. (Alpine events, slalom, and downhill were first recognized by skiing's international overseer, the Federation Internationale de Ski, in 1930, but didn't make it into the Olympic Games until 1936.)

The idea of adding turns to a downhill race, of setting a course around poles jammed in the snow, originated with Sir Arnold Lunn, a Britisher who was knighted for his contributions to skiing. Lunn's slalom races (the word was taken from the Norwegian, meaning "snake"), in the mid and late 1920s, became the standard form, along with downhill, of alpine—as opposed to nordic racing.

The 1930s was the decade when ski racing got a toehold around the world. The 1940s were dominated by the war. In the 1950s skiing exploded as if it had been holding its breath for a decade. Aspen leapt instantly onto the international map by hosting the first postwar World Championships in 1950. In 1952 American teenager Andrea Mead won two gold medals at the Oslo Olympics. Oslo also was the coming out for Stein Eriksen, the stylish (and very fast) Norwegian who came to embody skiing's grace and athleticism, and who would become the world's first skiing superstar. In 1958 the first World Championship for biathlon was held. Biathlon is cross-country skiing and target shooting, a natural outgrowth of the long history of infantry on skis, and the only Winter Olympic sport that uses firearms.

The French national team dominated alpine racing in the 1960s, led by the dashing Jean-Claude Killy. In 1966 French ski journalist Serge Lange put forth the idea for a World Cup, an international circuit of races to determine season-long championships. Today all the major branches of ski competition, alpine, cross-country, jumping, biathlon, freestyle, and speed skiing, have the World Cup as their top "amateur" circuit. (I put amateur in quotes because top racers have always been paid "under the table." Most are year-round athletes supported by equipment companies and their national teams. So-called amateur racers at the very top of the sport in the 1980s, racers like Sweden's Ingemar Stenmark and Switzerland's Maria Walliser, made millions of dollars from skiing, yet retained,

As a teenager, Andrea Mead Lawrence won two gold medals at the 1952 Olympics in Oslo. Here (in 1989) she shows that racing is not just for the young.

through convoluted FIS logic, their amateur status.)

The '60s also were a benchmark for citizen racing, truly amateur competition for ordinary citizens and weekend warriors. In 1968, former U.S. Team coach Bob Beattie started a recreational racing program called NASTAR, for National Standard Race. The genius of NASTAR was that every racer could, through a simple handicapping system, compare his time with the times of the fastest racers in the world. NASTAR caught on in a big way and is now offered at hundreds of resorts in at least thirty states. Other programs followed, but NASTAR is still the largest recreational racing program in the world

The '70s saw the birth of professional ski racing. It was the creative and driven Beattie again, this time orchestrating a pro circus called World Pro Skiing, complete with network television contracts and millions of dollars in purses. The pro-skiing format differed from the World Cup variety by having the racers ski side-

Citizen racing took off in the 1960s and '70s often adopting the dual, side-by-side format used by the men's and women's pro tours.

by-side in identical, parallel courses. One racer was eliminated and the survivor moved on to the next round. American audiences loved the *mano a mano* shoot-out quality of the competition. Beattie bowed out in 1981, but a new circuit, the U.S. Pro Tour, stepped in to fill the vacuum. Now there's also a women's professional tour.

The '70s were a decade of broken barriers and new freedoms. In 1976 taciturn Vermonter Bill Koch won the first-ever U.S. Olympic medal in cross-country, taking the silver in the 30 km race at Innsbruck. His feat almost single-handedly sparked the cross-country boom in this country. In 1978 American Steve McKinney broke through the almost mythical 200 kilometers-per-

hour boundary (124 mph) on the speed skiing course in Portillo, Chile. Speed skiers had been tantalizingly close for years, and some even thought the other side of 200 kph would bring strange revelations the way the sound barrier had been similarly regarded before its demystification. Of course McKinney, like Chuck Yeager before him, experienced no mirror realities on the other side, and he and his competition went on to set ever higher speed records. As France readied to host the 1992 Winter Olympics, with speed skiing on the program as a demonstration sport, top speeds were pushing 140 mph.

Freestyle skiing made it to the Olympics in 1988. Throughout the Seventies, freestyle, or

The urge to compete affects telemarkers as well, whose turn was born and bred for wild, backcountry snows. *Lori Adamski-Peek*

"hot-dogging" as it was known, was a free-spirited reaction to skiing conventions and conventional style. Hot-doggers attacked mogul fields with abandon, practiced multiple flips in the air, and donned super-short skis to perform gymnastic ballet moves. Today competition in the three disciplines, moguls, aerials, and ballet, is under the wing of the FIS.

THE COMPETITION HIERARCHY

Which brings me to the organizational pyramid of competitive skiing. I think it's useful to know how things stack up. Here's a look at skiing's "mountain" of officialdom from the top down.

Federation Internationale de Ski

Right at the summit is the FIS, with representatives from every skiing country and the power to determine the rules, the schedules, and the rankings for all amateur international competition. The exception is the Winter Olympics, which are run more or less by current FIS rules but are not organized by the Federation.

The FIS oversees the World Cup—both alpine and cross-country—the biennial World Championships (held in odd-numbered years sandwiched around the Olympiads), and the satellite, or minor-league, amateur circuits including Europa Cup and Can-Am (Canadian-American) Series races. It is also the final authority for amateur freestyle competition and its World Cup. Speed skiing, long a maverick, self-governing bunch of individualists (as you can imagine considering what these people do), is now under the FIS umbrella as well.

United States Ski Association

In America the United States Ski Association governs all amateur U.S. competition. USSA runs the national championships, funds the U.S. Ski Team (which competes on the World Cup, the Europa Cup, at the Olympic Games, etc.), as well as various developmental and junior squads. USSA- sanctioned races and training camps around the country are the stepping stones for young racers and freestylers on the way to the U.S. Team.   They also provide a way to stay in the sport competitively for masters-level (thirty and over) skiers all the way up to eighty years and over. Each winter season culminates with national championships at every level.

Youngsters starting out in racing usually test their wings first in club competitions or small-fry leagues like the USSA-sponsored Bill Koch Leagues. Few high schools offer interscholastic skiing, although clubs are very active at this age-group level, and many of the most gifted racers attend one of the ski academies sprinkled around the country, such as the Rowmark Academy in Salt Lake City and the Burke Mountain Academy in Vermont. USSA, P.O. Box 100, Park City, UT 84060. For help in locating ski clubs, contact the following: National Ski Club Newsletter, Rowil Publishing, P.O. Box 17385, Denver, CO 80217, or the Ski Club Finder, Action Sports Marketing, Box SKI, 12 Broadway, Rockville Center, NY 11570, or the U.S. Recreational Ski Association, P.O. Box 25469, Anaheim, CA 92825-5469.

Collegiate Racing

College ski racing is under the auspices of the National Collegiate Athletic Association (NCAA) and the National College Ski Association (NCSA). The NCAA's are by far the more serious competitions, involving the best college athletes in the country and some of the most venerable and heated rivalries: Dartmouth vs. the University of Vermont, the University of Utah vs. Denver University, Colorado vs. Wyoming.

The NCSA was founded in 1976 as a "fun club" racing program for college-age skiers of any and every ability. Some 15,000 collegians per year participate in over 200 NCSA events, both alpine

A bunch of happy club racers from the Minneapolis police department.

and cross-country. For more information: National College Ski Association, 9200 West North Ave., Suite 108, Milwaukee, WI 53226.

Citizen Racing

At the broad base of the pyramid are the myriad skiers who are anything but elite. They're not headed for the national team. They're not competing for sponsorship or a career. They're citizen racers. They may race only one NASTAR course in a winter, or they may run a ski marathon every weekend in a different part of the country. They may be young or old, getting faster or just in it for the fun. It'd be hard to count; there are probably on the order of two or three million citizen racers in the U.S.

Some of the venues include: NASTAR and its offshoots, recreational giant slalom races at designated alpine areas; the Marlboro Challenge coin-operated dual slalom courses at many alpine areas; local town leagues (akin to bowling leagues); corporate racing series involving teams from companies around the country; club racing. There's even a series just for chefs called the Grand Marinier Chef's Series. NASTAR, Grand Mariner, and the corporate and club series hold regional competitions throughout the winter, then stage their own national championships in the spring.

Citizen racing for cross-country skiers is almost as popular as recreational alpine racing. There aren't as many cross-country racers nationwide, but they make up for it in sheer numbers per event. The American Birkebeiner, the oldest ski marathon in this country, regularly attracts as many as 7,000 starters.

Most events are far smaller. Just about every touring center and ski town in snow country sponsors a race or two during the season. Races will be designated classical (diagonal stride technique only) or freestyle (at which almost everyone uses the faster skating techniques). Lengths vary from 5 to 55 kilometers, or about 3 to 33 miles.

The top series of cross-country citizen races is the Great American Ski Chase, a program of the USSA. The Chase consists of nine marathons, from 42 to 58 kilometers (with simultaneous shorter events of 20 to 30 kilometers) across the country. The Birkebeiner, which races over 55 km from the towns of Hayward to Cable in

Wisconsin, is one of the stops along the way. Anyone can enter these races; there's a generous eight-hour maximum finish time to have your place counted.

Citizen racers of all stripes might find it beneficial to join the USSA. Membership entitles you to a guide to all USSA-sanctioned events for the upcoming winter by region, with details on length, style, eligibility, entry fees, location, entry deadline, and contact people. Membership also brings a subscription to *Ski Racing*, the international newspaper of nordic and alpine racing published in Vermont. And finally, members have the right to compete in USSA National Championships, including special events for masters classes.

THE RACING "DISCIPLINES"

Each branch of skiing—alpine, nordic, freestyle, etc—has within it one or more disciplines, or separate events. For example, alpine racers enter downhill, giant slalom, super giant slalom, or slalom races. Each demands special skills, and in most cases at the top levels of competition, racers specialize in one or two disciplines.

ALPINE DISCIPLINES: Downhill

This is the granddaddy of alpine events, the one with the most risk, the most drama, and the most glory, especially in the downhill-crazy Alpine nations of Austria, Switzerland, Italy, Germany, and France.

In the 1930s, downhill consisted of a *geschmozzel* or mass start, where everyone lined up together at the top of the mountain, and at the starter's signal charged off downhill in a sea of edges and elbows. There was no predetermined path down the mountain; the racers could choose any route they wanted. The first one to the bottom was the winner. Falls were commonplace, even for the winner, whose time might have been on the order of nine minutes for a two-mile run.

Modern downhillers regularly clock runs of under two minutes for a two-mile course, averaging 60 mph from top to bottom and hitting maximum speeds of 80 mph. They must steer around a dozen or more control gates which both control their speed and provide specific terrain

Canadian downhiller Rob Boyd at full throttle. While most of us will never travel at 80 mph down a mountain, we can learn to use the sidecut of the ski to aid our turns just as the racers do. *Lori Adamski-Peek*

challenges, like jumps and difficult fall-away turns. Unlike the old days where snow conditions were essentially wild, modern courses are watered and smoothed to an icy perfection.

They ski on long boards (225 cm for the men, 215-222 cm for the women), very quiet and damp—that is, vibration-absorbing—with low-profile, aerodynamic tips so that the skis won't take off and fly. Downhillers' suits are skin-tight stretch nylons to reduce drag. Wax can be extremely important in these races; World Cup coaches spend hours every week taking the snow's temperature and testing various waxes before a race. Every bit of the streamlining is deemed worth it, however, as races are very often decided by mere hundredths of seconds.

What can we learn by watching downhillers? Downhillers etch beautiful, pure carved turns— when they're not in the air or scratching and clawing to hold on in a difficult sharp turn. Most of the turns they make on a course will leave a clean, curving line on the snow where the ski

simply followed its sidecut around. Watch for these turns. See how the racers edge their outside skis and set their bodies to the inside, for balance against the centrifugal force of the turn. Few of us will ever attempt to do it at these speeds, but the carving action is just as easily achieved— more easily, in fact—by skiers properly edging and weighting at 20 mph.

Slalom

Downhill is the fastest event; slalom is the slowest, and the quickest. There may be as many as seventy-five gates from start to finish on a one-and-one-half minute course. In the early 1920s slalom's inventor, Sir Arnold Lunn, used tree branches stuck in the snow as gates. Then for decades the poles were bamboo. Now they're hollow plastic, hinged at snow level and spring-loaded so they right themselves after being knocked down. In fact, slalom racers bump the gates so frequently (the shortest line to the finish

In slalom racing, the quickest alpine discipline, the gates come fast and furious. Swiss Vreni Schneider moves her quick feet below a calm center, a steady, anticipated upper body.

is the tightest line to the poles), their sweaters and pants are armored with plastic shields. Even their hands and heads sport special plastic deflectors for knocking poles away.

Slalom skis are relatively short (203 cm and under), lively and quick, designed for a short, snappy turn.

What can we learn by watching slalom racers? Few of us will ever be as quick foot-to-foot as a slalom racer, but we can borrow from the body position that allows them to be so nimble. Watch a slalom skier from below (as most television and film sequences are shot) and you will never see that skier's back, never even see his or her sides. All you see is the front of that sweater. Slalom skiers keep their upper bodies focused straight down the fall line, while their feet dart back and forth below. If they turned their whole bodies along with their skis, they'd never get everything around in time for even the second gate. That steady upper-body mass (what I have called anticipation) is the calm center from which precise, quick, short-radius turns emerge.

Giant Slalom

Giant slalom was introduced in the late 1930s (and became a separate Olympic event at the Oslo games in 1952) as a compromise between the straight rush of the downhill and the tight zig-zag of slalom. Giant slalom gates are spaced farther apart on the the hill than slalom gates resulting in higher speeds (30-40 mph on the top circuits)

The giant slalom racer, in this case Swiss Pirmin Zurbriggen, is skiing faster than slalom but not as fast as downhill, perhaps 40 mph. The key to his success on the course is the round, carved arc, with minimal skidding, a worthy goal for recreational skiers as well. *Lori Adamski-Peek*

and longer, rounder turns. But like slalom, a GS race is a two-run event. The best combined time from two runs on two different courses wins.

Most recreational race courses, like NASTAR, are considered GS courses. The gates are set rhythmically, back and forth across the hill with plenty of space between them for novices to maneuver at relatively slow speeds while at the same time providing a challenge for better skiers who ski the same course at faster speeds.

Giant slalom skis are, as you might expect, designed to make a long, round turn at medium to high speeds. They are usually much "damper" than slalom skis; that is, they smooth out the bumps in the snow, swallowing or dissipating vibrations. This makes for an elegant ride and it helps keep the edge in contact with the snow throughout the carving of a turn. The recreational incarnations of these skis are known as cruising skis. Not quite as versatile as slalom

skis, they nevertheless give a silky, stable ride especially on groomed snow.

What can we learn from watching giant slalom racers? Winning at giant slalom has everything to do with line, with the path chosen and executed around the gates. A line that swings way wide of the flags covers too much distance to be fast, but it is the way that skiers with lesser skills can navigate their way successfully down a course. Think of this line as a meandering river. At the same time it is possible to ski too tight a line. In an effort to shave distance a racer may point straight at the flags then have to jam a hard turn, skidding and losing speed, in order to "make" the next gate. (Miss a gate, of course—that is fail to get out around it—and your run is disallowed.) This kind of abrupt, Z-shaped line is disapprovingly known as "the mark of Zorro." The best line is a sensuous round one, not too wide but not too straight—call it a "braided rope." The skis are never braking; they are always moving forward on their edges, doing more carving than skidding through the corners.

Sweden's Ingemar Stenmark, the greatest GS racer of all time (he won eighty-six World Cup races between 1974 and 1990, forty-six more than his closest rival on the all-time list, Swiss Pirmin Zurbriggen), was so smooth he used to win races by two and three seconds, eons in a sport accustomed to margins measured in hundredths of seconds. While other racers charged and slashed and rammed the poles looking for speed, Stenmark skied crisp semicircles, rarely bumped a gate. His skis didn't throw up the rooster tails of spray the others' did because he didn't skid. And finally, where you could hear most of the other racers clattering down a course, Stenmark's skis were practically silent; the edges didn't scrape the snow, they hissed along in their own sidecut grooves.

Classical, or diagonal, stride racers on the Olympic track at Calgary, Alberta. We can learn much from the racer's ability to glide, which comes both from a powerful kick and a finely honed balance over the gliding foot.

Super G

From the late 1970s into the '80s, World Cup organizers tried a lot of different tricks to thwart Stenmark. If they didn't do something, they knew, he would win the overall trophy every year with ease. One of the things they did was create a new event, the super giant slalom, known as the super G. It was a cross between a downhill and a giant slalom, using the downhill, or single-run, format. Stenmark didn't race downhills—he was uncomfortable with the extreme speeds—so the super G was designed to help downhillers, who rarely did well in the quicker slalom and giant slalom, score more points. It worked. Stenmark continued to rack up victories in the gate races, but he never again took the overall after 1978.

The super G is not universally popular with the racers. Most see it as simply a slow downhill, and who wants to watch or race that? Fans have given it a similarly cool reception.

NORDIC DISCIPLINES: Classical

So-called classical races restrict competitors to the traditional diagonal stride. This was mandated in the late 1980s to prevent unfair competition by devotees of the newly discovered, and much faster, skating techniques. Traditional distances for the men are 15 and 30 kilometers. Women's classical distances are usually 10 and 15 kilometers, although 5 km sprints are sometimes included in a meet.

Skis, boots, and poles for classical technique look very much like skating gear, but there are subtle differences. The skis are longer for straight-ahead directional stability, and sport higher tips for guiding the skis down the preset grooves. Boots have a more flexible "hinge" at the ball of the foot for natural full-extension striding. And poles are just slightly shorter than skating poles, about chin height compared to nose height or higher with skating poles.

Racers dash to the front after a mass start skate race. Racers teach us to vary the skating cadence, quick and short for skiing uphill, long and flowing across the flats and downhills. *Lori Adamski-Peek*

What can we learn by watching classical racers? Glide. Glide. Glide. It's the name of the game in all cross-country racing, especially classical. Watch how the best racers coax a longer glide out of each stride than do the merely good. They do it with a powerful kick, but even more important with a finely honed balance, completely focused on riding one ski at a time, keeping that ski flat (not on edge) and humming down the track.

Skating

Normal skating distances are 10 and 50 kilometers for the men and 10 and 30 km for the women. Because skating is about 20 percent faster than striding, it is the preferred technique for the longer marathon distances. Although every once in a while, race organizers will schedule a 5-km skate sprint. Relay races, pitting four-member teams against one another over 5- or 10-km loops, are now exclusively skate races. These are intensely exciting for spectators especially in the hand-off areas where hurried touches sometimes result in spectacular crashes. Cross-country skaters can cover 5 kilometers in about 13 minutes for an average speed, up and down hills, of over 14 mph.

What can we learn watching the best skate racers? Cadence. Varying the rhythm to the terrain. Since skating skis have only glide wax on their bases, propulsion comes entirely from the skating push-off. Edge, push-off, and glide. Edge, push-off, and glide. The best skaters match the cadence of these elements to the terrain. On flats and slight downhills, they stretch the movements out until it almost looks as if they're working in slow motion. On gradual uphills, they step up the pace, gliding a shorter distance with each thrust. On steep uphills, their legs and arms become like pistons churning out short, staccato, rapid-fire steps with very little glide to each one.

Biathlon

In this country biathlon is a minor sport within the relatively minor sport of cross-country track racing. But it is very big in Europe, particularly eastern Europe and the Soviet Union. Racers ski distances similar to what classical and skate racers do. But they do it with specially made small-bore target rifles strapped to their backs. And every few kilometers along the way, they are required to stop, assume one of several firing positions (standing and prone), and squeeze off shots at five distant targets. Miss any of the targets and they must ski penalty loops around a small track nearby. Winners miss very few targets or ski incredibly fast to make up the penalty time.

We rarely see any biathlon coverage on

Biathlon demands both fast skiing and accurate target shooting, a fiendishly difficult challenge. *Lori Adamski-Peek*

Ski jumpers make an air foil of their bodies and their skis to literally ride the wind over distances as great as 200 meters.
Lori Adamski-Peek

television, even during an Olympiad. Nor is one likely to run into a biathlon team out on the practice loop. It's hard to imagine a national team in an Olympic sport that is smaller and poorer than our biathlon team. Be that as it may, I find it an extremely interesting sport for the excruciating dichotomy at its core. Which is this: On the trail, the biathlete is working at maximum heart rate, maximum oxygen uptake, etc. (It's well known that cross-country is the most aerobically demanding sport extant.) And then he is asked to stop, whip off his gun, and in a matter of seconds calm his breathing and heart to the point where he can shoot with Zen like control. The two activities are total opposites, and here they are combined in one fiendishly difficult challenge.

Nordic Combined

This is another little-known ski sport in America. It combines jumping competition with a cross-country race, usually on two consecutive days. It is a kind of throwback to the days when all-around skiers were the real heroes. Throughout the pre-WWII years, the real national champion was the winner of the "four-way" title, which included jumping, cross-country, a downhill, and a slalom. These days in skiing, as in most everything else, specialists have taken over. The nordic combined athlete, a master of multiple skills and training regimens, is seldom as revered as the individual event champions, even in Scandinavia, where the very first competitions were combineds.

Jumping

Jumping always gets a lot of air time during the Winter Games because it is so spectacular to watch. Jumpers dive onto a steep start ramp where they crouch through a rapid acceleration then launch themselves on long, parabolic arcs that resemble flying more than skiing. Then they touch down in a graceful telemark position. If all goes well, that is. There is perhaps an equal, morbid fascination with the inevitable mistakes, the crashes on landing and the awkward swimming in the air which may recall our own most frustrating flying dreams.

Jumpers are a special breed. They have to be to fly 70 and 90 meters (the two Olympic-caliber jumps). In a few places in Europe there are "ski flying" hills where jumps of 200 meters are not out of the question. Ski flying is not an Olympic event.

Jumping skis are very long and wide, often with multiple grooves in the bases to keep them running straight on the in-run. The jumpers use free-heel boots and bindings, both for the ankle freedom they need to spring off the ramp and because the ideal position in the air has the jumper lying well forward, his body parallel to his skis. In this way he creates an airfoil, like a wing. Skis and body together create lift, and the jumper hangs in the air far longer than it ever seems possible.

FREESTYLE SKIING

Jumping and freestyle are the only ski sports which are judged subjectively, like figure skating or gymnastics. Jumpers have relatively insignificant style points added to their distance numbers. In freestyle, everything is subjective.

The graceful and athletic Stein Eriksen was performing flips on skis two decades before freestyle skiing officially came into being. *Franz Berko*

Freestyle mogul competitions are judged objectively for time and subjectively for style by a panel of jurors at the finish line. *Wade McKoy*

Ballet skiing, set to music and judged like figure skating is, the most elegant of the freestyle disciplines. *Lori Adamski-Peek*

Aerial maneuvers have become infinitely more complex since Stein Eriksen's day. Some involve up to three somersaults and as many twists. Freestyle became a demonstration sport at the 1988 Winter Olympics. *Lori Adamski-Peek*

Moguls, ballet, and aerials are all scored on a combination of style and difficulty points.

Despite the inherent pitfalls in this system, freestyle boomed in the 1970s. It was not new then. Soon after gleaning Olympic gold in 1952, Stein Eriksen came to this country and dazzled everybody with his laid-out forward flips on skis. In the 1960s Stein and a whole crew of acrobatic skiers, including Art Furer and Tom LeRoy, invented a freestyle vocabulary out of outriggers and royal christies, elegant dances on one leg, the quick-swiveling mambo, and, of course, the flips. Sometimes they did them side-by-side, holding hands.

Then in the 1970s, trick skiing took on new, rebellious meaning and popular participation. Hot-doggers skied faster and wilder in the bumps, developed intricate spinning, ballet moves, and added dizzying twists to their double and even triple flips. Competitions took off on both professional and amateur circuits. Skiing had a new set of heroes in Airborne Eddie Ferguson, Wayne Wong, and Scotty Brooksbank.

But then disaster struck. There were a number of crippling injuries from accidents on inverted aerials. The free-spirited hot-doggers began to squabble among themselves about how to run the sport. Insurance skyrocketed. Ski areas shied away from freestyle competitions. The loosely formed world of freestyle fell apart and hot-dogging slunk into its dark ages.

But like a phoenix, freestyle came back. The staid, respected USSA took over the competition scene. Upside down (inverted) aerials were strictly controlled and banned outright for junior competitions. The FIS established a World Cup for freestyle's three events, moguls, ballet, and aerials. By 1988, what had once been an expression of skiing's counter-culture was button-down enough to be a demonstration sport at the Calgary Winter Olympics. Today competitive freestylers are often ex-gymnasts who work out their convoluted tricks on trampolines and dry-land ramps that dump skiers safely into swimming pools.

SPEED SKIING

At the other end of the spectrum, speed skiing is the only branch of the tree with a quantitative, ultimate record hovering like a mirage over every competition.

Like hot-dogging, speed skiing has had a turbulent and anarchistic history. But it goes back even further. Those miners racing in the California Sierra in the 1860s were, strictly speaking, speed skiers. They carefully measured the length of the courses and clocked their times. We can calculate rather precisely how fast they went. Tommy Todd's record run at La Porte in 1874 of 14 seconds down an icy 1,804-foot course translates to a speed of 88 mph. Fast by anybody's standards!

From the 1930s on, the most respected speed skiing meets were held on the Plateau Rosa on the Italian side of the Matterhorn. There skiers dove over the concave face of the glacier and through the Kilometro Lanciato, or Flying Kilometer. Speeds gradually inched upward toward the 200 kilometer per hour (124 mph) mark. Then in the late 1970s, a yawning crevasse across the top of the course, a fissure which had been spanned by a snow-covered wooden bridge, opened further and closed the run. American Steve McKinney broke the 200-km barrier on a hand-groomed track above the hotel in Portillo, Chile. The other two great modern tracks, places where new records have been set and which hold the potential for more, are the ones at Velocity Peak near Silverton, Colorado, and the one at Les Arcs, France.

The Les Arcs course will host speed skiing as a demonstration sport at the 1992 Winter Olympics. It is a near-perfect scoop for speed skiing. It starts high in a couloir on the Aiguille Rouge, a steep, snow-filled corridor between rock walls with a pitch approaching 50 degrees. Then the course plunges out in the open on a gradual, concave curve that drops 1,200 vertical feet over nearly a mile. The racers need the last quarter mile just to slow down and stop.

Speed skiers ride down these hills on skis almost as long and heavy as Tommy Todd's, about 240 cm long. They wear super-slick rubber body suits that they have to peel off and on. (Despite the tight fit, the suits are distorted by the wind at 120 mph and flap slightly, making a sound like rapidly frying bacon.) In order to cut drag behind their legs, they tape fin-shaped fairings to their calves, which together with the trout-face helmets give them a slippery, aquatic alien look. Everything for speed. And it works. The men's record is hovering right around 224 kph, or 139 mph, and the women's record is just over 125 mph. Speed skiers claim to be the fastest, non-motorized humans on earth.

In the mid 1980s speed skiing went public. Organizers of the big international events set up courses for citizen speedsters at ski areas around the country. If you had a helmet and a few dollars for a lift ticket and a one-day clinic, you could run a small-scale track with top speeds in the 60-80 mph range. Participants found after the experience that the rest of the mountain looked tame to them and that after seeking speed in a controlled environment they were more likely to dive into the fall line with élan. Everything about their free skiing improved.

Whether or not speed skiing will ever be mainstream, it will certainly be better known following its exposure during the Les Arcs Olympiad.

MOUNTAINEERING RACES

For decades the Swiss army has organized a one-day race from Zermatt to Verbier, up and down over half a dozen ridgelines and across the deep valleys that separate them. It's a grueling challenge without much appeal to either spectators or a citizen-racing public. But in recent years, a rash of new mountaineering-type races have emerged and attracted teams from all over Europe, Japan, and the U.S.

The oldest and best-known is *Le Raid Blanc,* the Steep White. Every winter five-person teams (one member must be a certified guide) race up and down for six days through some part of the Alps, linking mountain towns like Zermatt, Cervinia, and Courmayeur in Italy, Chamonix and Les Arcs in France. Sometimes they ride the trams and chairlifts to their high points then take off cross country. Other days they strap skins to their skis and climb where there are no lifts. And every day brings mammoth downhill runs through powder and wind crust, over glacial ice and through low-elevation trees and farmer's fields to the next village. Some of the descents cover 8,000 vertical feet. And at night, there are hot meals in pensions and mountain huts, and exhausted racers sleep the sleep of the dead.

Competition is heated at the top of the pack where teams routinely feature ski heroes like Olympians Patrick Russel and Jean-Noël Augert

Speed skier Kirsten Culver pierces the air at over 120 mph. Special helmet, body-hugging poles, and behind-the-leg fins known as fairings help reduce resistance on her straight-ahead run. Record speeds are approaching 140 mph. *Wade McKoy/Bob Woodall*

and mountaineering daredevil Jean Marc Boivin. But in the middle and back of the pack, competition is friendly; camaraderie and the spectacular skiing are the name of the game. For alpine tourers, *Le Raid Blanc* is the ultimate mountain rally.

TRAINING FOR RACING

Obviously, to improve at racing, you have to practice at it, train for it. The different disciplines require different kinds of training. Slalom racers, for example, use the same kind of fast-twitch, explosive muscle fibers that sprinters do. And marathon skaters need to focus their training on cardiovascular endurance, maintaining speed over long distances. And so on.

Race training is a bit beyond the scope of this chapter, which can only be an introduction to competition skiing in its numerous guises. Besides, there are excellent books and videotapes out there specifically aimed at helping you improve on the race course. Two of the best books for alpine racers are *How The Racers Ski*, by Warren Witherell, W.W. Norton and Co., 1972, and *World Cup Ski Technique*, by Olle Larson. The first is a timeless and unsurpassed explanation of the basic mechanics involved in making an efficient turn. The latter is a photographic study of the best racers in the world with Larson (who coaches at the Rowmark Academy in Salt Lake City) adding his expert commentary.

One of the best guides to cross-country (classical and skate) race technique is the video *World Cup Skiing from Falun and Holmenkollen*, 1988, A/S Video Productions, available from Nordic Equipment Inc., P.O. Box 997, Park City, UT 84060.

Training for skiing can mean anything from jogging a few miles and working out in the gym once or twice before heading for the hills, to a full-blown year-round training cycle preparing you for citizen-race fame. Neither is the "right" way to prepare. It all depends on your goals. Alpine skiers, by the very nature of the modern sport, can get by with a little heart/lung fitness and a modicum of muscle tone. On the other hand cross-country racers, like road runners, require a higher level of fitness just to finish an up-and-down race at elevation. Then again, alpine skiers who want to take full advantage of

the 100,000 vertical-foot guarantee that comes with most helicopter ski weeks, find it a lot more fun if they've prepared for a few weeks or months in advance. In all cases, the fitter you are, the better you will ski. A good book on the subject of ski fitness is Serious Training for Serious Athletes, by Rob Sleamaker, Leisure Press.

TIPS & TALES: My Race with Stein

Stein Eriksen attends dozens of celebrity fun races each winter. Ski areas put them on to raise money for charity, to call attention to themselves and to have a good time. President Gerald Ford sponsors one at Vail every year called the American Ski Classic. Aspen has one to benefit multiple sclerosis research. The town of Telluride, Colorado, used to stage an event called the Governor's Cup and Pioneers of Skiing. Governors came from all over, including then governor of New Hampshire John Sununu. Pioneers included inventor/genius Howard Head of the Head Ski Company, ski area visionaries Alf Engen (Sun Valley, Alta, Snowbasin) and Ernie Blake (Taos), and the incomparable stylemaster and promoter of skiing, Stein himself, probably the only person in skiing who doesn't need a last name.

The competition was to benefit Telluride's local medical clinic, and any business that contributed a certain amount earned the right to enter a team in the race. By stroke of luck I was able to join a team sponsored by the local lumber yard. The race was held on the NASTAR course, a gentle pitch with two parallel GS courses set down the middle, one with blue flags, one with green. They used the pro, or dual slalom, format, which means that two racers go at once. Each course is wired to register a separate elapsed time, but it looks like the two skiers are racing each other to the bottom of the hill.

Stein was nearly sixty years old, with nary a gray hair in his wavy, blond coiffe. And he was invincible. His back was ramrod straight and the famous smile beamed everywhere but in the start gate, where you could see a steely resolve drop like a mask over his features. Nobody had been able to stay with him all day.

When it was my turn to race Stein, I decided to let him go out first. I knew he'd beat me to the finish anyway, and I thought it might be less demoralizing to watch him from behind, and try to catch up, than to jump first and have him blow by me.

The race only took twenty seconds, but for a while in mid-course, I thought time had slowed to a crawl. Stein was off to my left about a gate ahead. For a little while there I matched his turns, skis slicing right then left then right, rooster tails of snow spraying out behind.

The timing lights showed my time to be within a couple tenths of Stein's, an eternity really on a short course like this, but a private victory nonetheless. Stein beamed his fabulous grin, still undefeated. It may have been a fluke on my part or on Stein's. I will never know which. But the moment stands as a high point in the always fragile landscape of self-esteem.

10

New Tools

It took about 7,000 years, but we finally have some new tools for sliding on snow. Monoskis and snowboards evolved out of surfing and have invigorated skiing with new movements and sensations. The Eighties have also seen a proliferation of vehicles for imitating skiing's movements *off* the snow, things like in-line skates, roller skis, side-to-side ski exercisers, and indoor ski decks.

OFF-SNOW SKIING

In-line skates, also known as Rollerblades after a major manufacturer (800-232-ROLL), have become indispensable dry-land training for cross-country skaters in particular and for any kind of skier in general. The in-line skates perform like an ice skate on asphalt. Three or four hard rubber wheels in line under a plastic, hockey-type boot behave much more like a ski than do old-fashioned four-wheel skates. These skates are very maneuverable and very fast. You can skate with poles or without, train over distances or slalom around a set of cones. Downhill control is a bit dicey. Some skates come with heel-pad brakes, others don't. But in any case, you must use caution on the hills. Wrist, elbow, and knee pads are recommended.

Roller skis do the same thing; they allow you to approximate cross-country skiing's movements on the road. The "ski" is a short aluminum shaft with a wheel at each end. The rear wheel is "clutched" to prevent backsliding (the way kick wax does on snow). Roller skis (available from ski manufacturer Karhu and the Finnish company Startex) work best for diagonal training. You can skate with them, but the in-line skates are so much more versatile and fun, they have all but eclipsed roller skis in that department.

When I wanted to train for alpine skiing, I used to set a cardboard box in the backyard and jump back and forth over it, from side to side, to approximate the active movements of short-radius turns. Now there are *indoor exercisers* that do the same thing with much lower impact for your aerobic investment. The best is the Skier's Edge (Scientific Sports Systems, 503 Seaport Ct., Port of Redwood City, CA 94063) an arched track with a sliding platform for your feet. Balancing your upper body with ski poles, you bounce back and forth over the arch while the platforms tilt to imitate the edge angle of a ski on snow. It's good cardiovascular exercise while at the same time it is training very ski-specific muscles.

In recent years a significant number of people have learned to ski without touching snow, or going outdoors. They're doing it on a revolving treadmill with a snowlike carpet called a *ski deck*. There are scores of them around the country in sporting goods stores, departments stores, malls, and health clubs.

A snowboarder surfs a snow wave at Jackson Hole, Wyoming. New tools are opening alternatives to traditional, two-legged skiing. *Wade McKoy*

In-line skates simulate skiing action on asphalt. Skate with or without poles. You can even run slalom gates. *Wade McKoy*

Cross-country skiers have long used roller skis to practice their diagonal stride. Four-wheeled mini skis let you kick and glide like the real thing. Downhills are scary, pavement being so much less forgiving than snow.
Wade McKoy

The decks offer a perfectly controlled learning environment; there is no wind, no cold, no need to bundle up, and no skier traffic. The deck can be adjusted for speed and slope pitch. You never stand in line or ride a lift. In fact, you can get in so many linked turns on the continuous deck, that half-hour lessons are roughly equivalent to a two-hour lesson on snow.

There are about two dozen deck ski schools located in Denver, Baton Rouge, Albuquerque, Oklahoma City, Dallas, Houston, and Jackson, Wyoming, among other cities. A lesson typically includes rental of short learning skis with teflon bases, boots and poles. While a plastic rug is no substitute for the feel of real, crystalline snow, for the sun and the bite of mountain air, deck skiers frequently make the move to snow with remarkable élan. It's like getting a head start, an early jump on the sensations of sliding and turning.

THE SURFING CONNECTION

Skis have been long and short, wide and skinny, chunks of wood or space-age laminations of titanium and fiberglass, but there has always been one per foot. Interestingly, the two new on-snow tools developed since the 1960s, the monoski and the snowboard, have their roots in surfing, where a single, wide-body board is the norm.

Monoskiing

In the early 1960s Californian Mike Doyle spent his summers surfing and his winters skiing. He saw both as water sports; with skiing it was just that the water was frozen. Doyle especially loved powder skiing, but he wished that he could float a little higher in the fluff the way a surfboard floated him in the waves. So Doyle built himself a single, extra-wide ski, mounted the bindings side-by-side in the middle and took off for the hills.

Riding the monoski was tricky at first. Edging on packed snow meant tilting the board up onto one edge or the other and weighting the *outside* of that foot, the exact opposite of two-ski technique where all your efforts are concentrated on the *inside* edge of the outside ski. Doyle also quickly realized what a challenge it was just moving around the base area or shuffling through a lift line. Once in the bindings he was effectively monolegged as well as monoskied.

But the payoff came, as he suspected it would, in fresh snow. Because of its much greater surface area, the board planed up high in the powder giving him a speed and fluidity in the liquid medium that he hadn't experienced before. There were no crossing tips, no submarining of one ski or the other; he was skimming the foam, throwing huge roostertails of spray in his wake.

Doyle's idea never really caught on in the U.S. But it flourished in the Alps, particularly in France. One can only speculate about the reasons. Perhaps it is because of the easy access via the lift systems in Europe to above-timberline, ungroomed snows, the mono's forte. Even more important probably, was the French sense of *la glisse,* which translates as the gliding or the slipping, but which has a broader meaning. The French have always championed the *avant garde,* and French mountain lovers are always looking for new ways to slide with gravity. Witness the French boom in downriver kayaking, in hang gliding and para-sailing. On snow, they have experimented with two skis, one ski (one foot behind the other like a water ski), even with riding the mountain in a surf kayak. And, of course, they have taken with enthusiasm to two American inventions, the monoski and the snowboard.

Mono skiers never have to worry about keeping their feet together. *Wade McKoy*

Snowboarding

In Europe snowboarding is known as *le surf.* It too has a surfing heritage and a long story of neglect in the country of its invention. But unlike the mono, snowboarding has returned home to become perhaps the fastest growing aspect of the ski scene.

We go back to the early Sixties again to the introduction by the Brunswick sporting goods company of the Snurfer, a plywood board shaped like a stubby surfboard and intended for backyard snow play. Unlike the monoski where you stood with feet together facing the tip of the board, on a Snurfer you stood sideways, one foot in front, one in back like a surfer.

The Snurfer lasted a couple of years, then the fad died out. But a few diehard kids wouldn't let go, most notably Long Island's Jake Burton Carpenter and Tom Sims of Santa Barbara, California, now the two largest manufacturers of snowboards in the U.S. Burton and Sims, quite independently of one another, tinkered with their boards, built their own versions, experimented with new shapes and materials and with various methods of securing their feet to the tops of the boards. Burton surfed the sand dunes of the East Coast and snuck onto the mountain at Stratton, Vermont, after the lifts closed in the afternoons. Snowboarders walked a lot. As in the early days of skiing, they had to earn their vertical one step at a time. But it was worth it as they swooped back down, feet spread fore and aft, bodies swaying up on the toes and back on the heels to bank their boards left and right against the soft resistance.

Slowly, small pockets of *aficionados* developed across the country, in the Sierra, Utah's Wasatch, and in New England. But snowboarding remained a fringe endeavor. Ski areas were not keen to allow riders on their slopes for a variety of stated reasons, most of which veiled a glacial conservatism. Underwriters weren't sure a snowboard was a "directional device" like a ski. Area operators worried that the lack of release

Snowboarding, known as *le surf* in Europe, has its roots in American surfing in the 1960s. Here a competitor in the half-pipe competition performs off a steeply banked, wavelike snow berm. *Wade McKoy*

bindings could mean injury and/or liability problems.

There were no such worries in Europe, where le surf took off like a cornice jumper after its introduction in the early '80s. Then, beginning about 1986, a few U.S. areas decided to give the new kid a try, to see if there might be a profitable new wave in the offing. Stratton, Breckenridge, and Purgatory in Colorado, and a handful of others opened the door a crack—and the flood was on.

Snowboarding appealed to kids, teenagers especially, who found skiing with their parents unacceptable. Skateboarders made the transition to snow surfing with ease. And a surprising number of veteran skiers tried it too. It was a new way to move, a new challenge (as telemarking had been a decade before), a new tool.

Snowboarding was seen as a radical alternative to skiing, complete with its own styles, its own clothing, and even its own language. Snowboarders speak of "shredding," or really tearing up the hill. Ski areas built "half-pipes" for the shredhead crowd—tall-sided, scooped out corridors where riders could swoop up the banks and perform aerial maneuvers. An in-air trick in which the rider grabs his board with one hand and twists into knee-torquing contortions is called "tweakage." "Gnarly tweakage" requires big air. And a really big jump is known as "nuclear air."

Snowboard Equipment

Snowboards, once just varnished wooden boards, are now as technically sophisticated as most skis. They have laminated wood or foam cores, glass wrapped and sandwiched, with full-length metal edges and P-Tex bases. The price is commensurate too. Expect to pay about the same for a snowboard as you would for an off-the-shelf recreational slalom ski.

There are two basic kinds of boards, freestyle boards and alpine boards. Freestyle boards are usually shorter (150-165 cm or so), have turned up tails (for spinning around and riding backwards as well as forwards), and symmetrical sidecuts. These boards are the preferred vehicle in moguls and in the half-pipes.

Alpine boards are sometimes, but not always, longer (up to 180 cm) and designed to carve turns rather than spin around and do tricks. They are stiffer than freestyle boards, and many are now designed with asymmetrical sidecuts. Because riders stand with their feet diagonally across the board, it is thought that the sidecut on the front side (toe side) should be skewed forward of the sidecut for backside (heel side) turns. Asymmetrical boards look like they've melted or been stretched out of shape while still warm, but riders swear that the configuration works hand-in-glove with the snowboarder's stance.

Snowboards are manufactured around the world now. Burton and Sims have been rewarded for their patience and are among the biggest. Some are built by long-time ski-industry companies like K2 and Look. Others are strictly into snowboarding and include Barfoot, Gnu, and Kemper. The venerable California surfboard manufacturer, Gordon and Smith, now has a snowboard line, and Mistral, the German

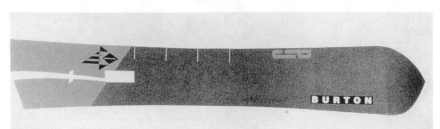

Freestyle (top) and alpine snowboards. The freestyle is shorter and flexed for tricks and general mountain boarding. The alpine board is asymmetrical (on the theory that toe- and heel-side turns have a different center) and flexed for long, carved turns. *Burton Snowboards*

sailboard and sportswear company, sells a lot of boards in Europe.

General rules of thumb: As you would with skiing, start out on a short board; they're easiest to learn on (many companies are now making extra-short boards for children); stiffer boards are for heavier and better riders; soft boards are better for beginners and for riding in powder.

Snowboard Boots and Bindings

There are two classes of boots and two types of bindings, but you'll not get them confused. Soft boots go with soft bindings, and hard boots go with hard bindings. Usually, but not always, you'll find soft bindings on freestyle boards and hard bindings on alpine boards. Freestyle riding requires lots of ankle flex and thus the soft setups. Hard boots and bindings provide the more rigid boot-to-board precision that high-speed carving and racing demand, and for which alpine boards are designed.

When snowboarding began, riders used their everyday leather-and-rubber pac boots, the most universally popular being the Canadian-made Sorels. Boots were clipped into simple plastic straps screwed into the board. That was part of the appeal in the beginning; you didn't need fancy ski boots or bindings. While Sorels are still a popular option, high technology (and business savvy) has naturally crept into this area as well. Board manufacturers often sell their own brand of boot as well, soft shell or hard. The snowboard-specific soft boots come with an alpine-style

bladder, or inner boot, and stiff soles to provide a closer fit and a little more stability than the undoctored Sorels.

Soft boots work with soft, or flexible, bindings, consisting of two or three buckle straps (two on the instep and one on the lower shin) and a plastic "spoiler" to support the calf and create leverage on heel side turns. The bindings don't release in a fall. No snowboard bindings do. While this may seem alarming at first, relatively few injuries are attributable to this locked-on situation. The majority of snowboarding injuries are to the hands and arms — trying to catch a fall. Nevertheless, some designers are working on a functional release system for snowboards.

The hard boot/binding concept came out of Europe during snowboarding's dark ages here. Euro-riders wanted more control than they got with the soft boots, so they looked for a way to ride in their hard-plastic mountaineering or alpine-touring boots. Some enterprising soul took the aluminum plates from a plate-style alpine binding, complete with toe bails and heel closures, and screwed them onto a board. Clamp the boot into the closure, and you have a nearly rigid setup. (Why not use regular alpine ski bindings? Because they'd extend well beyond the edges of the board, interfering with edging. As it is, boot toes and heels sometimes drag in a strongly edged turn.)

These plate systems have since become more snowboard-specific, with cants and leans and adjustable sizing, but the basic idea is unchanged. You can buy hard boots that double as

Soft binding (left) and soft boot are preferred by freestyle riders for their flexibility. *Burton Snowboards*

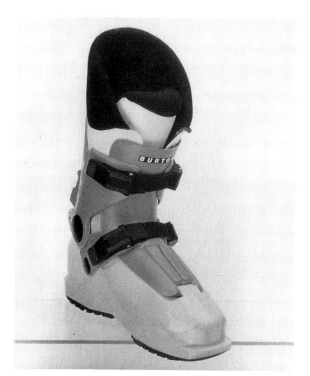 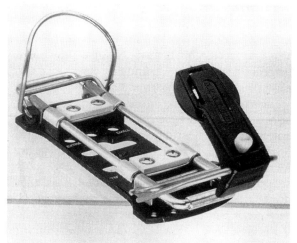

Hard boot (left) and hard binding. The boot evolved from plastic mountaineering boots which some riders preferred for their more precise transmission of turning forces. *Burton Snowboards*

mountaineering or ice climbing shoes, or for about the same money you can get something with a purely snowboarding stamp on it. Alpine equipment companies Rossignol, Kastinger, Raichle, and Alpina make specialized hard boots for snowboarding, as do snowboard-only companies Burton and Kemper.

Snowboarding Technique

Snowboarders don't use poles. That's because they rarely face straight down the fall line as an alpine skier does. Instead, they lead with one side of the body or the other. If you are like 70 percent of the population, you would lead with your left foot—it just feels right—and you would be known as a "regular foot." The other 30 percent are "goofy foots." They're more comfortable with their right foot in front. There is some correlation here with right- and left-handedness; many left-handed people are also goofy foot, but it's not necessarily so.

Either way, you have to learn to make toe-side and heel-side turns. For a skier with some years of experience, this can be disconcerting, as it was for me when I first tried snowboarding. Skiers work hard at not pressing forward on their toes or, even worse, back on their heels. The ideal is a neutral stance from which lateral movements edge the skis, knees and hips to the side. But in snowboarding the movements are primarily up and back along the foot's long axis.

Beginning Strategies

Beginners can rent appropriate boards at most ski areas and receive lessons from certified snowboard instructors. I highly recommend lessons at this stage.

Snowboarding is no more difficult to master than is skiing. In fact, many people think it is easier, but the first day is notoriously tough. You'll do a lot of falling—more than first-time skiers because your feet are stuck; you can't walk or step to save your balance. And you'll do a lot of just plain sitting in the snow, so wear good, waterproof pants. You may be bruised at the end of the day. My instructor told me he couldn't walk after his first day on a board. But don't be discouraged. Once you get the hang of traversing and skidding into rudimentary front side and back side turns—usually after just a day or two—

you're on your way, and continued progress is often rapid.

Like the mono skiers, you have to take one foot off the board to get around the lift line. Leave the front foot in the binding and scoot along pushing with the back foot. You ride the lift this way, slide down the ramp with the back foot on the board but unattached, then sit down out of the way and rebuckle the rear foot.

Start off with gentle traverses. Flex your knees and press down with your toes to engage the edge for a frontside traverse. Weight your heel and lift up slightly with your toes on the backside. Sit down to flip the board up and around to switch directions. Experiment with the amount of edge: Let the board go flatter to the hill to release it into a sideslip; tilt it up higher to slow down and stop, and to make the board hold a traverse line across the slope. With these two skills, traversing and sideslipping, you can descend most hills. You should feel comfortable with them before attempting downhill turns.

Toe Turns

Toe turns are usually easier to pick up than heel turns, perhaps because most of us are better at balancing up on our toes than we are up on our heels.

Begin in a backside traverse, knees flexed and weight centered between your feet. Release the uphill edge so the board flattens out. Now shift the majority of your weight to your front foot. It becomes the pivot point around which the back foot steers. Press the back foot around behind your front foot. At the same time pressure the new edge with weight on your toes and even deeper knee flexion.

Commit your body into the turn. The principle is the same as for a turn on skis; your center of mass must be inside the arc drawn by the board. Keep your front arm steady through the turn, pointing the way, drawing you down and through the arc. Don't flail your arms.

And finally don't drag the back hand in the snow as you come around. It may look cool, but it isn't functional. One of the best guides to basic snowboard instruction is the video *Don't Pat the Dog,* available from Motion Graphics, 8340 S.W. 39th Ave., Portland, OR 97219. The title refers to this habit of dragging the back hand during a turn: patting the dog. Snowboard rider and video

Toe-side or front-side turn. *Mount Bachelor*

narrator Chris Karol makes it crystal-clear that what is purely functional in this rhythmic, graceful dance is also the most beautiful.

This is a film of few words. Karol and producer/photographer Craig Adkins are rightly wary of explanations, of the seductive nature—for both teacher and student—of too many words. Instead they seek to imprint the subconscious with images and a few key phrases, repeated with almost hypnotic effect. On toe side turns, for example: "Commit your body into the turn. Dive into it. Stay low. Be powerful. Commit. Dive into it. Stay low. Be powerful."

Heel Turns

Heel turns are nearly a mirror image of toe turns: release the edge; pivot the back foot around the front; weight the heel edge and drive. There are two important added instructions. First, keep your knees bent and driving forward with the turn. Many beginners push the board away from

their bodies in a heel turn, straightening their legs in the process. Instinct tells them that that's the way to get the board on edge. Instead, drop your hips to the inside of the turn and drive with bent knees.

Second, keep your back arm down and forward. This helps keep your weight on your feet, over the heel edge. The tendency with many learners is to raise the rear arm high. Like patting the dog, it may look cool, but in fact, it pulls weight off your feet and too far to the inside of the turn. You may make it through that one arc, but then the transition to toe side again is difficult.

Transitions

In the beginning stages turns should be linked by traverses, so you can collect your balance and prepare mentally for the next turn. The most important preparation is selecting the best spot for a direction change. The crest of a small roll or

Heel-side or back-side turn. *Hubert Schriebl*

even a nascent mogul is better than a sidehill or a concave shape. As the slope falls away beneath you, there is less friction to overcome for the shift in edge and weight.

After a while you will want to link turns smoothly from toe side to heel side without traverses. Two things have to happen: you have to change edges, and you have to effectively weight the new turning edge. The best way to do this is to stand tall and momentarily weightless for the instant the board crosses beneath you into the new turn. Flex and drive through the "heavy" part of one turn, the end phase of the turn where you are well past the fall line and forces have built up under your edge. Finish the turn by standing up over the board; this unweights and flattens the board to the snow surface. Then, simultaneously flex at the knees to tilt the board into the new direction and transfer your weight to the new edge. It'll take some work to make the transition flow back and forth from one edge to the other. But keep at it, and the transitions—from one weighted edge to momentary weightlessness, to the next weighted edge—will begin to flow with that sinuous motion that is unique to *le surfing*.

TIPS & TALES: Cross Pollination

Fully-rigged, he would be a creature of hideous eclecticism. On one foot is the latest in adjustable, cantable, rear-entry alpine boots attached to a foam-core, titanium-and-fiberglass, vibration-swallowing slalom dancer. On the other foot there are but a few ounces of synthetic track shoe in Hawaiian-shirt colors rigged to an air-core, carbon-fiber, toothpick skate ski. One knee sports a telemarker's knee pad while the other leg is swaddled in red U.S. Team stretch pants. In one hand he grips an adjustable-length, convertible avalanche probe pole with self-arrest grips, while in the other he swings a slinky, curvy, body-hugging downhill model. One hand is muffed in Gore-Tex and Thinsulate, while the other flexes inside the snowy world's version of a driving glove. One side of the torso gets squeezed into day-glo, second-flesh stretch Lycra, while the other half is snug inside a water-proof/breathable, one-piece powder suit. On his wall at home are posters of track racer Gunde Svan, American alpine star Tamara McKinney, mogul master Airborne Eddie Ferguson, and extreme skier Patrick Vallençant.

This monster is me. Not literally, of course, but certainly in spirit, I believe in embracing all of skiing's diverse challenges. It wasn't always so. Growing up in the 1950s, there was downhill skiing and nothing else. You rode the T-bars at Mammoth Mountain or Stowe, and if you were good, you threw in a few christies down the hill.

Then in the 1970s I spent a few winters in a small California mountain town where huge snowfalls forced the closure of all the roads except the state highway. Nobody there minded; they just skied in and out from the road to their homes. My wife and I bought cross-country skis and quickly learned the beauty of quiet, self-propelled travel over snow. Cross-country veterans showed us the seeming magic of a wax that would grip the snow on our way up the buried streets and still glide back down them. We skied to the store in the evenings. We skied to the post office. One night we skied home from Thanksgiving dinner at a friend's cabin. There was no moon, only starlight, but that faint twinkling was enough to light our way slicing long strides between the pines.

Without really meaning to we were part of the telemark revival; that venerable turn was the only way to steer our skis on those pale night streets. We found that free-heel skiing in lightweight boots sharpened our balance and made us better alpine skiers. We learned to stand in balance on our feet and not depend on the high, stiff sides of our alpine boots for support.

Skiing off-track on our skinny skis, we learned about wild snow, how to be safe in it and how to turn downhill through it, lessons that carried over to our in-area alpine skiing. Our alpine skiing, in turn, taught us how to edge and steer our cross-country skis, how to anticipate and plant our poles to trigger a sinuous sequence of turns.

In-area, we raced the gates when we had a chance, and racing made us quicker. Moguls made us more supple, taught us to be pliant, to flow with the terrain rather than go against it. Powder taught us patience and a love of new snow in its myriad guises: wind-blown stiff or soft as foam, warm and heavy with Pacific moisture or cold and light as a carpet of dandelion fuzz.

Out on the track when skating burst on the scene in the '80s, we embraced the notion of glide. Pure glide and nothing but. Skating taught us about momentum and edging, balancing and aerobic fitness, lessons we applied to every other form of our skiing.

When the powder was all tracked up in-bounds, there was the lure of the outback, the endless backcountry, with it special responsibilities, self-sufficiency, and adventure.

All our skiing skills came into focus out there; our senses sharpened, our judgment honed. Those illuminations, in turn, made the lift-served skiing more fun, more playful, more of the lark it is.

And so on. Every day of skiing, every turn, whatever the gear or the technique, adds to the experience and the joy. If there's new snow sparkling in the light of a departing storm, I'll put on something wide, like telemark or alpine touring skis, or better yet, a snowboard, to float me high in the fluff. On the other hand if it hasn't snowed for weeks, that means the tracks will be slick as a polished rink for a skate around the meadow. If it's storming so hard you can't see across the street, I head for the lifts in my Gore-Tex cocoon, to slide around the empty, softening pistes, while others take their hot-buttered comfort indoors. And finally, when it's spring and the snow in the high country settles into that smooth, hard canvas known as corn, friends and I don climbing skins and ski valley-to-valley or hut-to-hut, staying out until the last bit of alpinglow fades from the peaks and we're skiing again on the blue snow of twilight.

It's all skiing. All magic.

Bibliography

Armstrong, Betsy and Knox Williams, *The Avalanche Book,* Fulcrum, 1986.

Atwater, Monty, *The Avalanche Hunters,* Macrae Smith Co., 1968.

Cochran, Barbara Ann and Lindy Cochran Kelly, *Teach Your Child to Ski,* Stephen Greene Press, 1989.

Cohen, Stan, *A Pictorial History of Downhill Skiing,* Pictorial Histories Publishing Co., 1985.

Gillette, Ned with John Dostal, *Cross-Country Skiing,* The Mountaineers, 1983.

La Chapelle, Edward R., *Field Guide to Snow Crystals,* University of Washington Press, 1969.

Needham, Richard, *Ski Fifty Years in North America,* Harry N. Abrams, 1987.

Parker, Paul, *Free-Heel Skiing,* Chelsea Greene, 1989.

Perla, Ronald I. and M. Martinelli, *Avalanche Handbook,* U.S. Department of Agriculture handbook No. 489, 1976.

Sleamaker, Rob, *Serious Training for Serious Athletes,* Leisure Press, 1989.

Tejada-Flores, Lito, *Backcountry Skiing,* Sierrra Club Books, 1983.

Wilkerson, James, *Medicine for Mountaineering,* The Mountaineers, 1967.

Witherall, Warren, *How the Racers Ski,* W.W. Norton, 1972.

APPENDIX

Appendix I

Ski Information

Auburn Ski Club Western America Skisport Museum, 19865 Boreal Ridge Rd., Soda Springs, CA 95728, (916) 426-3313.

Colorado Ski Museum/Ski Hall of Fame, P.O. Box 1976, Vail, CO 81658, (303) 476-1876.

Cross Country Ski Areas Association, 59 Bolton Rd., Winchester, NH 03470, (603) 239-4341.

Federation Internationale de Ski, Elfenstrasse 19, Postfach, CH-3000, Berne, Switzerland 16, Ph. 41-031-44-43-71.

National Handicap Sports and Recreation Association, 1145 19th St. N.W., Suite 717, Washington, D.C. 20036, (301) 652-7505.

National Ski Patrol System, 133 S. Van Gordon St., Suite 100, Lakewood, CO 80228, (303) 988-1111.

New England Ski Museum, P.O. Box 267, Franconia, NH 03580, (603) 823-7177.

Professional Ski Instructors of America, 133 S. Van Gordon St., Suite 240, Lakewood, CO 80228, (303) 987-9390.

United Ski Industries Association, 8377-B Greensboro Dr., McLean, VA 22102, (800) 742-7469.

U.S. Geologic Survey (topographic maps), Denver, CO 80225.

U.S. National Ski Hall of Fame, P.O. Box 191, Ishpeming, MI 49849, (906) 486-9281.

U.S. Recreational Ski Association, P.O. Box 25469, Anaheim, CA 92805, (714)634-1050.

U.S. Ski Association/U.S. Ski Team, P.O. Box 100, Park City, UT 84060, (801) 649-9090.

Equipment/Apparel Manufacturers

ALPINE

Allsop (poles), 4201 Meridian Rd., P.O. Box 23, Bellingham, WA 98225, (206) 734-9090.

Alpina Sports Corp. (boots), P.O. Box 23, Hanover, NH 03755, (603) 448-3101.

Atomic Ski USA, 4 Cote Ln., Bedford, NH 03102, (603) 668-8980.

Authier Skis, P.O. Box 217, Waitsfield, VT 05673, (802) 496-6900.

Barrecrafters (car racks), P.O. Box 158, Route 7, Shelburne, VT 05482, (802) 985-3321.

Bausch & Lomb (eyewear), 1400 N. Goodman St., Box 450, Rochester, NY 14692, (716) 338-6074.

Blizzard North America (skis), Airport Industrial Pk., P.O. Box 8100, West Lebanon, NH 03784, (603) 298-6000.

Bogner of America (skiwear), Bogner Dr., Newport, VT 05855, (802) 334-6507.

Bolle America (eyewear), 3890 Elm St., Denver, CO 80207, (303) 321-4300.

Brenco Enterprises (Munari boots, Kneissl skis), 7877 S. 180th St., Kent, WA 98032, (206) 251-5020.

Carrera International Corp. (eyewear), 35 Maple St., Norwood, NJ 07648, (201) 767-3820.

CB North America (skiwear), One Apollo Dr., Glens Falls, NY 12801, (518) 792-2121.

Colmar USA (skiwear), 605 N. Challenger Rd., Salt Lake City, UT 84116-2897, (801) 539-1411.

Dachstein (boots), Total Sports, 8610 Main St., Williamsville, NY 14221, (716) 632-7335.

Descente America (skiwear), 109 Inverness Dr. E., Englewood, CO 80112, (303) 790-1155.

Dynamic USA (skis), 2310 Laurel St. #2, Napa, CA 94558, (707) 255-9253.

Dynastar (skis, Lange boots, Kerma poles), Hercules Dr., Box 25, Colchester, VT 05446, (802) 655-2400.

Elan-Monarch (Elan skis, Dolomite boots, Geze bindings), P.O. Box 4279, Burlington, VT 05406, (802) 863-5593.

Ellesse USA (skiwear), 1430 Broadway, 18th Fl., New York, NY 10018, (212) 840-6111.

Fera International Corp. (skiwear), 20603 Earl St., Torrance, CA 90503, (213) 370-8538.

Fila Sports (skiwear), 145 Park Ln., Brisbane, CA 994005-1311, (415) 468-6800.

Fischer of America (skis and Dynafit boots), 35 Industrial Pkwy., Woburn, MA 01801, (617) 935-2452.

Hart Ski Manufacturing Co., P.O. Box 64049, 1410 Energy Park Dr. #9, St. Paul, MN 55108, (612) 644-1973.

Head Ski Division/Head Sports Inc., 4801 N. 63rd St., Boulder, CO 80301, (303) 530-2000.

K2 Corporation (skis), 19215 99th Ave., Vashon, WA 98070, (206) 463-3631.

Kastle USA (skis), P.O. Box 26947, Salt Lake City, UT 884126-0947, (801) 972-6226.

Kombi Ltd. (gloves), 102 Great Hill Rd., Naugatuck, CT 06770, (203) 723-7441.

Look USA (bindings), 8 Ave. D, Williston, VT 05495, (802) 863-7971..

Marker USA (bindings), P.O. Box 26548, Salt Lake City, UT 84126, (801) 972-2100.

Nevica USA/SD.C. (skiwear), 6330 Gunpark Dr. W., Boulder, CO 80301, (303) 530-3466.

Nils (skiwear), 11185 Condor Ave., Fountain Valley, CA 92708, (714) 241-8105.

Nishizawa USA (skis), 410 17th St., Suite 220, Denver, CO 80202, (303) 572-9559.

Nordica (boots), 6 Thompson Dr., Essex Junction, VT 05452, (802) 879-4644.

The North Face (skiwear), 999 Harrison St., Berkeley, CA 94710, (415) 527-9700.

Oakley (eyewear), 10 Holland, Irvine, CA 92718, (714) 951-0991.

Olin Skis, 31 Industrial Park Rd., Centerbrook, CT 06409, (800) 955-7547.

Pre Skis (and Scott poles and goggles), P.O. Box 2030, Sun Valley, ID 83353, (208) 726-4456.

Raichle Molitor USA (Raichle boots, Tyrolia bindings), Geneva Rd., Brewster, NY 10509, (914) 279-5121.

Reflex Sport Products (Reflex poles, Lacroix skis), 605 N. Challenger Rd., Salt Lake City, UT 84116-5037, (801) 539-8001.

Research Dynamics (RD skis), P.O. Box 303, 215 Lloyd Dr., Suite 202, Ketchum, ID 83340, (208) 726-4812.

Revo Sunglasses, 455 E. Middlefield Rd., Mountain View, CA 94043, (415) 962-0906.

Roffe (skiwear), 808 Howell St., Seattle, WA 98101, (206) 622-0456.

Rossignol Ski Co., Industrial Ave., P.O. Box 298, Williston, VT 05495, (802) 863-2511.

Salomon/North America (boots, skis, bindings), 400 E. Main St., National Northway Corp. Ofc. Park, Georgetown, MA 01833, (508) 352-7600.

Sanmarco USA (boots), 115 Atlantic Ave., Aspen CO 81611, (303) 925-5060.

Saranac Glove Co., P.O. Box 786, 1201 Main St., Green Bay, WI 54305, (414) 435-3737.

SKYR Skiwear, P.O. Box 486, Winchester, MA 01890-0686, (617) 729-4141.

Slalom Skiwear, Longview St., Newport, VT 05855, (802) 334-7958.

Smith Sport Optics (goggles and glasses), P.O. Box 2999, 191 5th St. E., Ketchum, ID 83340, (208) 726-4477.

Sport Obermeyer (skiwear), 115 Atlantic Ave., Aspen, CO 81611, (303) 925-5060.

Sypder Active Sports (skiwear), 3600 Pear St., Boulder, CO 80301, (303) 449-0611.

Sun Ice USA (skiwear), 300 Lind Ave. S.W., Renton, WA 98055, (206) 251-3544.

Tecnica USA (boots), P.O. Box 551, West Lebanon, NH 03784, (603) 298-8032.

Thule/Eldon Group America (car racks), 175 Clearbrook Rd., Elmsford, NY 10523, (914) 592-4812.

Tomic Golf and Ski Mfg. Co. (poles), 23102 Mariposa Ave., Torrance, CA 90502, (213) 534-2532.

Top Line Sports (Koflach boots), 2325 s. 2300 W., Salt Lake City, UT (801) 975-9011.

Uvex Winter Optical (goggles), 10 Thurber Blvd., Smithfield, RI 02917, (401) 232-1200.

Volant Ltd. (skis), 3280 Pearl St., Boulder, CO 80301, (303) 443-3378.

Volkl USA (skis), P.O. Box 206, Banner Elk, NC 28604, (704) 898-4536.

CROSS-COUNTRY

Alpina Sports Corp. (boots), P.O. box 23, Hanover, NH 03755, (603) 448-3101.

Atomic Ski USA, 4 Cote Ln., Bedford, NH 03102, (603) 668-8980.

Blizzard North America (skis), P.O. Box 8100, Airport Industrial Park, W. Lebanon, NH 03784, (603) 298-6000.

Brenco Enterprises, Inc. (Kneissl skis), 7877 S. 180th, Kent, WA 98032, (206) 251-5020.

CCM/Maska U.S., Inc. (Asnes and Morotto skis), P.O. Box 381, Bradford, VT 05033, (800) 451-4600.

Skis Dynastar, P.O. Box 25, Hercules Dr., Colchester, VT 05446, (802) 655-2400.

Elan Monark (skis), P.O. Box 4279, 208 Flynn Ave., Burlington, VT 05401, (802) 863-5593.

Exel, Inc. (Exel poles, Peltonen skis), 5 First Ave., Peabody, MA 01960, (508) 532-2226.

Fischer or America, Inc. (skis), 35 Industrial Parkway, Woburn, MA 01801, (617) 935-2452.

Helly-Hansen, Inc. (skiwear), 17275 N.E. 67th Court, Redmond, WA 98052, (206) 833-8823.

Jarvinen USA (skis), 844 Woburn St., Wilmington, MA 01887, (800) 343-6752.

K-Way USA (skiwear), 557 Long Rd., Pittsburgh, PA 15235, (412) 242-5903.

Karhu USA, Inc. (Karhu and Trak skis, Merrell boots), P.O. Box 4249, S. Burlington, VT 05401, (800) 222-1833.

Kastle USA (skis), 2250 S. 1300 W., Suite D, Salt Lake City, UT 84119, (800) 624-7540.

Kinder Binding, Bauer Cycle & Ski, 404 Third Ave. North, Minneapolis, MN 55401, (612) 333-2581.

The North Face (skiwear), 999 Harrison St., Berkeley, CA 94710, (800) 888-9991.

NorTur, Inc. (Landsem and Bonna skis), 3850 Annapolis Ln., Minneapolis, MN 55447, (800) 328-7436.

O.U. Sports, Inc. (Kazama skis), 1926 Third Ave., Seattle, WA 98101, (206) 728-4055.

Outdoor Research (gaiters), 1000 1st Ave. So., Seattle, WA 98134, (800) 421-2421.

Patagonia (skiwear), P.O. box 150, Ventura, CA 93002, (805) 643-8616.

REI, Inc. (skiwear, ski packages, and packs), P.O. Box 88127, Seattle, WA 98138-0127, (800) 426-4840.

Rossignol Ski Co., Inc., P.O. Box 298, Industrial Ave., Williston, VT 05495, (802) 863-2511.

Sierra Designs (skiwear, packs), 2039 Fourth St., Oakland, CA 94607, (800) 423-6363.

Swix Ski Waxes, Sport U.S.A., Inc., 261 Ballardvale St., Wilmington, MA 01887, (800) 343-8335.

Wild Country USA (skiwear), 27 Whitelaw Dr., Center Conway, NH 03813, (603) 356-9316.

Woolrich (skiwear), Woolrich, PA 17779, (717) 769-6464.

ALPINE TOURING

Alpine Research, Inc. (bindings, poles, skins, transceivers), 765 Indian Peaks Rd., Golden, CO 80403, (303) 499-4466.

Ascension Enterprises (skins), Boxholder, Ridgway, CO 81432, (303) 626-5612.

Aspen Expeditions (Petzl bindings), P.O. Box 2432, Aspen, Co 81612, (303) 925-7625.

Black Diamond Equipment Ltd. (skis, boots, bindings, poles), P.O. Box 110, Ventura, CA 93002, (805) 650-1395.

Coll-tex (skins), Alpine Crafts, San Francisco, CA.

Gregory Mountain Products (packs), 100 Calle Cortez, Temecula, CA 92390.

Life-Link International, Inc. (shovels, poles), 1240 Huff Ln., Jackson Hole, WY 83001, (800) 443-8620.

Lowe Alpine Systems (packs, crampons), P.O. Box 1449, Broomfield, CO 80038.

Appendix III

Ski Guides

Adirondack Alpine Adventures, Dept. 121, P.O. Box 179, Keene, NY 12942, (518) 576-9881.

American Alpine Institute Ltd., 1212 24th, C-22, Bellingham, WA 98225 (206) 671-1505.

American Professional Guides Association, P.O. Box 59, Bishop, CA 93514.

Colorado Outward Bound School, 945 Pennsylvania St., Dept. B90, Denver, CO 80203, (303) 837-0880.

Fantasy Ridge, Box 1679, Telluride, CO 81435, (303) 728-3546.

Mountain Ski Ventures, Dept. C P.O. Box 2974, Bellingham, WA 98227, (206) 647-0656.

National Outdoor Leadership School (NOLS), Dept. R, Box AA, Lander, WY 82520, (307) 332-6976.

Paragon Guides, P.O. Box 130-0, Vail, CO 81658, (303) 949-4272.

Timberline Mountain Guides, P.O. Box 464, Terrebonne, OR 97760, (503) 548-0749.

ABOUT THE AUTHOR

Peter Shelton worked as a ski instructor for eight years in Colorado and California, and as director of the Telluride Ski School in Telluride, Colorado. He is a three-time recipient of the National Association of Ski Journalism's "Ski Writer of the Year" award and writes regularly for *Ski, Powder*, and *Outside* magazines.